Joint Workshop on Social Dynamics and Personal Attributes in Social Media 2014

Held at ACL 2014

Baltimore, Maryland, USA
27 June 2014

ISBN: 978-1-63439-207-5

Printed from e-media with permission by:

Curran Associates, Inc.
57 Morehouse Lane
Red Hook, NY 12571

CURRAN ASSOCIATES INC. proceedings.com

Some format issues inherent in the e-media version may also appear in this print version.

Printed by Curran Associates, Inc. (2014)

For permission requests, please contact the Association for Computational Linguistics at the address below.

Association for Computational Linguistics
209 N. Eighth Street
Stroudsburg, Pennsylvania 18360

Phone: 1-570-476-8006
Fax: 1-570-476-0860

acl@aclweb.org

Additional copies of this publication are available from:

Curran Associates, Inc.
57 Morehouse Lane
Red Hook, NY 12571 USA
Phone: 845-758-0400
Fax: 845-758-2634
Email: curran@proceedings.com
Web: www.proceedings.com

Introduction

These proceedings contain papers presented at the Joint Workshop on Social Dynamics and Personal Attributes in Social Media. The workshop was held in Baltimore, Maryland, USA and hosted in conjunction with the 52nd Annual Meeting of the Association for Computational Linguistics.

This workshop was intended to serve as a forum for sharing research in:

I NLP and Social Dynamics: Language is a set of publicly agreed conventions that serves the purpose of inter-personal communication. Speakers (or writers) try to convey a message, instill an idea or make an impression on the listeners. Listeners (or readers), in turn, are affected by the message and may respond to it. Language, in that sense, is an important vehicle that shapes (and is shaped by) social dynamics.

Traditional NLP research, however, focuses on "documents" (either of full length or on the sentence level), rather than on the communication process as reflected by language use. Common examples of traditional NLP research are parsing, document classification, machine translation, and sentiment analysis at the sentence and document level without considering the social dynamics of the people who are writing and reading those texts. We propose to move beyond analyzing the informational aspect of documents and discuss ways in which NLP can contribute to gaining insights about the interplay between language use and various levels of social dynamics.

II Personal Attributes in Social Media: There are many important social science questions and commercial applications that are impacted by the large amounts of diverse personalized data emerging from social media. These data can reveal user interests, preferences and opinions, as well as trends and activity patterns for companies and their products.

The automatic prediction of latent attributes from discourse in social media includes topics such as: inferring user/customer demographic profiles (gender, age, religion, social status, race, ethnicity, origin); predicting user interests (sports, movies) and preferences (political favorites or product likes); classifying sentiment, personality, emotional states (onset of depression), and opinions held by an author; and analyzing general trends and influence for companies and products.

We invited original and unpublished research papers on all topics related to NLP and social dynamics and text-driven attribute prediction in social media, including but not limited to the topics listed below.

NLP and Social Dynamics:

- Emergence and diffusion of slang, neologisms and metaphors
- Emotion dynamics in social media conversation threads
- Evolution of word formation and word meaning
- Language coordination and lexical entrainment
- Language evolution through history and language variation across communities
- Linguistic and social factors in acceptance of new words and phrases
- Persuasive language and (online) campaigns
- Pragmatics of language

- Social dynamics in (blog/news story) comment threads

Personal Attributes in Social Media:

- Dynamic and streaming nature of social media data
- Data collection, sharing and labeling biases for personal analytics in social media
- Joint latent attribute prediction (e.g., age together with political preference)
- Emotional states, distress, mental condition classification in social networks
- Mood, sentiment, emotion and opinion analysis of authors in social media
- Multi-relational aspect of social media (e.g., networks of friends, followers, user mentions etc.)
- Scalability to other understudied languages and dialects in social media
- Security, identity and privacy issues for personal analytics in social media.

The Workshop Committee received 24 submissions. Three reviewers reviewed each submission. For the final workshop program, 15 regular papers, 5 to 11 pages each, were selected, 3 papers were rejected and 3 withdrawn. 3 papers have chosen to be non-archived. Authors affiliations include Computer and Information Science, Linguistics, Political Science, Nutrition and Health Promotion, History, English and Business and Management.

We would like to thank all Program Committee members and external reviewers for their effort in providing high-quality reviews. We thank all the authors who submitted their papers. Many thanks to our invited speakers and panel participants.

Alice Oh,
Benjamin Van Durme,
David Yarowsky,
Oren Tsur,
Svitlana Volkova

Organizers:

Alice Oh, Korea Advanced Institute of Science and Technology
Benjamin Van Durme, Johns Hopkins University
David Yarowsky, Johns Hopkins University
Oren Tsur, Harvard University, Northeastern University
Svitlana Volkova, Johns Hopkins University

Program Committee:

Abigail Jacobs, University of Colorado at Boulder, USA
Alan Ritter, Carnegie Mellon University, USA
Alejandro Jaimes, Yahoo Research, Barcelona
Alessandro Moschitti, Qatar Computing Research Institute, Qatar
Ancsa Hannak, Northeastern University, USA
Ari Rappaport, The Hebrew University, Israel
Aron Culotta, Illinois Institute of Technology, USA
Brendan O'Connor, Carnegie Mellon University, USA
Brian Keegan, Northeastern University, USA
Carlo Strapparava, FBK, Italy
Chin-Yew Lin, Microsoft Research Asia
Chris Dyer, Carnegie Mellon University, USA
Cristian Danescu-Niculescu-Mizil, Max Planck Institute SWS
Dan Jurafsky, Stanford University, USA
Daniel Romero, University of Michigan, USA
David Smith, Northeastern University, USA
Delip Rao, Amazon, USA
Derek Ruths, McGill University, Canada
Dong Nguyen, University of Twente, Netherlands
Eugene Kharitonov, Yandex, Russia
Francisco Iacobelli, Northeastern Illinois University, USA
Gideon Dror, Yahoo! Research, USA
Glen Coppersmith, Johns Hopkins University, USA
Haewoon Kwak, Qatar Computing Research Institute, Qatar
Idan Szpektor, Yahoo! Research, USA
Ilia Chetviorkin, Lomonosov Moscow State University, Russia
Ingmar Weber, QCRI, Qatar
Jacob Eisenstein, Georgia Institute of Technology, USA
James Caverlee, Texas University, USA
John Henderson, MITRE, USA
Margaret Mitchell, Microsoft Research, USA
Mark Dredze, Johns Hopkins University, USA
Michael Gamon, Microsoft Research, USA
Michael Paul, Johns Hopkins University, USA
Omri Abend, University of Edinburgh, UK
Patrick Pantel, Microsoft Research, USA

Paul Cook, University of Melbourne, Australia
Pavel Braslavski, KonturLabs, Russia
Pavel Sergyukov, Yandex, Russia
Philip Resnik, University of Maryland, USA
Rebecca Knowles, Johns Hopkins University, USA
Reut Tzarfati, Weizman Institute of Science, Israel
Rivka Levitan, Columbia University, USA
Roi Reichart, Israel Institute of Technology, Israel
Roy Schwartz, The Hebrew University, Israel
Saif Mohammad, National Research Council, Canada
Silviu-Petru Cucerzan, Microsoft Research, USA
Souneil Park, University of Michigan, USA
Vasileios Lampos, University College London, UK
Vivi Nastase, FBK, Italy
Yael Netzer, Ben Gurion University, Israel
Yoav Goldberg, Bar Ilan University, Israel
Yu-Ru Lin, University of Pittsburgh, USA
Yuval Pinter, Yahoo! Research, Israel

Invited Speakers:

Derek Ruths, McGill University
Henry Kautz, University of Rochester

Panelists:

Hanna Wallach, UMass Amherst
Jacob Eisenstein, Georgia Tech
Cristian Danescu-Niculescu-Mizil, Max Planck Institute SWS
Jimmy Lin, University of Maryland

Table of Contents

Conference Program

Friday, June 27, 2014

(8:40–8:50) Welcome Notes

8:50–9:50 Invited talk by Derek Ruths

Oral Session 1

Oral Session 2

11:30–12:30 Panel by Hanna Wallach, Jacob Eisenstein, Cristian Danescu-Niculescu-Mizil and Jimmy Lin

Oral Session 3

2:35–3:35 Invited talk

Friday, June 27, 2014 (continued)

Oral Session 4

3:45–4:00 *Generating Subjective Responses to Opinionated Articles in Social Media: An Agenda-Driven Architecture and a Turing-Like Test*
Tomer Cagan, Stefan L. Frank and Reut Tsarfaty

4:00–4:15 *A Semi-Automated Method of Network Text Analysis Applied to 150 Original Screenplays*
Starling Hunter

Poster Session

4:30–5:30 *Power of Confidence: How Poll Scores Impact Topic Dynamics in Political Debates*
Vinodkumar Prabhakaran, Ashima Arora and Owen Rambow

4:30–5:30 *As Long as You Name My Name Right: Social Circles and Social Sentiment in the Hollywood Hearings*
Oren Tsur, Dan Calacci and David Lazer

4:30–5:30 *Towards Tracking Political Sentiment through Microblog Data*
Yu Wang, Tom Clark, Jeffrey Staton and Eugene Agichtein

4:30–5:30 *Innovation of Verbs in Hebrew*
Ornan Uzzi

4:30–5:30 *User Type Classification of Tweets with Implications for Event Recognition*
Lalindra De Silva and Ellen Riloff

4:30–5:30 *Collective Stance Classification of Posts in Online Debate Forums*
Dhanya Sridhar, Lise Getoor and Marilyn Walker

Friday, June 27, 2014 (continued)

(5:30–5:40) Closing Remarks

Detecting sociostructural beliefs about group status differences in online discussions

Brian Riordan **Heather Wade**
Aptima, Inc.
3100 Presidential Drive
Fairborn, OH 45324
{briordan, hwade}@aptima.com

Afzal Upal
Defence R&D Canada Toronto
1133 Sheppard Ave W
Toronto, ON, M3K 2C9
Afzal.Upal@drdc-rddc.gc.ca

Abstract

Detection of fine-grained opinions and beliefs holds promise for improved social media analysis for social science research, business intelligence, and government decision-makers. While commercial applications focus on mapping landscapes of opinions towards brands and products, our goal is to map "sociostructural" landscapes of perceptions of social groups. In this work, we focus on the detection of views of social group status differences. We report an analysis of methods for detecting views of the legitimacy of income inequality in the U.S. from online discussions, and demonstrate detection rates competitive with results from similar tasks such as debate stance classification.

1 Introduction

Social media and the internet continue to be a vast resource for exploring and analyzing public opinion. While there has been a longstanding focus on detecting sentiment for commercial applications (Liu, 2012), in recent years there has been increased interest in detecting opinions and perspectives in politics and social science more generally (Grimmer & Stewart, 2013). Examples include analyzing people's perceptions of particular political issues by classifying debate stances (Hasan and Ng, 2013) and detecting the expression of ideology (Sim et al., 2013). Research has increasingly turned from detecting opinions and beliefs in general (Prabhakaran et al., 2010) to discerning particular types of opinions or beliefs for specific applications.

The goal of our work is to detect indicators of people's views of social conditions and intergroup perceptions in social media. Working within the framework of Social Identity Theory (Tajfel and Turner, 1979; Tajfel and Turner, 1986; Turner, 1999), we explore detection of the linguistic correlates of sociostructural beliefs. Sociostructural beliefs are abstract theoretical constructs in Social Identity Theory that underpin individual and social identity formation and individual actions that affect the relations between social groups.

For this study, we focus on class-based social groups and the views of individuals on the issue of income inequality. We seek to detect people's views of the legitimacy of the socio-economic structure that has resulted in increasing income inequality, particularly in the U.S. Our approach focuses on comments on news articles related to the issue of income inequality. We develop a series of supervised classifiers for detecting the expression of views on the legitimacy of income inequality. We show promising results comparable to detection rates for other studies of social and political perspectives.

2 Background

Social Identity Theory attempts to account for how subjectively perceived social structure can lead people to define themselves in terms of a shared social identity and thereby produce forms of intergroup behavior. Social identity – how people perceive their relations to the multiple groups to which they belong – is argued to be a crucial part of a person's self-concept. People invoke part of their social identities whenever they think of themselves as belonging to one gender, ethnicity, social class, religion, etc. Group membership and social identity play a role in shaping interpersonal interactions.

Social Identity Theory (as well as social categorization theory) holds that people are sensitive to group status differences and are motivated to view their own social groups positively. These two factors are key drivers of individuals' social identity management strategies. For example, membership

Proceedings of the Joint Workshop on Social Dynamics and Personal Attributes in Social Media, pages 1–6,
Baltimore, Maryland USA, 27 June 2014.

in a relatively low-status group may engender perceptions of deprivation, which in turn may result in individuals taking actions to increase their group's status or diminish the status of other groups (Tajfel and Turner, 1979; Tajfel and Turner, 1986). According to Social Identity Theory, a group member's expectations of rewards of group membership are importantly affected by sociostructural beliefs about the nature of group status differences. Group status differences are thought to be shaped by three types of these beliefs:

- *Legitimacy*: the degree to which people believe that group status differences are valid.
- *Stability*: people's sense of how likely the status hierarchy is to last into the future.
- *Permeability*: the perception of how easy it is for outsiders to enter or leave the group.

Based on these sociostructural beliefs and perceptions of the relative deprivation of one's group, people are motivated to take actions to maintain and enhance their group's image.

3 Detecting sociostructural beliefs

A central challenge for extracting sociostructural beliefs is determining where they are likely to occur in natural discourse on the internet. Sociostructural beliefs relate to group status differences – for example, in terms of wealth, power, or prestige. Hence, the most likely context for sociostructural belief expressions is discussions of issues that relate to such social differences.

While debate-focused websites (e.g., createdebate.com, debate.org) hold potential as a data source, we found that in practice such websites had few discussions of issues that might relate to sociostructural beliefs and, furthermore, the number of posts for each topic was generally small. In contrast, we found that highly relevant data can be harvested from comments on news or opinion articles from large newspapers or popular media websites. Articles and op-eds commonly generate hundreds of responses. We considered a variety of topics related to social differences in ethnicity, gender, religion, etc., but found the most data on the topic of income inequality in the U.S. We collected comments across several news articles and op-ed pieces that focused on income inequality.

In the context of income inequality, the social groups are hard to rigorously define, but in comments it was common to observe a dichotomy between "rich" and "poor," or "the 1 percent" and "everyone else". We observed comments on each of the three types of sociostructural beliefs – legitimacy, stability, permeability – but by far the most common topic of discussion was the legitimacy of a large income gap. Therefore, we focused on detecting expressions of legitimacy and leave the extraction of expressions of stability and permeability to future work.

In past survey research related to sociostructural beliefs (Kessler and Mummendey, 2002; Mummendey et al., 1999), participants were asked to respond to explicit statements reflecting sociostructural beliefs – for example, *It is [justified|right|legitimate|accurate|fair] that [proposition]*. However, we found no instances of such explicit expressions in our data. Nevertheless, beliefs about legitimacy are implicit in many instances. For example, consider this comment:

> *Now we are all victims and we should be given our fair share instead of earning our fair share. All the wealth should be redistributed. The wealthy are vilianized. The ones who have been able to rely on their vision, innovation, self motivation, sacrifice and wits are being called out by the envious.Like it or not, the one-percenters are the ones who have advanced humanity to the highest standard ofliving - ever.*

Although there is no explicit articulation of a belief that it is legitimate for income inequality to exist across social groups, for human annotators, it is not difficult to infer that this author likely believes that this is the case. Our goal is to uncover cases like this where sociostructural beliefs are strongly implicit.

We formulated the problem as staged text classification (cf. Lamb et al. (2013)):

1. Finding comments that implicity express the sociostructural belief in the legitimacy or illegitimacy of income inequality (+/-E);
2. Making a binary classification of the author's sociostructural belief (income inequality is legitimate or not) (+/-L).

4 Data Collection

We scraped more than 10,000 comments from articles from major internet media outlets related to the income inequality issue in the U.S., including *CNN*, *The New York Times*, *Daily Finance*, and marketwatch.com (*The Wall Street Journal*). For example, we collected comments from the CNN op-ed "Is income inequality 'morally wrong'?"[1], which had attracted several thousand comments at the time of data collection (and continues to receive more).

An initial set was randomly selected for annotation for +/-E and +/-L by one of the authors. Another author independently annotated a subset of these comments (N=100) and agreement was assessed. While the agreement was low for the +/-E label (κ = .282), for comments that the annotators agreed were +E, the inter-annotator agreement was high (κ = .916). After the annotators discussed and resolved differences in the +/-E annotation guidelines, the first annotator continued the annotation process to compile a final dataset. Table 1 gives a summary of the final corpus.

	+	-	Total
Expression related to legitimacy (E)	400	1,088	1,488
Support for legitimacy (L)	174	226	400

Table 1: Dataset annotation statistics.

5 Features

5.1 *N*-grams

As with similar tasks such as debate stance classification and sentiment tagging, token-level differences should provide a strong baseline for discriminating between the classes of belief expression (+/-E) and the belief in legitimacy (+/-L). Therefore, we explored a variety of combinations of *n*-gram features, including surface tokens, lemmas, and parts of speech.

5.2 Word classes

Beyond *n*-gram features, we expected that coherent sets of tokens would pattern together for implicit beliefs about legitimacy of status differences. One of the authors coded a total of 24 classes for the income inequality setting based on annotating a subset of about 100 comments. Examples are shown in Table 2. The classes reflected both semantic similarity and, for some, polarity of the sociostructural belief.

[1] http://www.cnn.com/2013/07/25/opinion/sutter-income-inequality-moral-obama/

Word class	Example words
income inequality	gap, widening, inequality
lack of income inequality	equal chance, never fair, free society
the non-rich (+)	the 99%, have-nots
the non-rich (+/-)	the poor, middle-class
the non-rich (-)	lazy, dumb
change (+)	fix, make changes
change (-)	redistribution, impose
greed	greed, exploit
hardship	can't afford, cost of living
rich – epithets	shameful, evil, no empathy
poor – epithets	soviet, communist, envy
rich individuals	Buffet, Gates, Bloomberg
society	safety net, playing field
business	companies, profit
money	wealth, income level, salary
the rich (+)	wealthy, those with means
the rich (+/-)	upper middle class
the rich (-)	extreme rich, the 1%
deserve	deserve, earn
work / effort	work harder, effort
success	success, fortune, move up
government	regulation, bloated
taxes	taxes, taxpayer, pay most of
lifestyle	save, budget, responsibility

Table 2: Example word classes.

5.3 Quotation-related features

Excerpts from other posters' comments and quotations of famous individuals are common in our dataset. For example:

> *"Everyone in America has an equal chance an equal opportunity to succeed." Dont know if Id go THAT far.*

The author quotes a previous post's words in order to explicitly disagree with a statement. In this case, *n*-gram features might indicate that the comment should be labeled +L (since comments discussing an "equal opportunity to succeed" typically expressed this belief). However, the second sentence expresses a negation of the ideas in the quoted text. This issue is common in dialogic social media settings, particularly when debating political or social issues, and poses a challenge to surface-oriented classifiers (Malouf and Mullen, 2008). To address this issue, *n*-gram features were computed specifically for text inside quotes ("quote features") and text outside quotes ("nonquote features"). In the quote above, the words *Everyone in America has an equal chance...* would contribute to the quote *n*-grams.

6 Experiments

For classification, we experimented with Naive Bayes and MaxEnt (via MALLET[2]) and SVMs (via LIBSVM[3]). Our baseline was a majority class predictor. We began by comparing the results of several different *n*-gram sets, including *n*-grams from surface text or lemmatization, binary labels or count features, combinations of unigrams, bigrams, trigrams, and 4-grams, and the inclusion or exclusion of stopwords. We found that the *n*-grams set of binary labels for unigrams, bigrams, trigrams, and 4-grams after lemmatization had the highest performance. The *inclusion* of stopwords generally afforded better performance; hence we do not remove stopwords.

We explored the hypothesis that this result was due to the inclusion of negation operators among stopwords. Negation may be useful to retain in *n*-grams to distinguish expressions such as *didn't earn* from *earned.* We removed negation operators from the stopword list. However, other than MaxEnt, performance was worse[4]. What stylometric features that stopwords capture to distinguish authors' beliefs in this task is left for future work.

Classifier	**+/-E**	**+/-L**
MLE	73.1	56.5
MaxEnt	79.9	66.0
Naive Bayes	75.9	**68.3**
SVM	**80.1**	66.3

Table 3: Comparison of classifiers by accuracy on the +/-E and +/-L task with a feature set of: unigram, bigram, trigram, and 4-gram lemma labels, stopwords included. MLE = majority class.

The results for both the +/-E and +/-L tasks are shown in Table 3. We report accuracy following previous related work. We only report results for the staged classifier setting (-E posts were not annotated for +/-L). For the +/-E task, absolute accuracy values were high due to the very unbalanced dataset (cf. Table 1). On the +/-L task, Naive Bayes achieved the highest accuracy score. Our dataset consisted of a mix of short and long comments (M = 45.4 tokens, SD = 37.5 tokens), which, interestingly, was not unfavorable to Naive Bayes (cf. Wang and Manning (2012)). All classifiers were significantly better than the baseline (by paired samples t-tests on accuracy across folds in cross-validation with $p < .05$) in both tasks. On +/-E, MaxEnt and SVM were not significantly different; both performed better than Naive Bayes. On +/-L, there were no significant differences.

Tables 4 and 5 report the results after adding the +/-L problem-specific features to the best *n*-gram set. The addition of the word class features provides a small improvement in accuracy across the classifiers. MaxEnt's performance approached significance compared to the others ($p < .1$) These results confirm that, for the task of detecting sociostructural beliefs about legitimacy in this domain, words tokens do tend to co-occur in topical and polarity-based word classes. However, it is likely that our word class feature set suffered from limited coverage relative to the diversity of expressions used in the domain.

Feature set	MLE	**ME**	**NB**	**SVM**
n-grams	56.5	66.0	68.3	66.3
+ WC counts	56.5	**70.8**	68.8	67.0
+ WC lab.	56.5	69.5	68.0	67.0
+ WC counts, lab.	56.5	69.8	68.8	66.8

Table 4: Classification accuracies for the +/-L task on variants of word class (WC) feature sets for MaxEnt, NB, and SVM. MLE = majority class.

Table 5 reports the results of adding quotation features. Performance improved with the addition of these features, most notably with the addition of both quote and nonquote features. While these results suggest that accounting for quotations is important, the inclusion of quotation-related features only differentiates between words appearing in quotations from those outside quotations, and does not represent any relationship between the two sets of features. The appearance of terms in a quotation that are typically not found in quotations and that are used by people expressing a particular stance is often a strong indicator that the opinion of the text surrounding the quotation is the opposite of that in the quotation a relationship found by Malouf and Mullen (2008)). Hence, more research that explores relations between terms in and outside of quotations would seem worthwhile.

[2]http://mallet.cs.umass.edu/

[3]http://www.csie.ntu.edu.tw/ cjlin/libsvm/

[4]ME = 66.5, NB = 65.8, SVM = 63.0

Finally, we experimented with combining both word class features and quotation features, but performance did not improve over the results for word class features or quote features alone.

Feature set	MLE	ME	NB	SVM
n-grams	56.5	66.0	68.3	66.3
+ Q count	56.5	67.0	68.3	66.8
+ Q labels	56.5	66.0	68.8	66.3
+ Q count & lab.	56.5	66.5	69.3	65.3
+ NQ labels	56.5	66.3	69.0	65.3
+ Q & NQ	56.5	67.3	70.0	66.3
repl. w/ Q & NQ	56.5	67.3	**70.5**	66.3

Table 5: Classification accuracies for the +/-L task on variants of quotation (Q, NQ) feature sets for MaxEnt, NB, and SVM. MLE = majority class.

7 Error analysis

7.1 Focus on a specific sub-issue

In discussions on income inequality, there are "sub-issues" that are repeatedly discussed in comments, including taxes, welfare, the U.S. economy, and business owners. The difficulty of classifying these kinds of comments stems from the difficulty of deciding whether the comments contain an implicit expression of a sociostructural belief, i.e. the +/- E classification problem. Inference based on world knowledge may be required to chain together the steps that link expressions to beliefs.

7.2 Personal stories used as examples

In discussions involving social status, we observed that people often use personal examples to support their positions.

> *My Dad slept in a dresser drawer on the floor with cotton stuffed under a sheet... He graduated with an engineering degree summa cum laude and has never been un-employed for 45 years because he always worked harder and made himself more valuable than his peers. No GI Bill No Pell Grants No Welfare...*

While a human annotator can usually infer which view on legitimacy such a story supports, the content can seem unrelated to the issue of interest. Similar behavior occurs on debate websites, where descriptions of personal experiences add material irrelevant to stance, often leading to misclassification (Hasan and Ng, 2013).

7.3 Importance of context

While we considered comments independently for our classification task, comments can refer to or reply to previous comments, such that the meaning of a comment can be obscured without the content of these related comments. To address this issue, techniques for incorporating other comments in dialog threads may be fruitful (Walker et al., 2012; Hasan and Ng, 2013).

8 Related Work

The goal of detection of sociostructural beliefs in the context of Social Identity Theory is similar to work in debate stance classification (Anand et al., 2011; Hasan and Ng, 2013; Somasundaran and Wiebe, 2009; Walker et al., 2012). For example, Hasan and Ng (2013) developed methods for classifying author postings on debate websites into binary classes reflecting opposing stances on political issues (e.g., gay marriage). Our setting differs in that "sides" of the issue are only hypothesized (i.e., legitimate/illegitimate) and not given, and stances are never explicitly observed. However, the behavior of posters appears to be similar across debate sites and comments on news articles.

The work here also fits into the increasing focus on content analysis for political and social science analysis (Grimmer and Stewart, 2013). Much recent work has focused on analysis of artifacts from the political arena, such as speeches, floor debates, or press releases (Gerrish and Blei, 2012; Sim et al., 2013; Thomas et al., 2006).

9 Discussion

This work explored the task of detecting latent author beliefs in social media analysis. We focused on the specific problem of detecting and classifying sociostructural beliefs from Social Identity Theory – beliefs about the legitimacy, stability, and permeability of social groups and their status. We collected and analyzed a dataset of social media comments centering on the issue of income inequality and sought to classify implicit author beliefs on the legitimacy of class-based income disparity. Because of the heavily implicit nature of sociostructural belief expression, we formulated the detection problem as a form of text classification. Our approach achieved classification accuracies competitive with results from similar tasks such as debate stance classification.

References

Anand, Pranav, Walker, Marilyn, Abbott, Rob, Tree, Jean. E. Fox, Bowmani, Robeson, and Minor, Michael. 2011. Classifying stance in online debate. In *Proceedings of the 2nd workshop on computational approaches to subjectivity and sentiment analysis.*

Gerrish, Sean M., and Blei, David M. 2012. How They Vote: Issue-Adjusted Models of Legislative Behavior. In *Advances in Neural Information Processing Systems.*

Grimmer, Justin, and Stewart, Brandon M. 2013. Text as data: The promise and pitfalls of automatic content analysis methods for political texts. *Political Analysis*, 21(3), 267297.

Hasan, Kazi Saidul, and Ng, Vincent. 2013. Frame Semantics for Stance Classification. *CoNLL-2013*, 124.

Kessler, Thomas, and Mummendey, Amélie. 2002. Sequential or parallel processes? A longitudinal field study concerning determinants of identity-management strategies. Journal of Personality and Social Psychology, 82(1), 75-88.

Lamb, Alex, Paul, Michael J., and Dredze, Mark. 2013. Separating fact from fear: Tracking flu infections on Twitter. In *Proceedings of NAACL-HLT.*

Liu, Bing. 2012. *Sentiment analysis and opinion mining.* Morgan & Claypool.

Malouf, Robert, and Mullen, Tony. 2008. Taking sides: User classification for informal online political discourse. *Internet Research*, 18(2), 177-190.

Mummendey, Amélie, Klink, Andreas, Mielke, Rosemarie, Wenzel, Michael, and Blanz, Mathias. 1999. Sociostructural characteristics of intergroup relations and identity management strategies: results from a field study in East Germany. *European Journal of Social Psychology*, 29(2-3), 259285.

Prabhakaran, Vinodkumar, Rambow, Owen, and Diab, Mona. 2010. Automatic committed belief tagging. In *Proceedings of COLING.*

Sim, Yanchuan, Acree, Brice, Gross, Justin H., and Smith, Noah A. 2013. Measuring ideological proportions in political speeches. In *Proceedings of EMNLP.*

Somasundaran, Swapna, and Wiebe, Janyce. 2009. Recognizing stances in online debates. In *Proceedings of the Joint Conference of the 47th Annual Meeting of the ACL and the 4th International Joint Conference on Natural Language Processing of the AFNLP.*

Tajfel, Henri and Turner, John C. 1979. An integrative theory of intergroup conflict. In W. G. Austin and S. Worchel (Eds.), *The social psychology of intergroup relations* (pp. 3347). Monterey, CA: Brooks-Cole.

Tajfel, Henri and Turner, John C. 1986. The social identity theory of intergroup behaviour. In S. Worchel, and W. G. Austin (Eds.), *Psychology of intergroup relations* (pp. 724). Chicago, IL: Nelson-Hall.

Thomas, Matt, Pang, Bo, and Lee, Lillian. 2006. Get out the vote: Determining support or opposition from Congressional floor-debate transcripts. In *Proceedings of EMNLP.*

Turner, John C. 1999. Some current issues in research on social identity and self-categorization thoeries In Ellemers, N., Spears, R., Doosje, B. *Social identity* (pp. 6-34). Oxford: Blackwell.

Walker, Marilyn A., Anand, Pranav, Abbott, Robert, and Grant, Ricky. 2012. Stance classification using dialogic properties of persuasion. In *Proceedings of NAACL-HLT.*

Wang, Sida I., and Manning, Christopher D. 2012. Baselines and Bigrams: Simple, Good Sentiment and Topic Classification. In *Proceedings of ACL.*

Using county demographics to infer attributes of Twitter users

Ehsan Mohammady and **Aron Culotta**
Department of Computer Science
Illinois Institute of Technology
Chicago, IL 60616
emohamm1@hawk.iit.edu, culotta@cs.iit.edu

Abstract

Social media are increasingly being used to complement traditional survey methods in health, politics, and marketing. However, little has been done to adjust for the sampling bias inherent in this approach. Inferring demographic attributes of social media users is thus a critical step to improving the validity of such studies. While there have been a number of supervised machine learning approaches to this problem, these rely on a training set of users annotated with attributes, which can be difficult to obtain. We instead propose training a demographic attribute classifiers that uses county-level supervision. By pairing geolocated social media with county demographics, we build a regression model mapping text to demographics. We then adopt this model to make predictions at the user level. Our experiments using Twitter data show that this approach is surprisingly competitive with a fully supervised approach, estimating the race of a user with 80% accuracy.

1 Introduction

Researchers are increasingly using social media analysis to complement traditional survey methods in areas such as public health (Dredze, 2012), politics (O'Connor et al., 2010), and marketing (Gopinath et al., 2014). It is generally accepted that social media users are not a representative sample of the population (e.g., urban and minority populations tend to be overrepresented on Twitter (Mislove et al., 2011)). Nevertheless, few researchers have attempted to adjust for this bias. (Gayo-Avello (2011) is an exception.) This can in part be explained by the difficulty of obtaining demographic information of social media users — while gender can sometimes be inferred from the user's name, other attributes such as age and race/ethnicity are more difficult to deduce. This problem of **user attribute prediction** is thus critical to such applications of social media analysis.

A common approach to user attribute prediction is supervised classification — from a training set of annotated users, a model is fit to predict user attributes from the content of their writings and their social connections (Argamon et al., 2005; Schler et al., 2006; Rao et al., 2010; Pennacchiotti and Popescu, 2011; Burger et al., 2011; Rao et al., 2011; Al Zamal et al., 2012). Because collecting human annotations is costly and error-prone, labeled data are often collected serendipitously; for example, Al Zamal et al. (2012) collect age annotations by searching for tweets with phrases such as "Happy 21st birthday to me"; Pennacchiotti and Popescu (2011) collect race annotations by searching for profiles with explicit self identification (e.g., "I am a black lawyer from Sacramento."). While convenient, such an approach likely suffer from selection bias (Liu and Ruths, 2013).

In this paper, we propose fitting classification models on *population-level* data, then applying them to predict user attributes. Specifically, we fit regression models to predict the race distribution of 100 U.S. counties (based on Census data) from geolocated Twitter messages. We then extend this learned model to predict user-level attributes. This *lightly supervised* approach reduces the need for human annotation, which is important not only because of the reduction of human effort, but also because many other attributes may be difficult even for humans to annotate at the user-level (e.g., health status, political orientation). We investigate this new approach through the following three research questions:

RQ1. **Can models trained on county statistics be used to infer user attributes?** We find that a classifier trained on county statis-

Proceedings of the Joint Workshop on Social Dynamics and Personal Attributes in Social Media, pages 7–16,
Baltimore, Maryland USA, 27 June 2014. ©2014 Association for Computational Linguistics

tics can make accurate predictions at the user level. Accuracy is slightly lower (by less than 1%) than a fully supervised approach using logistic regression trained on hundreds of labeled instances.

RQ2. **How do models trained on county data differ from those using standard supervised methods?** We analyze the highly-weighted features of competing models, and find that while both models discern lexical differences (e.g., slang, word choice), the county-based model also learns geographical correlates of race (e.g., city, state).

RQ3. **What bias does serendipitously labeled data introduce?** By comparing training datasets collected uniformly at random with those collected by searching for certain keywords, we find that the search approach produces a very biased class distribution. Additionally, the classifier trained on such biased data tends to overweight features matching the original search keywords.

2 Related Work

Predicting attributes of social media users is a growing area of interest, with recent work focusing on age (Schler et al., 2006; Rosenthal and McKeown, 2011; Nguyen et al., 2011; Al Zamal et al., 2012), sex (Rao et al., 2010; Burger et al., 2011; Liu and Ruths, 2013), race/ethnicity (Pennacchiotti and Popescu, 2011; Rao et al., 2011), and personality (Argamon et al., 2005; Schwartz et al., 2013b). Other work predicts demographics from web browsing histories (Goel et al., 2012).

The majority of these approaches rely on hand-annotated training data, require explicit self-identification by the user, or are limited to very coarse attribute values (e.g., above or below 25-years-old). Pennacchiotti and Popescu (2011) train a supervised classifier to predict whether a Twitter user is African-American or not based on linguistic and social features. To construct a labeled training set, they collect 6,000 Twitter accounts in which the user description matches phrases like "I am a 20 year old African-American." In our experiments below, we demonstrate how such serendipitously labeled data can introduce selection bias in the estimate of classification accuracy. Their final classifier obtains a 65.5% F1 measure on this binary classification task (compared with the 76.5% F1 we report below for a different dataset labeled with four race categories).

A related lightly supervised approach includes Chang et al. (2010), who infer user-level ethnicity using name/ethnicity distributions provided by the Census; however, that approach uses evidence from first and last names, which are often not available, and thus are more appropriate for population-level estimates. Rao et al. (2011) extend this approach to also include evidence from other linguistic features to infer gender and ethnicity of Facebook users; they evaluate on the fine-grained ethnicity classes of Nigeria and use very limited training data.

Viewed as a way to make individual inferences from aggregate data, our approach is related to *ecological inference* (King, 1997); however, here we have the advantage of user-level observations (linguistic data), which are typically absent in ecological inference settings.

There have been several studies predicting population-level statistics from social media. Eisenstein et al. (2011) use geolocated tweets to predict zip-code statistics of race/ethnicity, income, and other variables using Census data; Schwartz et al. (2013b) and Culotta (2014) similarly predict county health statistics from Twitter. However, none of this prior work attempts to predict or evaluate at the user level.

Schwartz et al. (2013a) collect Facebook profiles labeled with personality type, gender, and age by administering a survey of users embedded in a personality test application. While this approach was able to collect over 75K labeled profiles, it can be difficult to reproduce, and is also challenging to update over time without re-administering the survey.

Compared to this related work, our core contribution is to propose and evaluate a classifier trained only on county statistics to estimate the race of a Twitter user. The resulting accuracy is competitive with a fully supervised baseline as well as with prior work. By avoiding the use of labeled data, the method is simple to train and easier to update as linguistic patterns evolve over time.

3 Methods

Our approach to user attribute prediction is as follows: First, we collect population-level statistics, for example the racial makeup of a county. Second, we collect a sample of tweets from the same population areas and distill them into one feature vector per location. Third, we fit a regression model to predict the population-level statistics from the linguistic feature vector. Finally, we adapt the regression coefficients to predict the attributes of individual Twitter user. Below, we describe the data, the regression and classification models, and the experimental setup.

3.1 Data

We collect three types of data: (1) Census data, listing the racial makeup of U.S. Counties; (2) geolocated Twitter data from each county; (3) a validation set of Twitter users manually annotated with race, for evaluation purposes.

3.1.1 Census Data

The U.S. Census produces annual estimates of the race and Hispanic origin proportions for each county in the United States. These estimates are derived using the most recent decennial census and estimates of population changes (deaths, birth, migration) since that census. The census questionnaire allows respondents to select one or more of 6 racial categories: White, Black or African American, American Indian and Alaska Native, Asian, Native Hawaiian and Other Pacific Islander, or Other. Additionally, each respondent is asked whether they consider themselves to be of Hispanic, Latino, or Spanish origin (ethnicity). Since respondents may select multiple races in addition to ethnicity, the Census reports many different combinations of results.

While race/ethnicity is indeed a complex issue, for the purposes of this study we simplify by considering only four categories: Asian, Black, Latino, White. (For simplicity, we ignore the Census' distinction between race and ethnicity; due to small proportions, we also omit Other, American Indian/Alaska Native, and Native Hawaiian and Other Pacific Islander.) For the three categories other than Latino, we collect the proportion of each county for that race, possibly in combinations with others. For example, the percentage of Asians in a county corresponds to the Census category: "NHAAC: Not Hispanic, Asian alone or in combination." The Latino proportion corresponds to the "H" category, indicating the percentage of a county identifying themselves as of Hispanic, Latino, or Spanish origin (our terminology again ignores the distinction between the terms "Latino" and "Hispanic"). We use the 2012 estimates for this study.[1] We collect the proportion of residents from each of these four categories for the 100 most populous counties in the U.S.

3.1.2 Twitter County Data

For each of the 100 most populous counties in the U.S., we identify its geographical coordinates (from the U.S. Census), and construct a geographical Twitter query (bounding box) consisting of a 50 square mile area centered at the county coordinates. This approximation introduces a very small amount of noise — less than .02% of tweets come from areas of overlapping bounding boxes.[2] We submit each of these 100 queries in turn from December 5, 2012 to November 14, 2013. These geographical queries return tweets that carry geographical coordinates, typically those sent from mobile devices with this preference enabled.[3] This resulted in 5.7M tweets from 839K unique users.

3.1.3 Validation Data

Uniform Data: For validation purposes, we categorized 770 Twitter profiles into one of four categories (Asian, Black, Latino, White). These were collected as follows: First, we used the Twitter Streaming API to obtain a random sample of users, filtered to the United States (using time zone and the place country code from the profile). From six days' worth of data (December 6-12, 2013), we sampled 1,000 profiles at random and categorized them by analyzing the profile, tweets, and profile image for each user. Those for which race could not be determined were discarded (230/1,000; 23%).[4] The category frequency is Asian (22), Black (263), Latino (158), White (327). To estimate inter-annotator agreement, a second annotator sampled and categorized 120 users. Among users for which both annotators selected one of the four categories, 74/76 labels agreed (97%). There was some disagreement over when the category could be determined: for

[1] `http://www.census.gov/popest/data/counties/asrh/2012/files/CC-EST2012-ALLDATA.csv`

[2] The Census also publishes polygon data for each county, which could be used to remove this small source of noise.

[3] Only considering geolocated tweets introduces some bias into the types of tweets observed. However, we compared the unigram frequency vectors from geolocated tweets with a sample of non-geolocated tweets and found a strong correlation (0.93).

[4] This introduces some bias towards accounts with identifiable race; we leave an investigation of this for future work.

21/120 labels (17.5%), one annotator indicated the category could not be determined, while the other selected a category. For each user, we collected their 200 most recent tweets using the Twitter API. We refer to this as the **Uniform** dataset.

Search Data: It is common in prior work to search for keywords indicating user attributes, rather than sampling uniformly at random and then labeling (Pennacchiotti and Popescu, 2011; Al Zamal et al., 2012). This is typically done for convenience; a large number of annotations can be collected with little or no manual annotation. We hypothesize that this approach results in a biased sample of users, since it is restricted to those with a predetermined set of keywords. This bias may affect the estimate of the generalization accuracy of the resulting classifier.

To investigate this, we used the Twitter Search API to collect profiles containing a predefined set of keywords indicating race. Examples include the terms "African", "Black", "Hispanic", "Latin", "Latino", "Spanish", "Chinese", "Italian", "Irish." Profiles containing such words in the description field were collected. These were further filtered in an attempt to remove businesses (e.g., Chinese restaurants) by excluding profiles with the keywords in the name field as well as those whose name fields did not contain terms on the Census' list of common first and last names. Remaining profiles were then manually reviewed for accuracy. This resulted in 2,000 annotated users with the following distribution: Asian (377), Black (373), Latino (356), White (894). For each user, we collected their 200 most recent tweets using the Twitter API. We refer to this as the **Search** dataset.

Table 1 compares the race distribution for each of the two datasets. It is apparent that the Search dataset oversamples Asian users and undersamples Black users as compared to the Uniform dataset. This may in part due to the greater number of keywords used to identify Asian users (e.g., Chinese, Japanese, Korean). This highlights the difficulty of obtaining a representative sample of Twitter users with the search approach, since the inclusion of a single keyword can result in a very different distribution of labels.

	Uniform	Search
Asian	3%	19%
Black	34%	19%
Latino	21%	18%
White	42%	44%

Table 1: Percentage of users by race in the two validation datasets.

3.2 Models

3.2.1 County Regression

We build a text regression model to predict the racial makeup of a county (from the Census data) based on the linguistic patterns in tweets from that county. For each county, we create a feature vector as follows: for each unigram, we compute the proportion of users in the county who have used that unigram. We also distinguish between unigrams in the text of a tweet and a unigram in the description field of the user's profile. Thus, two sample feature values are (*china*, 0.1) and (*desc_china*, 0.05), indicating that 10% of users in the county wrote a tweet containing the unigram *china*, and 5% have the word *china* in their profile description. We ignore mentions and collapse URLs (replacing them with the token "http"), but retain hashtags.

We fit four separate ridge regression models, one per race.[5] For each model, the independent variables are the unigram proportions from above; the dependent variable is the percentage of each county of a particular race. Ridge regression is an L2 regularized form of linear regression, where α determines the regularization strength, $\mathbf{y}^i$ is a vector of dependent variables for category i, X is a matrix of independent variables, and β are the model parameters:

$$\hat{\beta}^i = \underset{\beta}{\text{argmin}} \, ||\mathbf{y}^i - X\beta^i||_2^2 + \alpha||\beta||_2^2$$

Thus, we have one parameter vector for each race category $\hat{\beta} = \{\hat{\beta}^A, \hat{\beta}^B, \hat{\beta}^L, \hat{\beta}^W\}$. Related approaches have been used in prior work to estimate county demographics and health statistics (Eisenstein et al., 2011; Schwartz et al., 2013b; Culotta, 2014).

Our core hypothesis is that the $\hat{\beta}$ coefficients learned above can be used to categorize individual users by race. We propose a very simple approach that simply treats $\hat{\beta}$ as parameters of a linear classifier. For each user in the labeled dataset, we construct a binary feature vector $\mathbf{x}$ using the same unigram vocabulary from the county regression task. Then, we classify each user according to

[5]Subsequent experiments with lasso, elastic net, and multi-output elastic net performed no better.

the dot product between this binary feature vector $\mathbf{x}$ and the parameter vector for each category:

$$\hat{y} = \underset{i}{\text{argmax}} \left(\mathbf{x} \cdot \hat{\beta}^i \right)$$

3.2.2 Baseline 1: Logistic Regression

For comparison, we also train a logistic regression classifier using the user-annotated data (either Uniform or Search). We perform 10-fold classification, using the same binary feature vectors described above (preliminary results using term frequency instead of binary vectors resulted in lower accuracy). We again use L2 regularization, controlled by tunable parameter α.

3.2.3 Baseline 2: Name Heuristic

Inspired by the approach of Chang et al. (2010), we collect Census data containing the frequency of racial categories by last name. We use the top 1000 most popular last names with their race distribution from Census database. If the last name in the user's Twitter profile matches names on this list, we categorize the user with the most probable race according to the Census data. For example, the Census indicates that 91% of people with the last name Garcia identify themselves as Latino/Hispanic. We would thus label Twitter users with Garcia as a last name as Hispanic. Users whose last names are not matched are categorized as White (the most common label).

3.3 Experiments

We performed experiments to estimate the accuracy of each approach, as well as how different training sets affect performance. The systems are:

1. **County**: The county regression approach of Section 3.2.1, trained only using county-level supervision.
2. **Uniform**: A logistic regression classifier trained on the Uniform dataset.
3. **Search**: A logistic regression classifier trained on the Search dataset.
4. **Name heuristic**: The name heuristic of Section 3.2.3.

We compare testing accuracy on both the Uniform dataset and Search datasets. For experiments in which systems are trained and tested on the same dataset, we report the average results of 10-fold cross-validation.

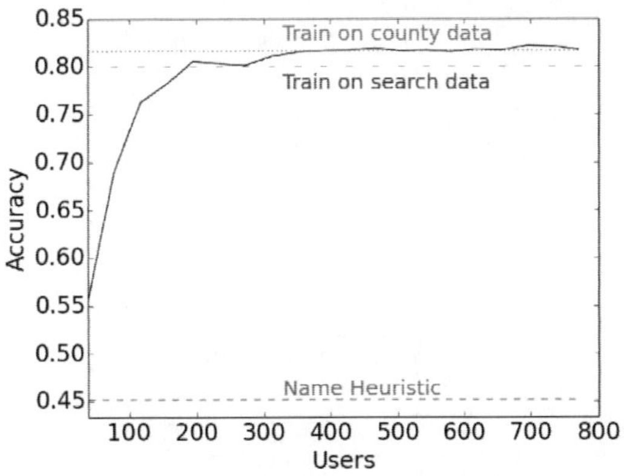

Figure 1: Learning curve for the Uniform dataset. The solid black line is the cross-validation accuracy of a logistic regression classifier trained using increasingly more labeled examples.

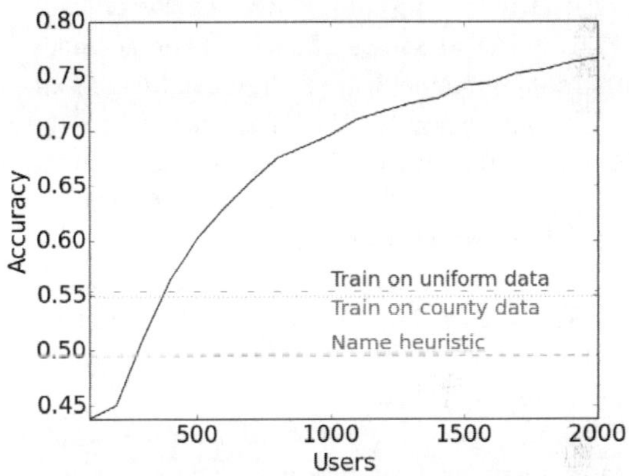

Figure 2: Learning curve for the Search dataset. The solid black line is the cross-validation accuracy of a logistic regression classifier trained using increasingly more labeled examples.

We tune the α regularization parameter for both ridge and logistic regression, reporting the best accuracy for each approach. Systems are implemented in Python using the `scikit-learn` library (Pedregosa and others, 2011).

4 Results

Figure 1 plots cross-validation accuracy on the Uniform dataset as the number of labeled examples increases. Surprisingly, the County model, which uses no user-labeled data, performs only slightly worse than the fully supervised approach (81.7% versus 82.2%). This suggests that the linguistic patterns learned from the county data can

Train \ Test	Search	Uniform
Search	0.7715	0.8000
Uniform	0.5535	0.8221
County	0.5490	0.8169
Name heuristic	0.4955	0.4519

Table 2: Accuracy of each system.

Train \ Test	Search	Uniform
Search	0.7650	0.8074
Uniform	0.4721	0.8130
County	0.4738	0.8050
Name heuristic	0.3838	0.3178

Table 3: F1 of each system.

Train \ Test	Search	Uniform
Search	0.7909	0.8250
Uniform	0.6659	0.8155
County	0.4781	0.7967
Name heuristic	0.5897	0.6886

Table 4: Precision of each system.

Train \ Test	County
Search	0.0190
Uniform	0.0361
County	0.0186
Name heuristic	0.0154

Table 5: Mean Squared Error of each system on the task of predicting the racial makeup of a county. Values are averages over the four race categories.

be transferred to make inferences at the user level.

Figure 1 also shows slightly lower accuracy from training on the Search dataset and testing on the Uniform dataset (80%). This may in part be due to the different label distributions between the datasets, as well as the different characteristics of the linguistic patterns, discussed more below.

The Name heuristic does poorly overall, mainly because few users provide their last names in their profiles, and only a fraction of those names are on the Census' name list.

Figure 2 plots the learning curve for the Search dataset. Here, the County approach performs considerably worse than logistic regression trained on the Search data. However, the County approach again performs comparable to the supervised Uniform approach. That is, training a supervised classifier on the Uniform dataset is only slightly more accurate than training only using county supervision (54.9% versus 55.3%). By F1, county supervision does slightly better than the Uniform approach. This again highlights the very different characteristics of the Uniform and Search datasets. Importantly, if we remove features from the user description field, then the cross-validation accuracy of the Search classifier is reduced from 77% to 67%. Since a small set of keywords in the description field were used to collect the Search data, the Search classifier simply recovers those keywords, thus inflating its performance.

Tables 2-4 show the accuracy, F1, and precision for each method (averaged over each class label). The relative trends are the same for each metric. The primary difference is the high precision of the Name heuristic — when users do provide a last name on the Census list, this heuristic predicts the correct race 69% of the time on the Uniform data, and 59% of the time on the Search data.

We additionally compute how well the different approaches predict the county demographics. For the County method, we perform 10-fold cross-validation, using the original county feature vectors as independent variables. For the logistic regression methods, we train the classifier on one of the user datasets (Uniform or Search), then classify each user in the county dataset. These predictions are aggregated to compute the proportion of each race per county. For the name heuristic, we only consider users who match a name in the Census list, and use the heuristic to compute the proportion of users of each race.

Table 5 displays the mean squared error between the predicted and true race proportions, averaged over all counties and races. The name heuristic outperforms all other systems on this task, in contrast to the previous results showing the name heuristic is the least accurate predictor at the user level. This is most likely because the name heuristic can ignore many users without penalty when predicting county proportions. The County method does better than the Search or Uniform methods, which is to be expected, since it was trained specifically for this task. It is possible that the Search and Uniform error can be reduced by adjusting for quantification bias (Forman, 2008),

Black	White	Latino	Asian
black	*white*	*spanish*	*asian*
african	*italian*	*latin*	asian
american	*irish*	*hispanic*	*filipino*
black	*british*	spanish	*korean*
the	*french*	*latino*	*chinese*
african	*german*	de	korean
young	*girl*	en	*japanese*
smh	*boy*	el	philippines
to	own	que	*vietnamese*
male	italian	latin	japanese
yall	*russian*	es	filipino
niggas	pretty	la	asians
woman	fucking	por	japan
rip	christmas	latino	chinese
man	buying	hispanic	many

Table 6: Top-weighted features for the classifier trained on the Search dataset. Terms from the description field are in italics.

Black	White	Latino	Asian
ain	makes	pizza	were
lmao	please	3rd	sorry
somebody	seriously	drunk	bit
tryna	guys	ti	hahaha
bout	whenever	gets	ma
nigga	snow	el	hurts
niggas	pretty	estoy	keep
black	literally	self	team
smh	thing	lucky	aw
tf	isn	special	food
lil	such	everywhere	sad
been	am	sleep	packed
real	red	la	care
everybody	glass	chicken	goodbye
gon	sucks	tried	forever

Table 7: Top-weighted features for the classifier trained on the Uniform dataset.

though we do not investigate this here.

4.1 Analysis of top features

Tables 6-8 show the top 15 features for each system, sorted by their corresponding model parameters. In both our training and testing process, we distinguish between words in the user description field and words in tweets. We also include a feature that indicates whether the user has any text at all in their profile description. In addition, we ignore mentions but retain hashtags. In these tables, words in description are shown in italics.

Because the Search dataset is collected by matching description keywords, in Table 6 many of these keywords are top-weighted features (e.g., 'black', 'white', 'spanish', 'asian'). However in Table 7, there is no top feature word from the description. This observation shows how our search dataset collection biases the resulting classifier.

The top features for the Uniform method (Table 7) tend to represent lexical variations and slang common among these groups. Interestingly, no terms from the profile description are strongly weighted, most likely a result of the uniform sampling approach, which does not bias the data to users with keywords in their profile.

For the County approach, it is less revealing to simply report the features with the highest weights. Since the regression models for each race were fit independently, many of the top-weighted words are stop words (as opposed to the logistic regression approach, which treats this as a multi-class classification problem). To report a more useful list of terms, we took the following steps: (1) we normalized the parameter vectors for each class by vector length; (2) from the parameter vector of each class we subtracted the vectors of the other three classes (i.e., $\beta^B \leftarrow \beta^B - (\beta^A + \beta^L + \beta^W)$). The resulting vectors better reflect the features weighted more highly in one class than others. We report the top 15 features per class.

The top features for the County method (Table 8) reveal a mixture of lexical variations as well as geographical indicators, which act as proxies for race. There are many Spanish words for Latino-American users, for example 'de', 'la', and 'que.' In addition there are some state names ('texas', 'hawaii'), part of city names ('san'), and abbreviations ('sfo' is the code for the San Francisco airport). Texas is 37.6% Hispanic-American, and San Francisco is 34.2% Asian-American. References to the photo-sharing site Instagram are found to be strongly indicative of Latino users. This is further supported by a survey conducted by the Pew Research Internet Project,[6] which found that while an equal percentage of White and Latino online adults use Twitter (16%), online Latinos were almost twice as likely to use Instagram (23% versus 12%). Additionally, the term

[6] http://www.pewinternet.org/files/2013/12/PIP_Social-Networking-2013.pdf

Black	White	Latino	Asian
follow	you	*texas*	ca
my	*NoDesc*	lol	san
be	and	la	hawaii
got	so	de	*hawaii*
up	*you*	que	hi
this	can	el	*http*
ain	re	*de*	*california*
university	have	no	haha
bout	is	*la*	francisco
get	*university*	tx	#hawaii
all	haha	*instagram*	*ca*
nigga	are	*tx*	beach
on	*justin*	*san*	*ig*
smh	to	en	*com*
niggas	would	*god*	sfo

Table 8: Top-weighted features for the regression model trained on the County dataset. Terms from the description field are in italics.

Truth	Predicted	Top Features
white	latino	de, la, que, no, *la*, el, san, en, amp, me
white	black	this, on, be, got, up, in, shit, at, the, all
black	white	you, and, to, *you*, the, is, so, of, have, re

Table 9: Misclassified by the County method.

"justin" in the user profile description is a strong indicator of White users – an inspection of the County dataset reveals that this is largely in reference to the pop musician Justin Bieber. (Recall that users typically do not enter their own names in the description field.)

We find some similarities with the results of Eisenstein et al. (2011) — e.g., the term 'smh' ("shaking my head") is a highly-ranked term for African-Americans.

4.2 Error Analysis

We sample a number of users who were misclassified, then identify the highest weighted features (using the dot product of the feature vector and parameter vector). Table 9 displays the top features of a sample of users in the Uniform dataset that were correctly classified by the Uniform method but misclassified by the County method. Similarly, Table 10 shows examples that were misclassified by the Uniform approach but correctly classified by the County approach.

Truth	Predicted	Top Features
black	white	makes, guys, thing, isn, am, again, haha, everyone, remember, very
black	white	please, guys, snow, pretty, literally, isn, am, again, happen, midnight
black	white	makes, snow, pretty, literally, am, again, happen, yay, beer, amazing

Table 10: Misclassified by the classifier trained on the Uniform dataset.

One common theme across all models is that because White is the most common class label, many common terms are correlated with it (e.g., the, is, of). Thus, for users that use only very common terms, the models tend to select the White label. Indeed, examining the confusion matrix reveals that the most common type of error is to misclassify a non-White user as White.

5 Conclusions and Future Work

Our results suggest that models fit on aggregate, geolocated social media data can be used estimate individual user attributes. While further analysis is needed to test how this generalizes to other attributes, this approach may provide a low-cost way of inferring user attributes. This in turn will benefit growing attempts to use social media as a complement to traditional polling methods — by quantifying the bias in a sample of social media users, we can then adjust inferences using approaches such as survey weighting (Gelman, 2007).

There are clear ethical concerns with how such a capability might be used, particularly if it is extended to estimate more sensitive user attributes (e.g., health status). Studies such as this may help elucidate what we reveal about ourselves through our language, intentionally or not.

In future work, we will consider richer user representations (e.g., social media activity, social connections), which have also been found to be indicative of user attributes. Additionally, we will consider combining labeled and unlabeled data using semi-supervised learning from label proportions (Quadrianto et al., 2009; Ganchev et al., 2010; Mann and McCallum, 2010).

References

F Al Zamal, W Liu, and D Ruths. 2012. Homophily and latent attribute inference: Inferring latent attributes of twitter users from neighbors. In *ICWSM*.

Shlomo Argamon, Sushant Dhawle, Moshe Koppel, and James W. Pennebaker. 2005. Lexical predictors of personality type. In *In proceedings of the Joint Annual Meeting of the Interface and the Classification Society of North America*.

John D. Burger, John Henderson, George Kim, and Guido Zarrella. 2011. Discriminating gender on twitter. In *Proceedings of the Conference on Empirical Methods in Natural Language Processing*, EMNLP '11, pages 1301–1309, Stroudsburg, PA, USA. Association for Computational Linguistics.

Jonathan Chang, Itamar Rosenn, Lars Backstrom, and Cameron Marlow. 2010. ePluribus: ethnicity on social networks. In *Fourth International AAAI Conference on Weblogs and Social Media*.

Aron Culotta. 2014. Estimating county health statistics with twitter. In *CHI*.

Mark Dredze. 2012. How social media will change public health. *IEEE Intelligent Systems*, 27(4):81–84.

Jacob Eisenstein, Noah A. Smith, and Eric P. Xing. 2011. Discovering sociolinguistic associations with structured sparsity. In *Proceedings of the 49th Annual Meeting of the Association for Computational Linguistics: Human Language Technologies - Volume 1*, HLT '11, pages 1365–1374, Stroudsburg, PA, USA. Association for Computational Linguistics.

George Forman. 2008. Quantifying counts and costs via classification. *Data Min. Knowl. Discov.*, 17(2):164–206, October.

Kuzman Ganchev, Joo Graca, Jennifer Gillenwater, and Ben Taskar. 2010. Posterior regularization for structured latent variable models. *J. Mach. Learn. Res.*, 11:2001–2049, August.

Daniel Gayo-Avello. 2011. Don't turn social media into another 'Literary digest' poll. *Commun. ACM*, 54(10):121–128, October.

Andrew Gelman. 2007. Struggles with survey weighting and regression modeling. *Statistical Science*, 22(2):153–164.

Sharad Goel, Jake M Hofman, and M Irmak Sirer. 2012. Who does what on the web: A large-scale study of browsing behavior. In *ICWSM*.

Shyam Gopinath, Jacquelyn S. Thomas, and Lakshman Krishnamurthi. 2014. Investigating the relationship between the content of online word of mouth, advertising, and brand performance. *Marketing Science*. Published online in Articles in Advance 10 Jan 2014.

Gary King. 1997. *A solution to the ecological inference problem: Reconstructing individual behavior from aggregate data*. Princeton University Press.

Wendy Liu and Derek Ruths. 2013. What's in a name? using first names as features for gender inference in twitter. In *AAAI Spring Symposium on Analyzing Microtext*.

Gideon S. Mann and Andrew McCallum. 2010. Generalized expectation criteria for semi-supervised learning with weakly labeled data. *J. Mach. Learn. Res.*, 11:955–984, March.

Alan Mislove, Sune Lehmann, Yong-Yeol Ahn, Jukka-Pekka Onnela, and J. Niels Rosenquist. 2011. Understanding the demographics of twitter users. In *Proceedings of the Fifth International AAAI Conference on Weblogs and Social Media (ICWSM'11)*, Barcelona, Spain.

Dong Nguyen, Noah A. Smith, and Carolyn P. Ros. 2011. Author age prediction from text using linear regression. In *Proceedings of the 5th ACL-HLT Workshop on Language Technology for Cultural Heritage, Social Scie nces, and Humanities*, LaTeCH '11, pages 115–123, Stroudsburg, PA, USA. Association for Computational Linguistics.

Brendan O'Connor, Ramnath Balasubramanyan, Bryan R. Routledge, and Noah A. Smith. 2010. From Tweets to polls: Linking text sentiment to public opinion time series. In *International AAAI Conference on Weblogs and Social Media*, Washington, D.C.

F. Pedregosa et al. 2011. Scikit-learn: Machine learning in Python. *Machine Learning Research*, 12:2825–2830. `http://dl.acm.org/citation.cfm?id=2078195`.

Marco Pennacchiotti and Ana-Maria Popescu. 2011. A machine learning approach to twitter user classification. In Lada A. Adamic, Ricardo A. Baeza-Yates, and Scott Counts, editors, *ICWSM*. The AAAI Press.

Novi Quadrianto, Alex J. Smola, Tibrio S. Caetano, and Quoc V. Le. 2009. Estimating labels from label proportions. *J. Mach. Learn. Res.*, 10:2349–2374, December.

Delip Rao, David Yarowsky, Abhishek Shreevats, and Manaswi Gupta. 2010. Classifying latent user attributes in twitter. In *Proceedings of the 2Nd International Workshop on Search and Mining User-generated Contents*, SMUC '10, pages 37–44, New York, NY, USA. ACM.

Delip Rao, Michael J. Paul, Clayton Fink, David Yarowsky, Timothy Oates, and Glen Coppersmith. 2011. Hierarchical bayesian models for latent attribute detection in social media. In *ICWSM*.

Sara Rosenthal and Kathleen McKeown. 2011. Age prediction in blogs: A study of style, content, and online behavior in pre- and post-social media generations. In *Proceedings of the 49th Annual Meeting of the Association for Computational Linguistics: Human Language Technologies - Volume 1*, HLT '11, pages 763–772, Stroudsburg, PA, USA. Association for Computational Linguistics.

Jonathan Schler, Moshe Koppel, Shlomo Argamon, and James W Pennebaker. 2006. Effects of age and gender on blogging. In *AAAI 2006 Spring Symposium on Computational Approaches to Analysing Weblogs (AAAI-CAAW)*, pages 06–03.

H Andrew Schwartz, Johannes C Eichstaedt, Margaret L Kern, Lukasz Dziurzynski, Stephanie M Ramones, Megha Agrawal, Achal Shah, Michal Kosinski, David Stillwell, Martin E P Seligman, and Lyle H Ungar. 2013a. Personality, gender, and age in the language of social media: the open-vocabulary approach. *PloS one*, 8(9):e73791. PMID: 24086296.

H Andrew Schwartz, Johannes C Eichstaedt, Margaret L Kern, Lukasz Dziurzynski, Stephanie M Ramones, Megha Agrawal, Achal Shah, Michal Kosinski, David Stillwell, Martin EP Seligman, et al. 2013b. Characterizing geographic variation in well-being using tweets. In *Seventh International AAAI Conference on Weblogs and Social Media*.

The Enrollment Effect: A Study of Amazon's Vine Program

Dinesh Puranam
Samuel Curtis Johnson
Graduate School of Management
Cornell University
dp457@cornell.edu

Claire Cardie
Department of Computer Science
Department of Information Science
Cornell University
cardie@cs.cornell.edu

Abstract

Do rewards from retailers such as free products and recognition in the form of status badges[1] influence the recipient's behavior? We present a novel application of natural language processing to detect differences in consumer behavior due to such rewards. Specifically, we investigate the "Enrollment" effect, i.e. whether receiving products for free affect how consumer reviews are written. Using data from Amazon's Vine program, we conduct a detailed analysis to detect stylistic differences in product reviews written by reviewers before and after enrollment in the Vine program. Our analysis suggests that the "Enrollment" effect exists. Further, we are able to characterize the effect on syntactic and semantic dimensions. This work has implications for researchers, firms and consumer advocates studying the influence of user-generated content as these changes in style could potentially influence consumer decisions.

1 Introduction

In 2007 Amazon introduced its Vine program[2]. According to Amazon, "Amazon invites customers to become Vine Voices based on their reviewer rank, which is a reflection of the quality and helpfulness of their reviews as judged by other Amazon customers. Amazon provides Vine members with free products that have been submitted to the program by participating vendors. Vine reviews are the "*independent opinions* of the Vine Voices."[3] There could be potential concerns as to whether this enrollment affects the way reviews are written, introducing, for example, a positive bias.[4]

In this work, we investigate whether enrollment in the Vine program results in changes in the linguistic style used in reviews. We investigate this by looking at reviews by individuals before and after enrollment in the program. Following Feng et al. (2012) and Bergsma et al. (2012), we conduct a stylometric analysis using a number of syntactic and semantic features to detect differences in style. We believe that detecting changes in consumer behavior due to intervention by a firm is a novel natural language processing task. Our approach offers a framework for analyzing text to detect these changes. This work is relevant for social scientists and consumer advocates as research suggests that product reviews are influential (Chevalier and Mayzlin, 2006) and changes in style could potentially influence consumer decisions.

2 Related Work

Our work lies at the intersection of research in four broad areas — Product Reviews, Product Sampling, Status and Stylometry.

Product Reviews Product reviews have received considerable attention in multiple disciplines including Marketing, Computer Science and Information Science. Research has addressed questions such as the influence of product reviews on product sales and on brands (Gopinath et al. (2014); Chevalier and Mayzlin (2006)), detection of deceptive reviews (Ott et al., 2011) and sentiment summarization (Titov and McDonald, 2008).

[1] A status badge is a special identification usually placed next to a username in online content.

[2] http://blog.librarything.com/main/2007/08/amazon-vine-and-early-reviewers/

[3] http://www.amazon.com/gp/vine/help, words italicized by authors.

[4] http://www.npr.org/blogs/money/2013/10/29/241372607/top-reviewers-on-amazon-get-tons-of-free-stuff.

Proceedings of the Joint Workshop on Social Dynamics and Personal Attributes in Social Media, pages 17–27,
Baltimore, Maryland USA, 27 June 2014.

This list is by no means comprehensive, but it is indicative of the extensive work in this domain.

Product Sampling Here, consumers receive products for free — as a marketing tactic. This is also a well-studied phenomenon. Research in this area has indicated that consumers value free products (Shampanier et al. (2007); Palmeira and Srivastava (2013)); that product sampling affects brand sales (Bawa and Shoemaker, 2004) and that sampling influences consumer behavior (Wadhwa et al., 2008).

Status Research shows that status can influence writing style. Danescu-Niculescu-Mizil et al. (2012) study discussions among Wikipedia editors and transcripts of oral arguments before the U.S. Supreme Court and show how variations in linguistic style can provide information about power differences within social groups.

Stylometry focuses on the recognition of style elements to identify authors (Rosen-Zvi et al., 2004), detect genders and even determine the venue where an academic paper was presented (Bergsma et al., 2012).

Our work draws from each of these research areas and in turn hopes to make a contribution to each in return. Our primary objective is to establish a framework to detect behavioral change due to a decision by a firm (in this case enrollment to the Vine program characterized by free products and Vine membership status) by analyzing product reviews. Further, we hope to understand the dimensions on which this behavior may have changed. Consequently, we pursue a novel stylometric task. This type of work is especially important when the traditional numerical measure (rating) suggests there is no difference in the review pre and post-enrollment (see Section 4).

3 Data & Pre-processing Steps

We gathered all reviews by the top 10,000 reviewers ranked by Amazon as of September, 2012. These rankings are partly driven by helpfulness and recency of reviews[5]. The data collected includes the review text, review title, rating assigned, date posted, product URL, product price, whether the reviewed product was received for free via the Vine program (also referred to as "Vine Review"), "helpfulness" votes and badges received by the reviewer .

We collected a total of 2,464,141 reviews of which 282,913 reviews were for products received for free via the Vine program. These reviews covered a total of 9,982 reviewers[6] of which 3,566 were members of the Vine program. Approximately half the reviews belonged to Vine members. We eliminated reviews that did not have a rating. We further excluded reviews where the review text was less than 20 words in length. We were left with 1,189,704 reviews by Vine members.

The date of enrollment to the Vine program for each reviewer is not explicitly available. We infer the date of enrollment in the following manner. We sort in ascending order all the "Vine Reviews" for each reviewer by posted date. We assume the earliest posted date for a "Vine review" is the enrollment date. This is an important assumption, as potentially reviewers could have moved in and out of the program at varying points of time. Reviewers can be moved out of the program for reasons such as not posting a "Vine Review" within 30 days of receipt of the product. In our data set we found 47,510 "Vine Reviews" by 163 reviewers who were not actively on the Vine program [7]. We can view these reviewers as having been dropped from the Vine program. Given the small volume of this type of reviews and reviewers, our assumption on date of enrollment appears reasonable.

Member Type	Free/ Paid	Enrollment Timing	Review Count
Non Vine	Paid	NA	1,169,561
Non Vine	Free	NA	47,510
Vine	Paid	Post	452,729
Vine	Paid	Pre	503,688
Vine	Free	Post	233,287

Table 1: Data Summary

4 Enrollment Effect

This research seeks to answer the question: does enrollment in the Vine program change the writing styles of reviewers. One naive theory is that

[5] http://www.amazon.com/review/guidelines/top-reviewers.html/

[6] During the crawling, ranks changed resulting in fewer than 10,000 reviewers in our data set.

[7] As these reviewers were not enrolled to Amazon's Vine Program as of September, 2012, they are excluded from our analysis.

perhaps receiving products for free and receiving status badges will result in Vine members posting more positive reviews. Interestingly, the average rating for reviews by Vine members posted before enrollment is 4.22 and after enrollment is 4.21 and this difference is not statistically significant. In contrast, the length of reviews significantly increased from 251 words prior to enrollment to 306 words post-enrollment. Natural language techniques are the only option to further investigate possible effects of enrollment. Consequently we focus on the review text posted by Vine members.

4.1 Approach

Following Ashok et al. (2013) and Bergsma et al. (2012) we construct features that represent writing style from each review (discussed in more detail in the next section). We incorporate these features in a classification algorithm that attempts to classify each review as having been written pre or post-enrollment to the Vine program. We report whether the difference in accuracy for this classifier vs. a majority vote classification is statistically significant or not. In order to detect differences in style pre and post-enrollment, we need to address certain confounding factors — Reviewer Specificity , Product Specificity and Time Specificity.

Reviewer Specificity It may be possible that certain users post more reviews post-enrollment than pre-enrollment. Consequently the classifier may simply end up learning the differences in style *between* reviewers. To avoid this, we construct a balanced sample where we randomly select 25 reviews for each reviewer prior to and post-enrollment (see Table 2). This also sets our baseline accuracy at 50%.

Product Specificity As the program started in 2007, the post-enrollment reviews are likely to predominantly contain products released in after 2007. This might result in the classifier simply learning the differences *between* products (say I Phone vs Palm). Given our focus on style, we do not use word tokens as such - thus avoiding the use of product specific features. However, for some products, the product specific details may result in the use of specific syntactic structures. We assume this is not a significant contributor to the prediction performance. A post-hoc analysis of the top features supports this assumption. A second source of change in writing style could be due to simply whether the product was bought or received for free. We exclude "Vine Reviews" [8] to eliminate this confounding factor.

Time Specificity A similar concern as *Product Specificity* exists for date references. By focusing on syntactic and semantic style, we avoid the use of time specific features.

Another concern is that perhaps post enrollment, reviewers receive writing guidelines from Amazon. This does not appear to be the case, as the writing guidelines [9] appear to be for all members.We now turn to the extraction of style features.

Data Type	Number of Reviews	Number of Reviewers
Training	113,250	2,265
Test	2,500	50

Table 2: Experiment Data

4.2 Feature Extraction

We consider three different features — "Bag of words/ unigrams", "Parse Tree Based Features" and an umbrella category consisting of genre and semantic features (see Section 4.2.3).

4.2.1 Bag of Words

Bag of Words/Unigrams (UNIGRAMS) Unigrams have often been found to be effective predictive features (Joachims, 2001). In our context, this serves as a competitive baseline for the classification task.

4.2.2 Parse Tree Based Features

Following Feng et al. (2012) and Ashok et al. (2013) we use Probabilistic Context Free Grammar (PCFG) to construct a parse tree for each sentence. We then generate features from this parse tree and aggregate features to a review level.

All Production Rules (Γ) This set of features include all production rule features for each review, including the leaves of the parse tree for

[8] Reviews where product was received for free via the Vine program.

[9] http://www.amazon.com/gp/community-help/customer-reviews-guidelines

each sentence in the review. This effectively represents a combination of production rules and unigrams as features and represents an additional competitive baseline.

Non Terminal Production Rules (Γ^N) This excludes the leaves and hence restricts the feature set to non-terminal production rules. This allows us to investigate purely syntactic features from the text.

Phrasal/ Clausal Nodes (PHR/CLSL) We also investigate features that incorporate phrasal or clausal nodes of the parse trees. Please see Table 5 and Table 6 for examples of these features.

Parse Tree Measures (PTM) We construct a set of measures for each sentence based on the parse tree. These measures are maximum height of parse tree, maximum width of the parse tree and the number of sentences in each review.

Latent Dirichlet Allocation (LDA) We also apply Latent Dirichlet Allocation (Blei et al., 2003) to the production rules extracted from the Probabilistic Context Free Grammar. We use the topics generated as features in our prediction task. Our objective was to determine whether certain co-occurring production rules offered better classification accuracy. Our implementation includes hyper-parameter optimization via maximum likelihood. The number of topics is selected by maximizing the pairwise cosine distance amongst topics. We used the Stanford Parser (Klein and Manning, 2003) to parse each of the reviews and the Natural Language Toolkit (NLTK) (Bird et al., 2009) to post process the results.

4.2.3 Genre and Semantic Features

Style Metrics (STYLE) This includes three distinct types of metrics. *Character Based* - This includes counts of uppercased letters, number of letters, number of spaces and number of vowels. *Word Based* - This includes measures such as number of short words (3 characters or less), long words (8 characters or less), average word length and number of different words. *Syntax Based* - This includes measures such as number of periods, commas, common conjunctions, interrogatives, prepositions, pronouns and verbs.

Parts of Speech (POS) features have often been surprisingly effective in tasks such as predicting deception (Ott et al., 2011). Consequently we test this feature set as well.

Domain-independent Dictionary We make use of the Linguistic Inquiry and Word Count (LIWC) categorization (Tausczik and Pennebaker, 2010). One key advantage of this categorization is that it is domain independent and emphasizes psycho-linguistic cues. We run two variants of this set of features. The first (LIWC ALL) includes all the categories — both sub-ordinate and super-ordinate categories. The second (LIWC SUB CATEG.) only includes the sub-ordinate categories, thus ensuring the features are mutually exclusive.

Subjectivity Measures (OPINION) We measure number of subjective, objective and other (neither subjective nor objective) sentences in each review. We use the "OpinionFinder System" (Wiebe et al., 2005) to classify each sentence with these measures. We aggregate the count of subjective, objective and other sentences at the review level and use these aggregates as features.[10] We also report results on experiments where multiple feature types are included simultaneously in the model.

5 Experimental Methodology

All experiments use the Fan et al. (2008) implementation of linear Support Vector Machines (Vapnik, 1998). The linear specification allows us to infer feature importance. We learn the penalty parameter via grid search using 5 fold cross-validation and report performance on a held-out balanced sample of reviews from 50 randomly selected users (all of whom were excluded from the training set) from the group of reviewers with at least 25 reviews in pre and post enrollment periods. While reporting the results, for some features we report the threshold (Thr) value set to exclude the least frequent features. These thresholds were also learned via the 5 fold cross validation process. Finally, text features can be binarized, mean centered and/or normalized. Each of these options were also selected via 5 fold cross validation.

6 Results & Analysis

All of the feature sets perform statistically better[11] than a majority vote (50%).

Baselines Unsurprisingly, the feature set containing all production rules (Γ) yields the best ac-

[10] One drawback is that the classifiers are trained on sentences from the MPQA corpus. Domain specificity is likely to yield poorer classification performance on our data.

[11] as indicated by a paired t-test at p=0.05 on the held out sample

Baselines		
Style Features	**Feature Count**	**Accuracy**
UNIGRAMS	796,826	60.9 %
Γ (Thr =50)	29,362	62.0 %
By Feature Type		
Style Features	**Feature Count**	**Accuracy**
Γ^N (Thr=200)	2,730	59.2 %
PHR/CLSL	23	57.4 %
PTM	3	55.8 %
LDA	200	54.0 %
STYLE	26	57.6 %
POS	45	57.5 %
LIWC ALL	76	59.8 %
LIWC SUB CATEG.	67	60.3 %
OPINION	3	56.3 %
Feature Combinations		
Style Features	**Feature Count**	**Accuracy**
Γ^N (THR=200) + STYLE	2,756	57.9 %
Γ^N (THR=200) + OPINION	2,733	56.2 %
PHR/CLSL + OPINION	26	58.0 %
PHR/CLSL + STYLE	49	57.5 %
LIWC + STYLE	93	60.2 %
LIWC + PHR/CLSL	90	60.2 %
LIWC + Γ^N (Thr=200)	2,797	59.1 %
LIWC + OPINION	70	60.3 %
PTM + OPINION	6	57.2 %
STYLE + OPINION	29	58.7 %
STYLE + PTM	29	57.4 %
LIWC +STYLE+PHR/CLSL	116	60.1 %

Table 3: Experiment Results

curacy (62.0 %). Unfortunately, as expected, the top features all included terminal production rules that signal time or product specificity. For example in the pre-enrollment reviews the top 10 features for Γ include NNP $\rightarrow$ 'Update', CD $\rightarrow$ '2006', NNP $\rightarrow$ 'XP' and NNP $\rightarrow$ 'Palm'. In the post-enrollment reviews the top 10 features include CD $\rightarrow$ '2012',CD $\rightarrow$ '2011', NN $\rightarrow$ 'iPad' and NN $\rightarrow$ 'iPhone'. We observe the same issue with the UNIGRAMS feature set. This supports our contention that the analysis should restrict itself to style and domain-independent features. The best performing style feature set is LIWC SUB CATEG. followed by Non Terminal Production Rules (Γ^N). OPINION is the most parsimonious feature set that performs significantly better than a majority vote.

Non Terminal Production Rules (Γ^N) Table 7 presents the top Non Terminal Production Rules. We observe the following: First, pre-enrollment reviews have noun phrases(NP) that contain fewer leaf nodes than in the post-enrollment reviews. This appears to be due to the inclusion of determiners (DT), adjectives (JJ), comparative adjectives (JJR), personal pronouns (PRP $) or simply more nouns (NN). This might indicate that topics are discussed with more *specifics* in post-enrollment reviews. Second, clauses(S) begin with action oriented verb phrases (VP) in the pre-enrollment reviews. In contrast in the post-enrollment reviews clauses connect two clauses using coordinating conjunctions(CC) or prepositions(IN). One possibility is that reviewers are offering more *detail/concepts per sentence* (where each clause is a detail/concept) in the post-enrollment reviews. Finally, we observe that pre-enrollment reviews include adjectival phrases (ADJP) connect to superlative adverbs (RBS)which convey *certainty*. We will revisit this finding when we review the results from the LIWC model below.

Phrasal/Clausal (PHR./CLSL.) Tables 5 and 6 suggest that post-enrollment reviews emphasize information using *descriptive phrases* — adjectival phrases (ADJP) and adverbial phrases (ADVP) — and *quantifier phrases* (QP). Pre-enrollment reviews appear to have more *complex* clause structures (SBAR, SINV, SQ, SBARQ - see table 5 for definitions).

Parse Tree Metrics (PTM) The three features used are number of sentences, maximum height of parse tree and the maximum width of the parse tree, listed here in descending order of importance for the post-enrollment reviews. As mentioned earlier in section 4 the *average review length* is higher in the post-enrollment reviews so the finding that the number of sentences predict post-enrollment reviews is consistent. Maximum tree width predicts the pre-enrollment reviews. This flat structure indicates a more *complex* communication structure.

Latent Dirichlet Allocation (LDA) This model did not perform very well, being statistically marginally better than majority vote. As mentioned before, we selected the number of topics by maximizing the average cosine distance amongst topics. Even with 200 topics, this measure was 0.39, suggesting that the topics were themselves not well separated. In the limit, each topic would be a non-terminal production rule. This is the same as Non Terminal Production Rules (Γ^N) feature set discussed earlier in this section.

Predicts PRE Enrollment
'number of different words', 'uppercase', 'alphas', 'vowels' , 'short words', 'words per sentence', 'to be words' , 'punctuation symbols', 'long words', 'common prepositions'
Predicts POST Enrollment
'average word length', 'spaces', 'verbs are', 'chars per sentence' , 'verbs be', 'common conjunctions', 'verbs were', 'personal pronouns' , 'verbs was', 'verbs am'

Table 4: Style Metrics: Top Features

Style (STYLE) Table 4 presents the top features for this feature set. The features suggest that reviewers used a more varied vocabulary (number of different words), more words per sentence (words per sentence) and more long words (long words) in pre-enrollment than in post-enrollment reviews. This might indicate that sentences in the pre-enrollment reviews were longer and more *complex*. Interestingly, the average word length did go up in the post-enrollment reviews as did the characters per sentence. In addition, more personal pronouns and conjunctions are used — a finding replicated in the model using LIWC features (see below).

Parts of Speech (POS) The top features for post-enrollment are commas, periods, comparative adjectives, verb phrases and coordinating conjunctions. The top features for pre-enrollment are nouns, noun phrases, determiners , prepositions and superlative adverbs. These results are more difficult to interpret though the use of comparative adjectives suggest more *comparisons* between different objects in the post enrollment reviews.

LIWC SUB CATEG. The top 10 LIWC features are shown in Table 8. LIWC features are categories that are contained in broader categories. For example POSEMO (see Table 8, first feature for "Predicts POST enrollment") refers to the class of positive emotion words. POSEMO itself is contained in a category called "Affective Features" which in turn is classified as a Psychological Process (abbreviated to Pscyh.). The analysis of the categories of features is in itself interesting. Psych./ Cognitive Features occur higher up in features predictive of pre-enrollment reviews than in the features predictive of post-enrollment reviews. "Psych./ Affective Features" occurs as a top feature for the post-enrollment reviews. The actual feature from the "Psych./ Affective Features" category is POSEMO suggesting that the *positive emotion* is more strongly conveyed in the post-enrollment reviews than in the pre-enrollment reviews. Interestingly the corresponding negative feature NEGEMO is in the top 10 features predicting the pre-enrollment reviews. This is especially intriguing since the average rating for reviews in the pre and post-enrollment reviews is the same (see 4). We were concerned that possibly our sampling had induced a bias in the ratings. But the average ratings in our sample are 4.18 and 4.19 pre and post-enrollment respectively (difference is not statistically significant).

FUNCTION WORDS occur extensively in the post-enrollment reviews. We also observe that inclusive (INCL) and exclusive (EXCL) terms are used more in the post-enrollment reviews. Its possible that reviewers are seeking to be more *balanced*. Products are described in personal (I), perceptual (FEEL) and relativistic (SPACE) terms. Pre-enrollment reviews discuss personal concerns (LEISURE, RELIG) , indicate a level of *certainty* (CERTAIN) and opinions are presented in terms of thought process (INSIGHT). Interestingly, the pre-enrollment reviews address the reader (YOU).

Opinions (OPINION) Features predicting post-enrollment are number of objective sentences, number of subjective sentences and finally number of other (neither subjective nor objective) sentences. This suggests that reviewers try to write somewhat more objectively in the post-enrollment reviews.

Feature Combinations With the exception of the combinations STYLE + OPINION , PHR/CLSL +OPINION and PTM + OPINION which improve on either feature set used alone, none of the other combinations improved performance over all component feature sets modeled individually. Overall, none of the combinations improved over LIWC SUB CATEG. Hence we do not delve further into features from these models.

Summary Overall pre-enrollment reviews are more complex (complex clauses, wide parse trees, varied vocabulary, more words per sentence), have fewer concepts per sentence, contain negative emotions, addresses the reader directly and are more certain. Post-enrollment reviews are longer, more descriptive, contain comparisons, contain quantifiers, have more positive emotion and describe the product experience in physical and personal terms.

Predicts PRE Enrollment	
1 NP (Noun Phrase)	6 LST (List marker. Includes surrounding punctuation)
EXAMPLE 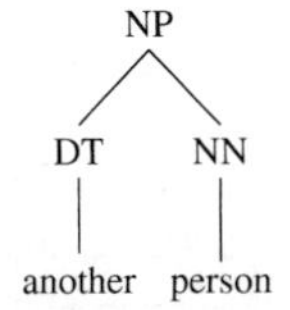	EXAMPLE (3)
2 SBAR (Clause introduced by a (possibly empty) subordinating conjunction)	7 VP (Verb Phrase)
EXAMPLE 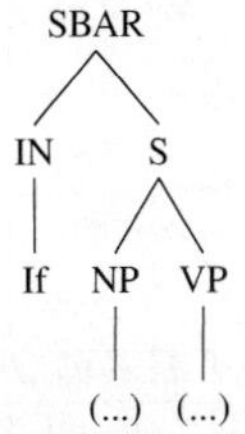	EXAMPLE 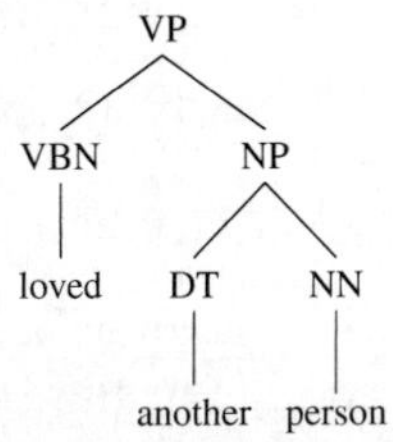
3 SQ (Inverted yes/no question, or main clause of a wh-question, following the wh-phrase in SBARQ)	8 PRN (Parenthetical)
EXAMPLE 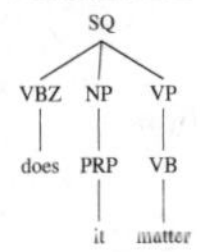	EXAMPLE (p. 73)
4 NAC (Not a Constituent; used to show the scope of certain prenominal modifiers within an NP)	9 SINV (Inverted declarative sentence, i.e. one in which the subject follows the tensed verb or modal)
EXAMPLE 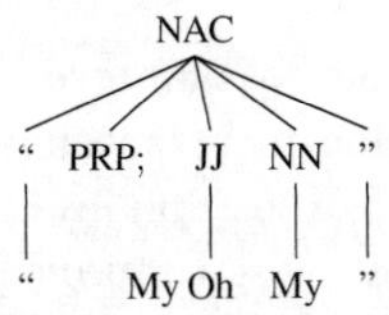	EXAMPLE 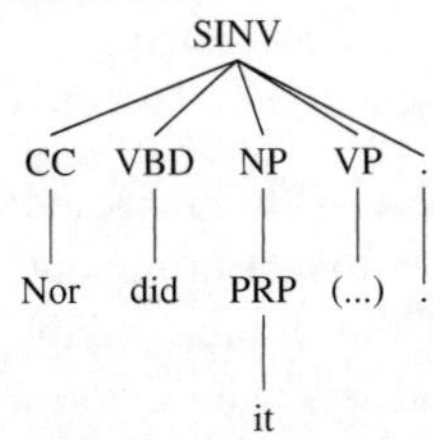
5 SBARQ (Direct question introduced by a wh-word or a wh-phrase)	10 NX (Used within certain complex NPs to mark the head of the NP)
EXAMPLE 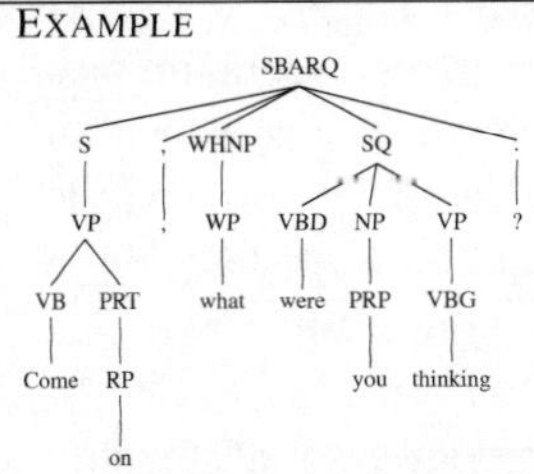	EXAMPLE 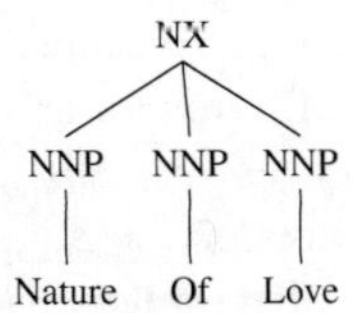

Table 5: Phr/Clsl: Top Features PRE

Predicts POST Enrollment	
1 S (Simple declarative clause)	6 FRAG (Fragment)
EXAMPLE 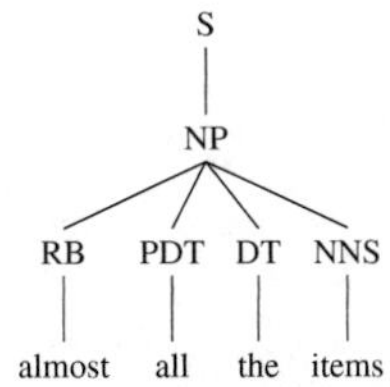	EXAMPLE 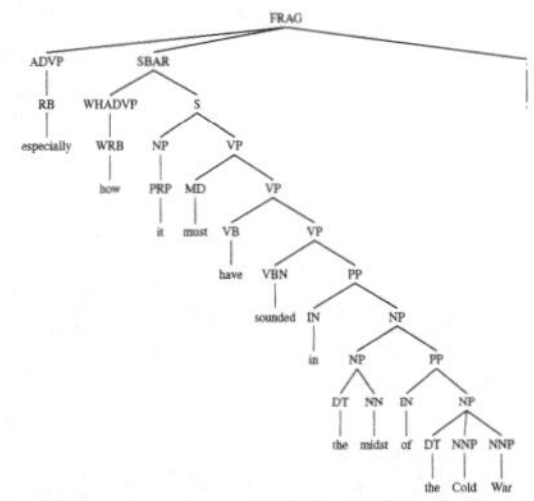
2 ADJP (Adjective Phrase)	7 QP (Quantifier Phrase)
EXAMPLE 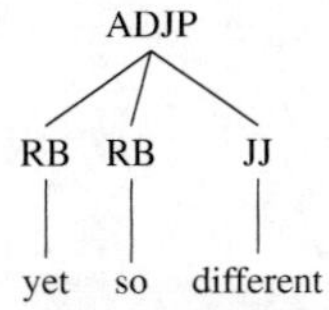	EXAMPLE 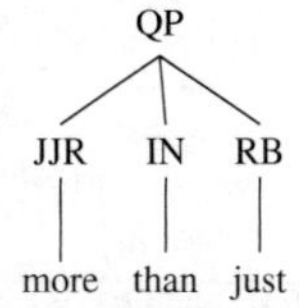
3 PRT (Particle. Category for words that should be tagged RP)	8 WHNP (Wh-noun Phrase)
EXAMPLE 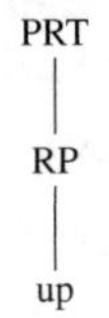	EXAMPLE 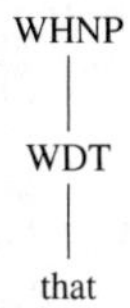
4 ADVP (Adverb Phrase)	9 UCP (Unlike Coordinated Phrase)
EXAMPLE 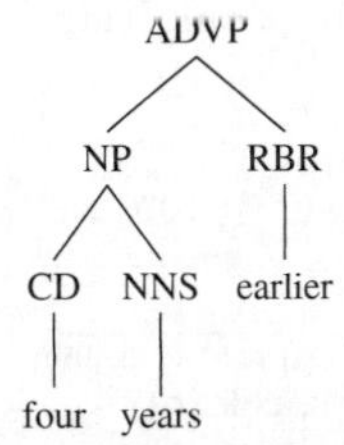	EXAMPLE 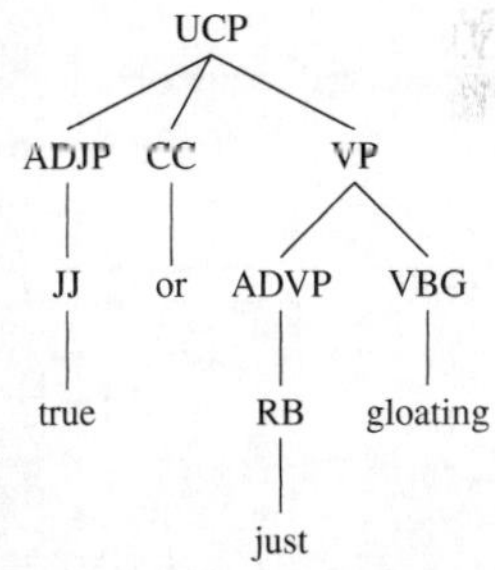
5 X (Unknown, uncertain, or unbracketable)	10 CONJP (Conjunction Phrase)
EXAMPLE 	EXAMPLE 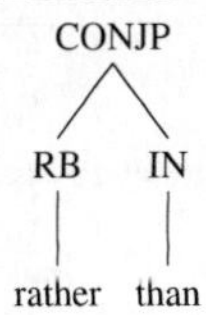

Table 6: Phr/Clsl: Top Features POST

Predicts PRE Enrollment	
Feature	**Examples**
ROOT → S	(1) And nearly every single item seemed cute and usable to me. (2) Look closely, (...) overwhelming personal and cultural upheaval.
NP → NNP NNP	(1) Tim Bess (2) Jennifer Fitch
PP → IN NP	(1) for its psychological and emotional richness (2) of loyalty
NP → DT NN	(1) the price (2) a book
NP → NNP POS	(1) Frost 's (2) Clough 's
ADJP → RBS JJ	(1) most assuredly (2) most entertaining
WHNP → WP	(1) who (2) what
NP → NNP	(1) Blessed (2) India
PP → TO NP	(1) to the crime (2) to me
S → VP	(1) linking Pye to the crime scene (2) Gripping due to (...)
Predicts POST Enrollment	
Feature	**Examples**
S → S , IN S .	(1) It is functionally the same as Apple's 10 watt charger which outputs 2.1 A , so it is also suitable for charging the iPad. (2) It has 3 levels of trays that spread as you open the box, so you can easily access contents in all trays.
S → IN NP VP .	(1) So I don't think the investment in graphics (...) enjoyability in the game. (2) So we decided to try it again this year.
ROOT → NP	(1) Some kind of (...) disorder ? (2) Proper Alignment and Posture; This segment (...) .
S → S CC S .	(1) Mage and Takumo (...) but lacking in depth.(2) The light feature is great and it powers off (...).
NP → PRP$ NNP NN	(1) your Alpine yodeling (2) my MacBook Pro
S → VP .	(1) Enough negativity. (2) Suffice it to say that (...) .
NP → DT JJR NN	(1) a better future (2) a slower flow
NP → DT JJ , JJ NN	(1) an immediate , visceral reaction (2)a roots-based, singer-songwriter effort
NP → DT NNP NNP NNP NNP	(1) the Post-Total Body Weight Training (2) The Gunfighter DVD Gregory Peck
WHADVP → WRB RB	(1) How far (2) how well

Table 7: Γ^N : Top Features (PCFG Non Terminal)

Predicts PRE Enrollment		
Feature	**Category**	**Examples**
leisure	Personal Concerns	Cook, chat, movie
verb	Function words	Walk, want, see
certain	Psych./Cognitive Processes	always, never
insight	Psych./Cognitive Processes	think, know, consider
negemo	Psych./Affective Processes	Hurt, ugly, nasty
exclam	Exclamation	!
period	Period	.
you	Function words	2nd person , you, your
preps	Function words	to, with, above
relig	Personal Concerns	2nd synagogue, sacred
Predicts POST Enrollment		
Feature	**Category**	**Examples**
posemo	Psych./Affective Processes	Love, nice, sweet
article	Function words	a, an, the
i	Function words	1st person singular.
space	Psych./Relativity	Down, in, thin
ingest	Psych./Biological Processes	Dish, eat, pizza
ipron	Function words	Impersonal Pronouns, it its , those
incl	Psych./Cognitive Processes	Inclusive, and, with , include
conj	Function words	and, but, whereas
excl	Psych./Cognitive Processes	Exclusive but, without, exclude
feel	Psych./Perceptual Processes	feels , touch

Table 8: LIWC Sub Category : Top Features

These reviews are are specific, balanced and contain more objective sentences as well.

Discussion on Readability One possibility is that the "Enrollment" effect leads to reviewers writing more readable reviews. To test this hypothesis we performed a paired t-test between readability scores for pre and post-enrollment reviews. Table 9 suggests that indeed this is the case. Flesch Reading Ease is the only measure where a higher score indicates simpler text. For the rest of the measures a higher score implies more complex text. All of the measures are within the average readability range and the magnitude of the differences are small. Nevertheless, these differences are statistically significant [12] with one exception lending support to the idea that "Enrollment" effect might lead to reviewers writing more readable reviews.

[12]The cell size for each class is 57,875, making the modest difference in magnitude statistically significant.

Reading Measure /Cite	Pre Mean	Post Mean	t Value
ARI /(Senter and Smith, 1967)	9.16	9.15	(0.45)
Coleman Liau /(Coleman and Liau, 1975)	8.76	8.68	(6.39)*
Flesch Kincaid /(Kincaid et al., 1975)	8.75	8.71	(2.19)*
Flesch Reading Ease /(Kincaid et al., 1975)	65.63	66.18	6.61*
Gunning Fog /(Gunning, 1952)	11.75	11.70	(2.18)*
LIX /(Anderson, 1983)	38.24	38.07	(2.89)*
RIX /(Anderson, 1983)	3.74	3.71	(3.05)*
SMOG /(McLaughlin, 1969)	10.59	10.56	(2.56)*
* Significant at 5% level			

Table 9: Readability Measures

7 Discussion

So far we have ignored the possibility that writing styles of reviewers may simply continuously evolve with experience and we are simply detecting a difference due to this underlying trend. [13] To address this question we investigated the sub-periods within the the pre and post enrollment periods.

We split the post enrollment period (i.e. from date of enrollment to the date the most recent review was posted) further into two equal time periods for each reviewer. As before, we learn a classifier to discriminate between the sub periods. Interestingly the classifier performed the same as chance at p=0.05 (Test Accuracy= 51.0%).[14] [15] However a similar analysis in the pre-enrollment period results in a test set accuracy of 63.3% (significant at p=0.05). So there is a change in writing style within the pre-enrollment period, but there is no continued change post-enrollment. This is not consistent with the continuous style evolution hypothesis. One account would be that Amazon enrolls reviewers whose styles have stabilized. This remains a possibility as Amazon actively selects the members (and we are not aware of the specific rules used by Amazon). The trends (see Figure 1)suggest that there are changes right upto the enrollment dateand some levelling out in the post enrollment period , providing some evidence against this hypothesis.

[13] Ideally, if a) the enrollment date had been the same for all reviewers and b) the enrollment was random, we would have a clean experimental framework to detect whether a similar trend exists for non-vine reviewers. Unfortunately, this is not the case.

[14] We report the results only on POS for conciseness. The other feature sets performed similarly.

[15] As before the test sample includes 50 users. However we sampled only 10 reviews in each sub period. Corresponding down sampled performance for Pre vs Post enrollment accuracy is 57.5% (significant at p=0.05)using POS features.

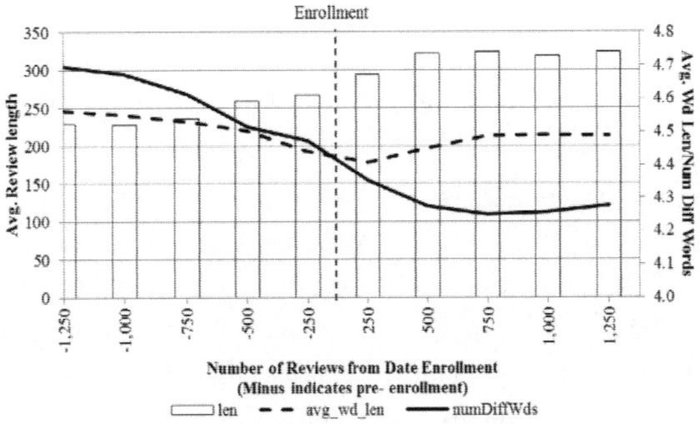

Figure 1: Feature Trends

	Train Size	Test Size	Accuracy
Within Pre-Enrollment	44,800	1000	63.3%
Within Post-Enrollment	59,250	1000	51.0%
Pre vs Post Enroll. Down Sampled	53,840	1000	57.5%

Table 10: Sub Period Results

8 Conclusion

We view this work as a first step toward investigating this phenomenon further. In particular, we plan to test the robustness of our results w.r.t. product specificity, to investigate stylistic differences (a) between reviews for purchased products versus for products received for free amongst Vine members and (b) between reviews by Vine reviewers and non-Vine reviewers. Another line of inquiry involves decomposing the "Enrollment" effect into a reputation/status effect (the influence of the status badge - Vine membership) and a product sampling effect (the influence of receiving goods for free). Finally, investigating the temporal dynamics of style for these reviewers might prove interesting as would determining whether these subtle differences in style affect the *readers* and influence purchase decisions.

9 Acknowledgements

We would like to thank our reviewers for insightful comments that we sought to address here. We would also like to thank Myle Ott for generously sharing the data.

References

Jonathan Anderson. Lix and rix: Variations on a little-known readability index. *Journal of Reading*, pages 490–496, 1983.

Vikas Ganjigunte Ashok, Song Feng, and Yejin Choi. Success with style: Using writing style to predict the success of novels. *Poetry*, 580(9): 70, 2013.

Kapil Bawa and Robert Shoemaker. The effects of free sample promotions on incremental brand sales. *Marketing Science*, 23(3):345–363, 2004.

Shane Bergsma, Matt Post, and David Yarowsky. Stylometric analysis of scientific articles. In *Proceedings of the 2012 Conference of the North American Chapter of the Association for Computational Linguistics: Human Language Technologies*, pages 327–337. Association for Computational Linguistics, 2012.

Steven Bird, Ewan Klein, and Edward Loper. *Natural Language Processing with Python*. O'Reilly Media, 2009.

David M Blei, Andrew Y Ng, and Michael I Jordan. Latent dirichlet allocation. *the Journal of machine Learning research*, 3:993–1022, 2003.

Judith A Chevalier and Dina Mayzlin. The effect of word of mouth on sales: Online book reviews. *Journal of marketing research*, 43(3): 345–354, 2006.

Meri Coleman and TL Liau. A computer readability formula designed for machine scoring. *Journal of Applied Psychology*, 60(2):283, 1975.

Cristian Danescu-Niculescu-Mizil, Lillian Lee, Bo Pang, and Jon Kleinberg. Echoes of power: Language effects and power differences in social interaction. In *Proceedings of the 21st international conference on World Wide Web*, pages 699–708. ACM, 2012.

Rong-En Fan, Kai-Wei Chang, Cho-Jui Hsieh, Xiang-Rui Wang, and Chih-Jen Lin. Liblinear: A library for large linear classification. *The Journal of Machine Learning Research*, 9: 1871–1874, 2008.

Song Feng, Ritwik Banerjee, and Yejin Choi. Characterizing stylistic elements in syntactic structure. In *Proceedings of the 2012 Joint Conference on Empirical Methods in Natural Language Processing and Computational Natural Language Learning*, pages 1522–1533. Association for Computational Linguistics, 2012.

Shyam Gopinath, Jacquelyn S Thomas, and Lakshman Krishnamurthi. Investigating the relationship between the content of online word of mouth, advertising, and brand performance. *Marketing Science*, 2014.

Robert Gunning. Technique of clear writing. 1952.

Thorsten Joachims. A statistical learning learning model of text classification for support vector machines. In *Proceedings of the 24th annual international ACM SIGIR conference on Research and development in information retrieval*, pages 128–136. ACM, 2001.

J Peter Kincaid, Robert P Fishburne Jr, Richard L Rogers, and Brad S Chissom. Derivation of new readability formulas (automated readability index, fog count and flesch reading ease formula) for navy enlisted personnel. Technical report, DTIC Document, 1975.

Dan Klein and Christopher D Manning. Accurate unlexicalized parsing. In *Proceedings of the 41st Annual Meeting on Association for Computational Linguistics-Volume 1*, pages 423–430. Association for Computational Linguistics, 2003.

G Harry McLaughlin. Smog grading: A new readability formula. *Journal of reading*, 12(8):639–646, 1969.

Myle Ott, Yejin Choi, Claire Cardie, and Jeffrey T Hancock. Finding deceptive opinion spam by any stretch of the imagination. In *Proceedings of the 49th Annual Meeting of the Association for Computational Linguistics: Human Language Technologies-Volume 1*, pages 309–319. Association for Computational Linguistics, 2011.

Mauricio M Palmeira and Joydeep Srivastava. Free offer$\neq$ cheap product: A selective accessibility account on the valuation of free offers. *Journal of Consumer Research*, 40(4):644–656, 2013.

Michal Rosen-Zvi, Thomas Griffiths, Mark Steyvers, and Padhraic Smyth. The author-topic model for authors and documents. In *Proceedings of the 20th conference on Uncertainty in artificial intelligence*, pages 487–494. AUAI Press, 2004.

RJ Senter and EA Smith. Automated readability index. Technical report, DTIC Document, 1967.

Kristina Shampanier, Nina Mazar, and Dan Ariely. Zero as a special price: The true value of free products. *Marketing Science*, 26(6):742–757, 2007.

Yla R Tausczik and James W Pennebaker. The psychological meaning of words: Liwc and computerized text analysis methods. *Journal of Language and Social Psychology*, 29(1):24–54, 2010.

Ivan Titov and Ryan McDonald. A joint model of text and aspect ratings for sentiment summarization. In *Proceedings of ACL-08: HLT*, pages 308–316, Columbus, Ohio, June 2008. Association for Computational Linguistics.

Vladimir N. Vapnik. *Statistical Learning Theory*. Wiley-Interscience, 1998.

Monica Wadhwa, Baba Shiv, and Stephen M Nowlis. A bite to whet the reward appetite: The influence of sampling on reward-seeking behaviors. *Journal of Marketing Research*, 45 (4):403–413, 2008.

Janyce Wiebe, Theresa Wilson, and Claire Cardie. Annotating expressions of opinions and emotions in language. *Language resources and evaluation*, 39(2-3):165–210, 2005.

Discourse Analysis of User Forums in an Online Weight Loss Application

Lydia Manikonda[1], Heather Pon-Barry[1], Subbarao Kambhampati[1], Eric Hekler[2]
David W. McDonald[3]
[1]School of Computing, Informatics, and Decision Systems Engineering, Arizona State University
[2]School of Nutrition and Health Promotion, Arizona State University
[3]The Information School, University of Washington
{lmanikon, ponbarry, rao, ehekler}@asu.edu, dwmc@uw.edu

Abstract

Online social communities are becoming increasingly popular platforms for people to share information, seek emotional support, and maintain accountability for losing weight. Studying the language and discourse in these communities can offer insights on how users benefit from using these applications. This paper presents a preliminary analysis of language and discourse patterns in forum posts by users who lose weight and keep it off versus users with fluctuating weight dynamics. Our results reveal differences about how the types of posts, polarity of sentiments, and semantic cohesion of posts made by users vary along with their weight loss pattern. To our knowledge, this is the first discourse-level analysis of language and weight loss dynamics.

1 Introduction and Related Work

Obesity is a major public health problem; the number of people suffering from obesity has risen globally in the last decade (Das and Faxvaag, 2014). Many of these people are trying to lose weight as the multifactorial diseases such as metabolic syndromes, respiratory problems, coronary heart disease, and psychological challenges are all closely associated with obesity (Rippe et al., 1998; Must et al., 1999). More obese people are trying to lose weight by using weight-loss applications and other people interested in using these applications are trying to avoid gaining weight. Many internet services are becoming increasingly popular for supporting weight loss as they provide users with the opportunities to seek information by asking questions, answering questions, sharing their experiences and providing emotional support. Also, the internet provides many attributes that can help people feel more comfortable with openly expressing their problems and concerns (Ballantine and Stephenson, 2011; Hwang et al., 2010).

Most of the existing studies (Saperstein et al., 2007; Johnson and Wardle, 2011; Hwang et al., 2010; Ballantine and Stephenson, 2011; Leahey et al., 2012; Das and Faxvaag, 2014) focused on why people participate in online weight loss discussion forums and how the social support can help them to lose weight. These studies are conducted from the perspective of medical and psychology domains, where the data are collected via interviews or a small set of online forum data that are manually analyzed by human experts. Their primary focus is on measuring the social support by collecting views/opinions of people through surveys; less attention is given to understanding the natural language aspects of users' posts on these online communities. Unlike choosing a small subset of a dataset, our work is novel in automating the process of language analysis that can handle a larger dataset. Automating the process can also help classify the user type based on the language efficiently. This work also considers weekly check-in weights of users along with the study of their language.

In this paper, we study the user's language in correlation with their weight loss dynamics. To this end, we analyze a corpus of forum posts generated by users on the forum of a popular weight loss application. The forum from which we obtained the data is divided into several threads where each thread consists of several posts made by different users. From the overall dataset we identify two preliminary patterns of weight dynamics: (1) users who lose weight and successfully maintain the weight loss (*i.e.*, from one week to the next, weight is lost or weight remains the same) and (2) users whose weight pattern fluctuates (*i.e.*, from one week to the next, weight

Proceedings of the Joint Workshop on Social Dynamics and Personal Attributes in Social Media, pages 28–32,
Baltimore, Maryland USA, 27 June 2014.

changes are erratic or inconsistent). While there are many possible groupings that we could have utilized, we chose this grouping because of the known problems with "yo-yo" dieting compared to a more steady weight-loss. We study how the user's language in these two groups varies by measuring the semantic cohesion and sentiment of posts made by them.

Our main contributions include understanding the types of posts users make on different threads with a main focus on question-related posts, the type of language they use by measuring the semantic cohesion and sentiment by correlating with users' weight loss patterns. From the empirical analysis we find that users who lose weight in a fluctuating manner are very active on the discussion forums compared to the users who follow a non-increasing weight loss pattern. We also find that users of non-increasing weight loss pattern mostly reply to the posts made by other users and fluctuating users post more questions comparatively. Both the users from these two clusters differ in terms of the way their posts cohere with previous posts in the threads and also in terms of the sentiment associated with their posts.

2 Dataset

We obtain a text corpus of online discussion forums from *Lose It!*, a popular mobile and web-based weight loss application. Along with the text corpus, we also obtain weekly weight check-in data for a subset of users. The entire corpus consists of eight different forums that are subdivided into conversation topic threads. Each thread consists of several posts made by different users. The forum data in our corpus consists of 884 threads, with a median length of 20 posts per thread. The posts were made between January 1, 2010 and July 1, 2012. We identify the subset of users for whom we have weight check-in data and who made at least 25 weight check-ins during this time period. This results in a total of 2,270 users.

The interesting feature of this weight loss application is that users are encouraged to set goals to regularly log their weight, diet, and exercise. For a subset of users, Lose It! has provided a weekly weight "check-in", an average of the user's weight check-ins during the week, for the January 1, 2010 through July 1, 2012 period. This allows us to juxtapose the weekly weights of the users with their posts on the discussion forums.

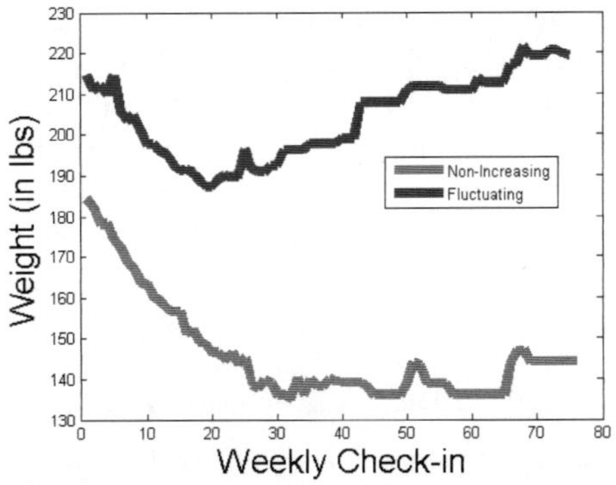

Figure 1: Example weight loss patterns from two individual users: non-increasing (bottom line), and fluctuating (top line). The x-axis ranges from the 1st through the 80th weekly check-in; the y-axis shows the weight, measured in lbs.

We partition the users into two groups based on their dynamic weight loss patterns: a *non-increasing* group and a *fluctuating* group.

1. **Non-increasing**: For each week j, the user's check-in weight w_j is less than or equal to their past week's weight w_{j-1}, within a small margin Δ. That is, $w_j \leq (1+\Delta)w_{j-1}$.

2. **Fluctuating**: If the difference between two consecutive weekly check-in weights do not follow the non-increasing constraint, users are grouped into this category.

We empirically set $\Delta = 0.04$ to divide the users in our dataset into two groups of similar size. To illustrate the two patterns of weight change, Figure 1 shows the weekly weight check-ins of two individual users, one from each group. This grouping is coarse, but is motivated by studies (Kraschnewski et al., 2010; Wing and Phelan, 2005) acknowledging that approximately 80% of people who set out to lose weight are successful at long-term weight loss maintenance, where successful maintenance is defined as losing 10% or more of the body weight and maintaining that for at least an year. In the future for further analysis, we aim to separate users less coarsely, e.g., users who maintain their weight neither gaining nor losing weight, users who lose weight and maintain it and finally, users who gain weight.

2.1 Characteristics of Online Community

The Lose It! application helps users set a personalized daily calorie budget, track the food they are eating, and their exercise. It also helps users to stay motivated by providing an opportunity to connect with other users who want to lose weight and support each other. Example snippets (paraphrased) from forum threads are shown below. The *"Can't lose weight!"* thread demonstrates users supporting each other and offering advice. The *"Someday I will"* thread highlights the complex relationship between text, semantics, and motivation in the forums.

Example thread: "Can't lose weight!"

User 1: *"I gained over 30 lbs in the last year and am stressed about losing it. I eat 1600 calories a day and burn more than that in exercise, but I havent lost any weight. I am so confused."*

User 2: *"You've only been a member for less than 2 months. I suggest you relax. Set your program to 1 pound weight loss a week. Adjust your habits to something you can live with... long term."*

User 3: *"You sound just like me. I think your exercise is good but maybe you are eating more than you think. Try diligently logging everything you consume."*

User 1: *"Thanks for the suggestions! I am going to get back to my logging."*

Example thread: "Someday I will..."

User 1: *"Do a pull-up :-)"*

User 2: *"... actually enjoy exercising."*

User 3: *"Someday I will stop participating in the lose it forums, but obviously not today."*

User 4: *"I hope you fail :-)"*

3 Empirical Analysis

In this section, we present preliminary observations on how the language and discourse patterns of forum posts vary with respect to weight loss dynamics. As an initial step, part-of-speech (POS) tagging is performed on all forum posts using the Stanford POS Tagger (Toutanova et al., 2003).

From the weekly check-in data we identified the number of users and the number of posts from each weight-loss pattern cluster which are shown in Table 1. We see that the average number of posts by fluctuating users is greater than the average number of posts by non-increasing users. This suggests that fluctuating users are more active in participation. Our data also suggest that posts made by non-increasing users are shorter compared to those made by fluctuating users.

	Weight Pattern	
	Non-increasing	Fluctuating
# Total users	1127	1143
# Forum users	29	68
# Forum posts	99	1279
Posts per user	3.5	18.2
Words per post	49.1	77.3

Table 1: Statistics of users and forum posts.

3.1 Asking Questions

Previous studies (Bambina, 2007; Langford et al., 1997) revealed that people on online health communities mainly engage in two activities: (*i*) seeking information, and (*ii*) getting emotional support. People usually ask questions to other community members or just browse through the community forums to get information while seeking information. Below is an example (paraphrased) showing how a users ask and respond to questions.

Example thread: "New user"

User 1: *"Did anyone upgrade to the premium app? What do you like about it?"*

User 2: *"I upgraded to the premium. I LOVE the functionality to log food in advance. I can track and set goals that are not related to weight like how much I sleep, how much water I drink, etc."*

User 3: *"I upgraded my account to premium too. I really liked the added features because it helped me keep track of my steps and participate in challenges."*

We are interested in knowing whether users in the two clusters are actively involved in posting questions. We deem a forum post to be a question if it meets one of these two conditions:

1. ***Wh*-question words:** If a sentence in the post starts with a question word: *Wh-Determiner (WDT), Wh-pronoun (WP), Possessive wh-pronoun (WP$), Wh-adverb (WRB).*

2. **Punctuation:** If the post contains a question mark symbol ('?').

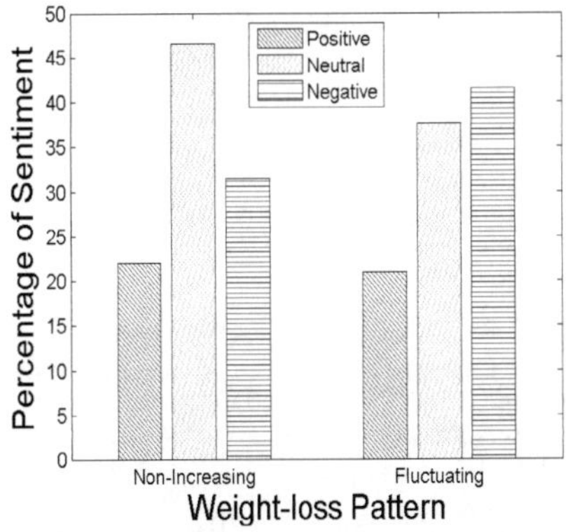

Figure 2: Proportion of sentiments for the two weight-loss patterns. For non-increasing users, percentage of posts with *Positive*, *Neutral* and *Negative* sentiments are: *22%*, *46.5%* and *31.5%* respectively. For fluctuating users, the percentage of posts with *Positive*, *Neutral* and *Negative* sentiments are: *20.9%*, *37.6%* and *41.5%* respectively.

We computed the ratio of question-oriented posts made by each user in the two clusters. After averaging these ratio values across all the users in each cluster separately, we found that on average, **32.6%** of the posts made by non-increasing users were questions ($SE = 0.061$). And, **37.7%** of the posts made by fluctuating users were questions ($SE = 0.042$). This shows that on an average fluctuating users post relatively more number of questions than the non-increasing users.

3.2 Sentiment of Posts

Analyzing the sentiment of user posts in the forums can provide a suprisingly meaningful sense of how the loss of weight impacts the sentiment of user's post. In this analysis, we report our initial results on extracting the sentiments of user's posts. In order to achieve this, we utilized the Stanford Sentiment Analyzer (Socher et al., 2013). This analyzer classifies a text input into one of five sentiment categories—from *Very Positive* to *Very Negative*. We merge the five classes into three: *Positive*, *Neutral* and *Negative*. In future, we may consider specific (health and nutrition) sentiment lexicons.

We analyzed the sentiment of posts contributed by the users from the two clusters. As shown in Figure 2, posts of users belonging to the non-increasing cluster are more *neutral* whereas the posts made by users from the fluctuating cluster are mainly of *negative* sentiment. This gives an interesting intuition that the fluctuating group of users might require more emotional support as they use more negative sentiment in their posts.

3.3 Cohesion with Previous Posts

Cohesion is the property of a well-written document that links together sentences in the same context. Several existing models measure the cohesion of a given text with applications to topic segmentation or multi-document summarization (Elsner and Charniak, 2011; Barzilay and Lapata, 2005; Soricut and Marcu, 2006). In this analysis, we want to find out if there is any correlation between the cohesiveness of posts made by users and their pattern of weight loss. We are mainly interested in measuring the similarity of a user's post with respect to the previous posts in a thread. This can help identify users who elaborate on previous post versus those who shift the topic.

We focus on content words: verbs and nouns (part-of-speech tags *VB*, *VBZ*, *VBP*, *VBD*, *VBN*, *VBG*, *NN*, *NNP*, *NNPS*). Next, we use WordNet (Miller, 1995) to identify synonyms of the content words. Then, we compute similarity between the current post and previous posts of other users in the thread, in terms of commonly shared verbs and nouns including synonyms. In our current, preliminary analysis, we consider this similarity score to be the measure of cohesion.

In this step, we consider all posts that are not thread-initial. To approximate whether a post is cohesive, we compare the nouns and verbs of the current post to the list of nouns and verbs (plus synonyms) obtained from the previous posts of the thread. Our analysis finds that posts made by fluctuating users have an average cohesion score of **0.42** ($SE = 0.008$), whereas posts made by non-increasing users have an average cohesion score of **0.51** ($SE = 0.027$). This suggests that non-increasing users may be more focused when participating in forums whereas the fluctuating users are more prone to make posts that have less in common with the previous posts in a thread.

4 Conclusions and Future Work

In this paper, we analyze how the language changes based on the weight loss dynamics of users who participate in the forum of a popular weight-loss application. Specifically, this analysis revealed four interesting insights about the two types of users who lose weight in a non-increasing manner and who lose weight in a fluctuating manner. Firstly, fluctuating users are more active in participation compared to the other set of users. Secondly, fluctuating users post more question-oriented posts compared to the non-increasing users. Thirdly, non-increasing users contribute posts that are more cohesive with respect to the previous posts in a given thread. Fourthly, posts contributed by fluctuating users have more negative sentiment compared to the posts made by non-increasing users. This observation hints that fluctuating users may need more emotional support to continue using this weight loss application and lose weight in an effective manner.

While this work is preliminary, our analyses provide a valuable early "proof of concept" for providing insights on how user behavior within online weight loss forums might impact weight outcomes. These sorts of analyses, particularly when replicated, could provide valuable insights for developing refined online weight loss forums that might facilitate more effective interactions for weight loss. It could also provide valuable insights for improving behavioral theories about behavior change (Hekler et al., 2013).

In the future, we plan to focus on a larger corpus from an extended time period, aligned more closely with weekly check-in weight data. Other directions for consideration are the temporal aspect of forum posts and gender-based analyses of user behavior.

Acknowledgments

We would like to thank Fit Now, Inc., makers of Lose It!, for providing us with the data to conduct this research. We thank the anonymous reviewers for their helpful suggestions. This research is supported in part by the ARO grant W911NF-13-1-0023, the ONR grants N00014-13-1-0176 and N0014-13-1-0519, and a Google Research Grant.

References

Paul W. Ballantine and Rachel J. Stephenson. 2011. Help me, I'm fat! Social support in online weight loss networks. *Journal of Consumer Behaviour*, 10(6):332–337.

Antonina D. Bambina. 2007. *Online Social Support: The Interplay of Social Networks and Computer-Mediated Communication*. Cambria Press.

Regina Barzilay and Mirella Lapata. 2005. Modeling local coherence: An entity-based approach. In *Proceedings of the Association for Computational Linguistics*, ACL '05, pages 141–148.

Anita Das and Arild Faxvaag. 2014. What influences patient participation in an online forum for weight loss surgery? *Interactive Journal of Medical Research*, 3(1).

Micha Elsner and Eugene Charniak. 2011. Disentangling chat with local coherence models. In *Proceedings of the Association for Computational Linguistics: Human Language Technologies - Volume 1*, HLT '11, pages 1179–1189.

Eric Hekler, Predrag Klasnja, Jon E. Froehlich, and Matthew P. Buman. 2013. Mind the theoretical gap: Interpreting, using, and developing behavioral theory in HCI research. In *Proceedings of the SIGCHI Conference on Human Factors in Computing Systems*.

Kevin O. Hwang, Allison J. Ottenbacher, Angela P. Green, M. Roseann Cannon-Diehl, Oneka Richardson, Elmer V. Bernstam, and Eric J. Thomas. 2010. Social support in an internet weight loss community. *I. J. Medical Informatics*, 79(1):5–13.

Fiona Johnson and Jane Wardle. 2011. The association between weight loss and engagement with a web-based food and exercise diary in a commercial weight loss programme: a retrospective analysis. *International Journal of Behavioral Nutrition and Physical Activity*, 8(1):1–7.

J L Kraschnewski, J Boan, J Esposito, N E Sherwood, E B Lehman, D K Kephart, and C N Sciamanna. 2010. Long-term weight loss maintenance in the united states. *International Journal of Obesity*, 34(11):1644–1654.

Catherine Penny Hinson Langford, Juanita Bowsher, Joseph P. Maloney, and Patricia P. Lillis. 1997. Social support: A conceptual analysis. *Journal of Advanced Nursing*, 25(1):145–151.

Tricia M. Leahey, Rajiv Kumar, Brad M. Weinberg, and Rena R. Wing. 2012. Teammates and social influence affect weight loss outcomes in a team-based weight loss competition. *Obesity*, 20(7):1413–1418.

George A. Miller. 1995. Wordnet: A lexical database for english. *Communications of the ACM*, 38(11):39–41.

Aviva Must, Jennifer Spadano, Eugenie H. Coakley, Alison E. Field, Graham Colditz, and Dietz William H. 1999. The disease burden associated with overweight and obesity. *JAMA*, 282(16):1523–1529.

James M. Rippe, Suellyn Crossley, and Rhonda Ringer. 1998. Obesity as a chronic disease: Modern medical and lifestyle management. *Journal of the American Dietetic Association*, 98(10, Supplement):S9 – S15.

S. L. Saperstein, N. L. Atkinson, and R. S. Gold. 2007. The impact of internet use for weight loss. *Obesity Reviews*, 8(5):459–465.

Richard Socher, Alex Perelygin, Jean Wu, Jason Chuang, Christopher D. Manning, Andrew Y. Ng, and Christopher Potts. 2013. Recursive deep models for semantic compositionality over a sentiment treebank. In *Proceedings of the EMNLP*, pages 1631–1642, October.

Radu Soricut and Daniel Marcu. 2006. Discourse generation using utility-trained coherence models. In *Proceedings of the COLING/ACL on Main Conference Poster Sessions*, COLING-ACL '06, pages 803–810.

Kristina Toutanova, Dan Klein, Christopher D. Manning, and Yoram Singer. 2003. Feature-rich part-of-speech tagging with a cyclic dependency network. In *Proceedings of the NAACL HLT - Volume 1*, pages 173–180.

Rena R. Wing and Suzanne Phelan. 2005. Long-term weight loss maintenance. *The American Journal of Clinical Nutrition*, 82(suppl):222S–5S.

A Unified Topic-Style Model for Online Discussions

Ying Ding, Jing Jiang, Qiming Diao
School of Information Systems
Singapore Management University
{ying.ding.2011, jingjiang, qiming.diao.2010}@smu.edu.sg

Abstract

Forums have become major places for online communications for many years, where people often share and express opinions. We observe that, when editing posts, while some people seriously state their opinions, there are also many people playing jokes and writing meaningless posts on the discussed topics. We design a unified probabilistic graphical model to capture both topic-driven words and style-driven words. The model can help us separate serious and unserious posts/users and identify slang words. An extensive set of experiments demonstrates the effectiveness of our model.

1 Introduction

With the fast growth of the popularity of online social media, people nowadays are very used to sharing their thoughts and interacting with their friends on the Internet. Large online social network sites such as Facebook, Twitter and Flickr have attracted hundreds of millions of users. Among these online social media platforms, forums have always played an important role with its special characteristics. Unlike personal blogs, forums allow many users to engage in online conversations with a topic focus. Unlike Facebook, forums are usually open to public and users who post in forums do not need to reveal too much personal information. Unlike Wikipedia or Freebase, forums encourage users to exchange not only factual information but more importantly subjective opinions. All these characteristics make online forums a valuable source from which we can retrieve and summarize the general public's opinions about a given topic. This is especially important for businesses who want to find out how their products and services have been received and policy makers who are concerned about people's opinions on social issues.

While the freedom with which users can post in online forums has promoted the popularity of online forums, it has also led to the diversity in post quality. There are posts which contribute positively to a discussion by offering relevant, serious and meaningful opinions, but there are also many posts which appear irrelevant, disrespectful or meaningless. These posts are uninformative, hard to consume and sometimes even destructive. Let us look at some examples. Table 1 shows two forum posts in response to a piece of news about GDP bonuses for senior civil servants in Singapore. We can see that User A's post is clearly written. User B's post, on the other hand, is hard to comprehend. We see broken sentences, many punctuation marks such as "?" and colloquial expressions such as "ha." User B is not seriously contributing to the online discussion but rather trying to make a joke of the issue. Generally speaking, User B's post is less useful than User A's post in helping us understand the public's response to the news.

	Senior civil servants to get bumper GDP bonuses
User A	let us ensure this will be the LAST time they accord themselves ceiling salary scales and bonuses. i suspect MANY citizens are eagerly looking forward to the GE.
User B	Fever night, fever night, fe..ver.. Fever like to do it Got it?????? Ha..ha..ha...

Table 1: Two example online posts.

In this work, we opt for a fully unsupervised approach to modeling this phenomenon in online discussions. Our solution is based on the observation that the writing styles of serious posts and unserious posts are different, and the writing styles are often characterized by the words used in the posts. Moreover, the same user usually exhibits

Proceedings of the Joint Workshop on Social Dynamics and Personal Attributes in Social Media, pages 33–41,
Baltimore, Maryland USA, 27 June 2014. ©2014 Association for Computational Linguistics

User	Post
User A	*Re: Creativity, Art in the eyes of beholder. your take?* The difference is, the human can get tired or sick, and then it will affect his work, but the robot can work 24 hours a day 365 days a year and yet produce the same every time.
	Re: Diesel oil spill turns Manila Bay red, poses risk to health - ST The question is, will this environmental hazard turn up on the shores of it neighbors? And maybe even affect Singapore waters?
User B	*Re: Will PAP know who i vote in GE?* Hey! Who are you??? You make. ha..ha..ha.. he..he..he.. very angry lah
	Re: Gender discrimination must end for Singapore to flourish, says AWARE Hao nan bu gen nu dou Let you win lah ha..ha..ha..

Table 2: Sample posts of two example users.

the same writing style in most of his posts. For example, Table 2 shows two example users, each with two sample posts. We can see that their writing styles are consistent in the two posts. If we treat each writing style as a latent factor associated with a word distribution, we can associate observed words with the underlying writing styles. However, not all words in a post are style-driven. Many words in forum posts are chosen based on the topic of the corresponding thread. Our model therefore jointly considers both topics and writing styles.

We apply our topic-style model to a real online forum dataset from Singapore. By setting the number of styles to two, we clearly find that one writing style corresponds to the more serious posts while the other corresponds to posts that are not so serious. This topic-style model also automatically learns a meaningful slang lexicon. Moreover, we find that topics discovered by our topic-style model are more distinctive from each other than topics produced by standard LDA.

Our contributions in this paper can be summarized as follows: 1) We propose a principled topic-style model to jointly model topics and writing styles at the same time in online forums. 2) An extensive set of experiments shows that our model is effective in separating the more serious posts and unserious posts and identifying slang words.

2 Related Work

Latent Dirichlet Allocation (LDA) (Blei et al., 2003) has been shown to be useful for many applications. Many extensions of LDA have been designed for different tasks, which are not detailed here. Our model is also an extension of LDA. We introduce two types of word distributions, one representing topics and the other representing writing styles. We use switch variables to alternate between these two types of word distributions. We also assume an author-level distribution over writing styles. It is worth pointing out that although our model bears similarity to a number of other LDA extensions, our objectives are different from existing work. E.g., the author topic model (Rosen-Zvi et al., 2004) also assumes an author-level distribution over topics, but the author-level distribution is meant to capture an author's topical interests. In contrast, our user-level distribution is over writing styles and is meant to identify serious versus unserious users. Similar to the models by Mei et al. (2007) and Paul et al. (2010) , we also use switch variables to alternate between different types of word distributions, but our goal is to identify words associated with writing styles instead of sentiment words or perspective words.

Another body of related research is around studying text quality, formality and sarcasm. Pitler and Nenkova (2008) investigated different features for text readability judgement and empirically demonstrated that discourse relations are highly correlated with perceived readability. Brooke et al. (2010) applied Latent Semantic Analysis to determine the formality level of lexical items. Agichtein et al. (2008) presented a general classification framework incorporating community feedback to identify high quality content in social media. Davidov et al. (2010) proposed the first robust algorithm for recognition of sarcasm. González-Ibáñez et al. (2011) took a closer look at sarcasm in Twitter messages and found that automatic classification can be as good as human classification. All these studies mainly rely on supervised techniques and human annotation needs to be done, which is very time consuming. Our method is fully unsupervised, which can automatically uncover different styles and separate serious posts from unserious posts.

Our work is also related to spam/spammer detection in social media, which has been studied over different platforms for a few years. Jindal and Liu (2008) first studied opinion spam in online reviews and proposed a classification method for opinion spam detection. Bhattarai et al. (2009)

investigated different content attributes of comment spam in the Blogsphere and built a detection system with good performance based on these attributes. Ding et al. (2013) proposed to utilize both content and social features to detect spams in online question answer website. Existing work on spam detection need annotated data to learn the spam features but our model does not as it is fully unsupervised.

3 A Topic-Style Model

Writing styles can be reflected in many different ways. Besides choices of words or expressions, many other linguistic features such as sentence length, sentence complexity and use of punctuation marks may all be associated with one's writing style. In this work, however, we try to take an approach that does not rely on heavy linguistic analysis or feature engineering. Part of the reason is that we want our approach to be independent of language, culture or social norms so that it is robust and can be easily applied to any online forum.

To this end, we represent a writing style simply as a distribution over words, much like a topic in LDA. We assume that there are S latent writing styles shared by all users contributing to a forum. Meanwhile, we also assume a different set of T latent topics. We mix writing styles and topics to explain the generation of words in forum posts.

A key assumption we have is that the same user tends to maintain a consistent writing style, and therefore we associate each user with a multinomial distribution over our latent writing styles. This is similar to associating a document with a distribution over topics in LDA, where the assumption is that a single document tends to have focused topics. Another assumption of our model is that each word in a post is generated from either the background or a topic or a writing style, as determined by a binary switch variable.

3.1 Model Description

We now formally describe the topic-style model we propose. The model is depicted in Figure 1. We assume that there are T latent topics, where ϕ_t is the word distribution for topic t. There are S latent writing styles, where ψ_s is the word distribution for writing style s. There are E threads, where each thread e has a topic distribution θ_e, and there are U users, where each user u has a writing style distribution π_u.

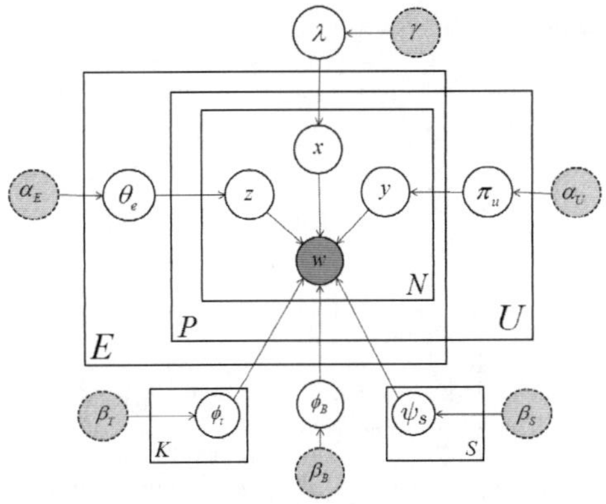

Figure 1: Topic-Style Model

Notation	Description
$\gamma, \alpha_E, \alpha_U, \beta_B, \beta_T, \beta_S$	Hyper-parameters of Dirichlet distributions
λ	A global multinomial distribution over switching variables x
θ_e, π_u	Thread-specific topic distributions and user-specific style distributions
ϕ_B, ϕ_t, ψ_s	Word distributions of background, topics and styles
$x_{e,p,n}$, $y_{e,p,n}$, $z_{e,p,n}$	Hidden variables: $x_{e,p,n}$ for switching, $y_{e,p,n}$ for style of style words, $z_{e,p,n}$ for topic of topic words
e, p, n	Indices: e for threads, p for posts, n for words
$E, P_e, U, N_{e,p}$	Number of threads, numbers of posts in threads, number of users and numbers of words in posts
S, K, V	Numbers of styles, topics and word types

Table 3: Notation used in our model.

For each word in a post, first a binary switch variable x is sampled from a global Bernoulli distribution parameterized by λ. If $x = 0$, we draw a word from the background word distribution. Otherwise, if $x = 1$, we draw a topic from the corresponding thread's topic distribution; if $x = 2$, we draw a writing style from the corresponding user's writing style distribution. We then draw the word from the corresponding word distribution.

The generative process of our model is described as follows. The notation we use in the model is also summarized in Table 3.

- Draw a global multinomial switching variable distribution $\lambda \sim$ Dirichlet(γ).
- Draw a multinomial background word distribution $\phi_B \sim$ Dirichlet(β_B).
- For each topic $t = 1, 2, \ldots, T$, draw a multinomial topic-word distribution $\phi_t \sim$ Dirichlet(β_T).
- For each writing style $s = 1, 2, \ldots, S$, draw a multinomial style-word distribution $\psi_s \sim$ Dirichlet(β_S).
- For each user $u = 1, 2, \ldots, U$, draw a multinomial style distribution $\pi_u \sim$ Dirichlet(α_u).
- For each thread $e = 1, 2, \ldots, E$

- draw a multinomial topic distribution $\theta_e \sim \mathrm{Dir}(\alpha_E)$.
- for each post $p = 1, 2, \ldots, P_e$ in the thread, where $u_{e,p} \in \{1, 2, \ldots, U\}$ is the user who has written the post
  * for each word $n = 1, 2, \ldots, N_{e,p}$ in the thread, where $w_{e,p,n} \in \{1, 2, \ldots, V\}$ is the word type
    · draw $x_{e,p,n} \sim \mathrm{Multinomial}(\lambda)$.
    · If $x = 0$, draw $w_{e,p,n} \sim \mathrm{Multinomial}(\phi_B)$
    · If $x = 1$, draw $y_{e,p,n} \sim \mathrm{Multinomial}(\pi_{u_{e,p}})$, and then draw $w_{e,p,n} \sim \mathrm{Multinomial}(\psi_{y_{e,p,n}})$.
    · If $x = 2$, draw $z_{e,p,n} \sim \mathrm{Multinomial}(\theta_e)$, and then draw $w_{e,p,n} \sim \mathrm{Multinomial}(\phi_{z_{e,p,n}})$.

3.2 Parameters Estimation

We use Gibbs sampling to estimate the parameters. The sampling probability that assign the nth word in post p of thread e to the background topic is as follows:

$$P(x_{e,p,n} = 0 | \boldsymbol{W}, \boldsymbol{U}, \boldsymbol{X}^{-i}, \boldsymbol{Y}^{-i}, \boldsymbol{Z}^{-i})$$
$$\propto (\gamma + n_0) \times \frac{\beta_B + n_B^{w_{e,p,n}}}{V\beta_B + n_0}$$

where n_0 is the number of words assigned as background words and $n_B^{w_{e,p,n}}$ is the number of times word type of $w_{e,p,n}$ assigned to background. The probability to assign this word to style s is as follows:

$$P(x_{e,p,n} = 1, y_{e,p,n} = s | \boldsymbol{W}, \boldsymbol{U}, \boldsymbol{X}^{-i}, \boldsymbol{Y}^{-i}, \boldsymbol{Z}^{-i})$$
$$\propto (\gamma + n_1) \times \frac{\alpha_U + n^s_{u_{e,p}}}{S\alpha_U + n^*_{u_{e,p}}} \times \frac{\beta_S + n_s^{w_{e,p,n}}}{V\beta_S + n_s^*}$$

where n_1 is the number of words assigned as style words, $n^*_{u_{e,p}}$ and $n^s_{u_{e,p}}$ are the number of words written by user $u_{e,p}$ and assigned as style words, and the number of these words assigned to style s, respectively. n_s^* and $n_s^{w_{e,p,n}}$ are the number of words assigned to style s and the number of times word type of term $w_{e,p,n}$ assigned to style s. The probability to assign this word topic t is as follows:

$$P(x_{e,p,n} = 2, z_{e,p,n} = t | \boldsymbol{W}, \boldsymbol{U}, \boldsymbol{X}^{-i}, \boldsymbol{Y}^{-i}, \boldsymbol{Z}^{-i})$$
$$\propto (\gamma + n_2) \times \frac{\alpha_E + n_e^t}{K\alpha_E + n_e^*} \times \frac{\beta_T + n_t^{w_{e,p,n}}}{V\beta_T + n_t^*}$$

where n_2 is the number of words assigned as topic words, n_e^* is the number of words in thread e assigned as topic words, n_e^t is the number of words in thread e assigned to topic t, n_t^* is the number of words assigned to topic t, and $n_t^{w_{e,p,n}}$ is the number of times word type of $w_{e,p,n}$ is assigned to topic t.

After running Gibbs sampling for a number of iterations, we can estimate the parameters based on the sampled topic assignments. They can be calculated by the equations below:

$$\phi_t^w = \frac{\beta_T + n_t^w}{V\beta_T + n_t^*} \qquad \phi_s^w = \frac{\beta_S + n_s^w}{V\beta_S + n_s^*}$$

$$\theta_e^t = \frac{\alpha_E + n_e^t}{K\alpha_E + n_e^*} \qquad \theta_u^s = \frac{\alpha_U + n_u^s}{S\alpha_U + n_u^*}$$

4 Experiment

4.1 Data Set and Experiment Setup

To evaluate our model, we use forum threads from AsiaOne[1], a popular online forum site in Singapore. We crawled all the threads between January 2011 and June 2013 under a category called "Singapore," which is the largest category on AsiaOne. In the preprocessing stage, we removed the URLs, HTML tags and tokenized the text. Emoticons are kept in our data set as they frequently occur and indicate users' emotions. All stop words and words occurring less than 4 times are deleted. We also removed users who have fewer than 8 posts and threads attracting fewer than 21 posts. The detailed statistics of the processed dataset are given in Table 4.

#Users	#Words	#Tokens	#Posts/User	#Posts/Thread
580	29,619	2,940,886	205.3	69.5

Table 4: Detailed statistics of the dataset.

We fix the hyper-parameters $\gamma, \alpha_E, \alpha_U, \beta_T$ and β_S to be $10, 1, 1, 0.01$ and 0.01 respectively. we set $\beta_{B,v}$ to be $H \cdot p_B(v)$, where H is set to be 20 and $p_B(v)$ is the probability of word v as estimated from the entire corpus. The number of topics K is set to be 40 empirically.

4.2 Model Development

Before we evaluate the effectiveness of our model, we first show how we choose the number of styles to use. Note that although we are interested in separating serious and unserious posts, our model can generally handle any arbitrary number of writing styles. We therefore vary the number of writing styles to see which number empirically gives the most meaningful results.

Assuming that different styles are characterized by words, we expect to see that the discovered

[1] http://www.asiaone.com

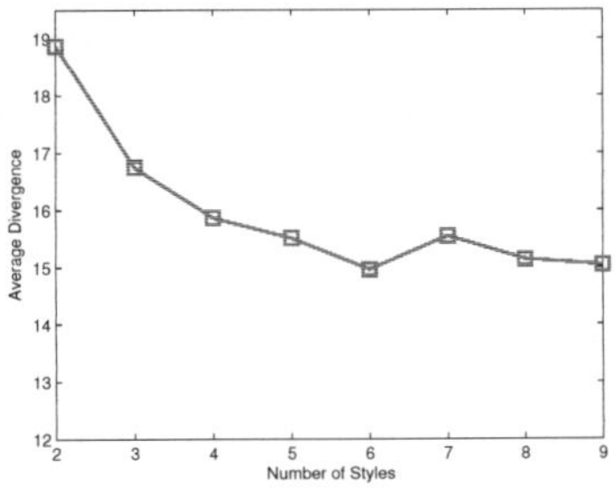

Figure 2: Average Divergence over different numbers of styles.

	Style No.	Top Words
2 styles	Style 1	singapore, people, years, government
	Style 2	BIGGRIN, TONGUE, lah, ha
3 styles	Style 1	people, make, WINK, good
	Style 2	singapore, years, government, mr
	Style 3	BIGGRIN, TONGUE, lah, ha
4 styles	Style 1	ha, lah, WINK, dont
	Style 2	singapore, year, mr, years
	Style 3	people, good, make, singapore
	Style 4	BIGGRIN, TONGUE, EEK, MAD

Table 5: Sample style words

word distributions for different styles are very different from each other. To measure the distinction among a set of styles, we define a metric called Average Divergence (AD) based on KL-divergence. Average Divergence can be calculated as follows.

$$AD(\boldsymbol{S}) = \frac{2}{N(N-1)} \sum_{i \neq j} S_{\text{KL}}(s_i || s_j),$$

where $\boldsymbol{S}$ is a set of style-word distributions, N is the size of $\boldsymbol{S}$ and s_i is the i-th distribution in $\boldsymbol{S}$. $S_{\text{KL}}(s_i || s_j)$ is the symmetric KL divergence between s_i and s_j (i.e., $D_{\text{KL}}(s_i || s_j) + D_{\text{KL}}(s_j || s_i)$). The higher Average Divergence is, the more distinctive distributions in $\boldsymbol{S}$ are.

Figure 2 shows the Average Divergence over different numbers of styles. We can clearly see that the Average Divergence reaches the highest value when there are only two styles and decreases with the increase of style number. This means the styles are mostly distinct from each other when the number is 2 and their difference decreases when there are more styles.

To get a better understanding of the differences of using different numbers of styles, we compare the top words in each style when the number of styles is set to be 2, 3 and 4. The results are shown in Table 5 where all uppercase words represent emoticons. From the top words of the first row, we can see that Style 1 is dominated by formal words while Style 2 is dominated by emoticons like BIGGRIN and slang words like "lah" and "ha." These two styles are well distinguished from each other and humans can easily tell the difference between them. Also, Style 2 is an unserious style characterized by emoticons, slang and urban words. Table 6 shows the top words of these 2 styles excluding emoticons. From this table, we can observe that Style 2 has many slang words with high probability while top words in Style 1 are all very formal. However, styles in the second and third rows of Table 5 are not easily distinguishable from each other. In these results, there often exist two styles very similar to the styles in row 1 while the other styles look like the combination of these two styles and humans cannot tell their meanings very clearly. Based on these observations, we fix the number of styles to 2 in the following experiments.

Serious Style	Unserious Style
singapore	lah
people	ha
years	dont
government	stupid
time	leh
made	ah
year	lor
public	liao

Table 6: Top words of different styles

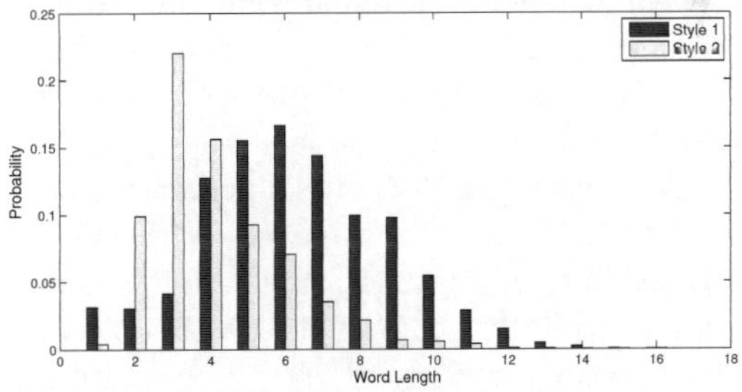

Figure 3: Word length distribution

One previous work uses word length as an indicator of formality (Karlgren and Cutting, 1994). Here, we borrow this idea and compare the word length of Style 1 and Style 2. We calculate the distributions of word length and show the results in Figure 3. It shows that the majority of words in Style 1 are longer compared with those in Style 2. To have a quantitative view of the difference between the word lengths of these two styles, we heuristically extract words labeled with Style 1 and Style 2 in our dataset in the final iteration of Gibbs sampling and apply Mann-Whitney U test on these two word length populations. The null hypothesis that the two input populations are the same is rejected at the 1% significance level. This verifies the intuition that serious posts tend to use longer words than unserious posts.

4.3 Post Identification

Our model can also be used to separate serious posts and unserious posts. We treat this as a retrieval problem and use precision/recall for evaluation.

We use a simple scoring function, which is the proportion of words assigned to the unserious style when we terminate the Gibbs sampling at the 800-th iteration, to score each post. When applying this method to our data, emoticons are all removed. For comparison, we rank post according to the number of emoticons inside a post as the baseline. After getting the result of each method, we ask two annotators to label the first and last 50 posts in the ranking list. The first 50 posts are used for evaluation of unserious post retrieval and the last 50 post are used for evaluation of serious post retrieval. This evaluation is based on the assumption that if a method can separate serious and unserious posts very well, posts ranked at the top position should be unserious ones and those ranked near to the bottom should be serious ones. The results are shown in Table 7 where our method is denoted as TSM and the baseline method is denoted as EMO. In serious post retrieval, the baseline have a perfect performance and our method is competitive. We can see that EMO has a perfect performance in identifying serious posts. When posts are ranked in reverse order according to the number of emoticons they contain, the last 50 ones do not contain any emoticons. They can be regarded as a random sample of posts without emoticons. Compared with identifying serious posts, identifying unserious posts looks much more difficult. EMO's poor performance on this task tells us that emoticon is not a promising sign to detect unserious posts. However, the word style a post uses matters more, which also proves the value of our proposed model.

4.4 User Identification

In this section, we evaluate the performance of TSM on identifying serious and unserious users. This identification task is very important as many research tasks such as opinion mining and expert finding are more interested in the serious users. We treat this task as a retrieval problem as well, which means we will rank users by a scoring function and do evaluation on this ranking result.

We rank user according to their style distribution π_u and pick the first 50 and last 50 users for evaluation. For each user, 10 posts are sampled to be shown to the annotators. We mix these 100 users and ask two graduate students to do the annotations. The evaluation strategy is the same as that in Section 4.3. We choose a simple baseline which ranks users by the number of emoticons they use per post. The evaluation result is shown in Table 8 for serious and unserious user retrieval respectively.

In both serious and unserious user retrieval tasks, our method gets almost perfect performance, which is better than the baseline. This means the user style distributions learned by our model can help separate serious and unserious users.

		P@5	P@15	P@25	P@35
Serious	EMO	1.0	1.0	1.0	**1.0**
	TSM	1.0	1.0	1.0	0.97
Unserious	EMO	0.4	0.67	0.64	0.6
	TSM	**1.0**	**0.93**	**0.96**	**0.97**

Table 7: Precision for Serious and Unserious Post Retrieval. P@N stands for the precision of the first N results in ranking list.

		P@5	P@15	P@25	P@35
Serious	Baseline	0.6	0.8	0.8	0.83
	TSM	**1.0**	**1.0**	**1.0**	**0.94**
Unserious	Baseline	1.0	0.87	0.92	0.91
	TSM	1.0	**1.0**	**1.0**	**1.0**

Table 8: Precision for serious and unserious user retrieval.

4.5 Perplexity

Perplexity is a widely used criterion in statistical natural language processing. It measures the predictive power of a model on unseen data, which is algebraically equivalent to the inverse of the geometric mean per-word likelihood. A lower perplexity means the test data, which is unseen in the training phase, can be generated by the model with a higher probability. So it also indicates that the model has a better generalization performance.

In this experiment, we leave 10% data for testing and use the remaining 90% data for training. We choose LDA as a baseline for comparison and treat each thread as a document. The perplexity for both models is calculated over different numbers of topics, which ranges from 10 to 100. The result is show in Figure 4. We can clearly see that our proposed model has a substantially lower perplexity than LDA over different numbers of topics. This proves that our model fits the forum discussion data better and has a stronger generalization power. It also indicates that separating topic-driven words and style-driven words can better fit the generation of user generated content in forum discussions.

4.6 Topic Distinction

In traditional topic modeling, like LDA, all words are regarded as topic-driven words, which are generated by mixture of topics. However, this may not be true to user-generated content in online forums as not all words are driven by discussed topics. Take the following post for example:

- Okay lah. Let them be. I mean its their KKB right? Let it rot lor.

In this post, the words "lah" and "lor" are not related to the topics under discussion. They appear in the post because the authors are used to using these words, which means these words are style driven. Style-driven words are related to a user's characteristics and should not be clustered into any topic. Without separating these two types of words, style-driven words may appear in different topics and make topics less distinct to each other.

Figure 5 compares the Average Divergence among discovered topics between TSM (Topic Style model) and LDA over different numbers of topics. We can clearly see that the Average Divergence of TSM is substantially larger than that of LDA over different numbers of topics. This proves that in TSM, the learned topics are more distinct from each other. This is because LDA mixes these two kinds of words, which introduces noise into the learned topics and decreases their distinction between each other. But topic driven words and style driven words are well separated in TSM. Figure 5 also plots the Average Divergence between the learned two styles, which is the curve denoted by DIFF. We can see the AD between different styles is even larger than that among topics in TSM. Different topics may still have some overlap in frequently used words but styles may share few words with each other. So AD of styles can get higher value. This also proves the effectiveness of our model in identifying writing styles and uncovering more distinct topics.

	P@5	P@10	P@20	P@30	P@40	P@50
E	0	0.2	0.25	0.23	0.225	0.2
T	**0.8**	**0.9**	**0.8**	**0.8**	**0.675**	**0.62**

Table 9: Slang identification precision. E: Emoticon; T:TSM.

	#Word/Post	#Post
Formal User	34.9	158.3
Informal User	14.5	381

Table 10: Mean Value of average post length and number of post for different type of users

4.7 Discovering Slang

By looking at Table 5, we notice that the unserious style contains many slang words with high probability. This indicates that the unserious style in the dataset we use is also characterized by slang words. In this section, we will show the usefulness of our model in slang discovery. The baseline method is denoted as Emoticon as it ranks words according to their probability of occurring in a post containing emoticons. We ask two Singaporean annotators to help us identify Singaporean slang in the top 50 words. The result is shown in Table 9. It tells us the unserious style learned in our model has very good performance in identifying local slang words. For people preferring unserious writing style, they would write posts in a very flexible way and use many informal words, abbreviations and slang expressions. So our unserious style will be characterized by these slang words and performs very well in identifying these slang words.

4.8 Analysis of Users

In this subsection, we analyze users in our dataset based on the result learned by TSM. Figure 8 shows the distribution of the histogram of serious style probability. The majority of users have a high serious style probability, which means most users in our dataset are more eager to give serious comments and express their opinions. This satisfies our observation that most people use forums mainly to discuss and seek knowledge on different topics and they are very eager to express their thoughts in a serious way.

We heuristically split all users into two sets according to user-style probability by setting 0.5 as threshold. Users with probability of serious style

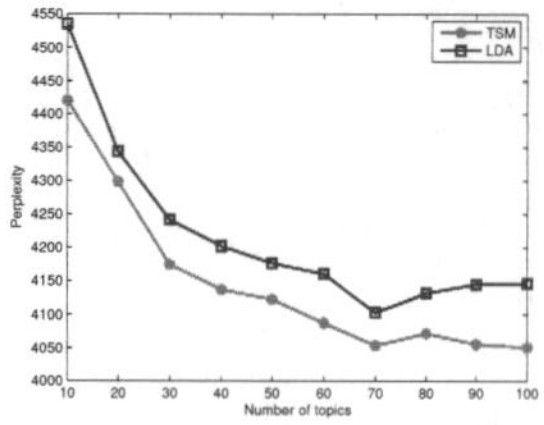

Figure 4: Perplexity

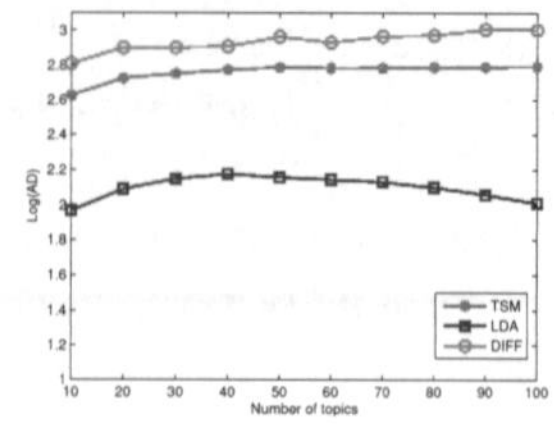

Figure 5: Average Divergence

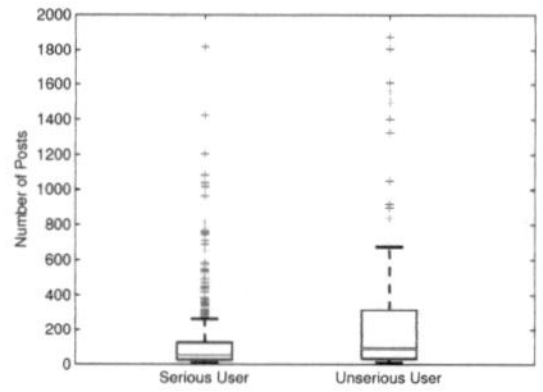

Figure 6: Box plot of post number for serious and unserious users

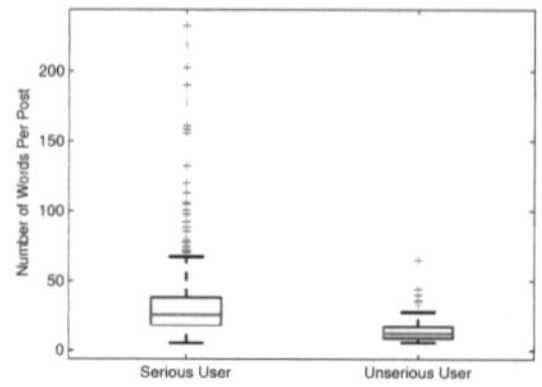

Figure 7: Box plot of average post length for serious and unserious users

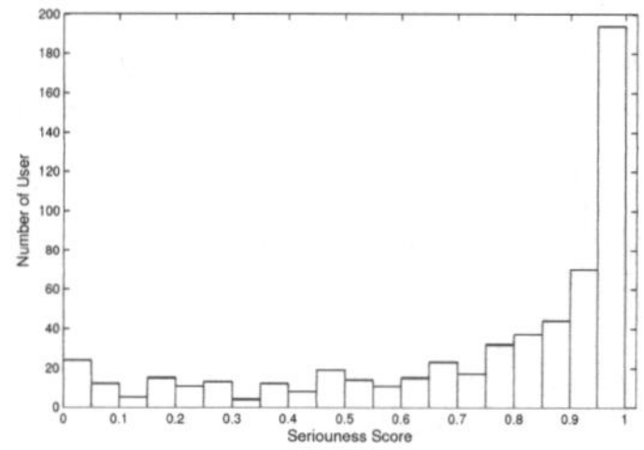

Figure 8: Seriousness Score of Users

larger than 0.5 are regarded as serious users and the remaining are unserious users. Next, we extract the number of posts each user edit and the average number of words per post for each user and compare the difference between these two user sets. Figure 6 and Figure 7 show the box plots of post number and average post length respectively. We can see that serious users edit fewer posts but use more words in each post. To see the difference between serious and unserious users more clearly, we apply Mann-Whitney U test on the post number populations and average post length populations. The Mann-Whitney U test on both data set reject the null hypothesis that two input populations are the same at the 1% significance level. The mean value for post number and average post length are also computed and shown in Table 10. We can find that serious users tend to publish fewer but longer posts than unserious users. This result is intuitive as serious users often spend more effort editing their posts to express their opinions more clearly. However, for unserious users, they may just use a few words to play a joke or show some emotions and they can post many posts without spending too much time.

5 Conclusions

In this paper, we propose a unified probabilistic graphical model, called Topic-Style Model, which models topics and styles at the same time. Traditional topic modeling methods treat a corpus as a mixture of topics. But user-generated content in forum discussions contains not only words related to topics but also words related to different writing styles. The proposed Topic-Style Model can perform well in separating topic-driven words and style-driven words. In this model, we assume that writing style is a consistent writing pattern a user will express in her posts across different threads and use a latent variable at user level to capture the user specific preference of writing styles. Our model can successfully discover writing styles which are different from each other both in word distribution and formality. Words belonging to different writing styles and user specific style distribution are captured by our model at the same time. An extensive set of experiments shows that our method has good performances in separating serious and unserious posts and users. At the same time, the model can identify slang words with promising accuracy, which is proven by our experiments. An analysis based on the learned parameters in our model reveal the difference between serious and unserious users in average post length and post number.

References

Eugene Agichtein, Carlos Castillo, Debora Donato, Aristides Gionis, and Gilad Mishne. 2008. Finding high-quality content in social media. In *Proceedings of the 2008 International Conference on Web Search and Data Mining*, pages 183–194, New York, NY, USA. ACM.

Archana Bhattarai, Vasile Rus, and Dipankar Dasgupta. 2009. Characterizing comment spam in the blogosphere through content analysis. In *Computational Intelligence in Cyber Security, 2009. CICS'09. IEEE Symposium on*, pages 37–44. IEEE.

David M. Blei, Andrew Y. Ng, and Michael I. Jordan. 2003. Latent dirichlet allocation. *J. Mach. Learn. Res.*, 3:993–1022, March.

Julian Brooke, Tong Wang, and Graeme Hirst. 2010. Automatic acquisition of lexical formality. In *Proceedings of the 23rd International Conference on Computational Linguistics: Posters*, pages 90–98, Stroudsburg, PA, USA. Association for Computational Linguistics.

Dmitry Davidov, Oren Tsur, and Ari Rappoport. 2010. Semi-supervised recognition of sarcastic sentences in twitter and amazon. In *Proceedings of the Fourteenth Conference on Computational Natural Language Learning*, pages 107–116, Stroudsburg, PA, USA. Association for Computational Linguistics.

Zhuoye Ding, Yeyun Gong, Yaqian Zhou, Qi Zhang, and Xuanjing Huang. 2013. Detecting spammers in community question answering. In *Proceeding of International Joint Conference on Natural Language Processing*, pages 118–126, Nagoya, Japan. Association for Computational Linguistics.

Roberto González-Ibáñez, Smaranda Muresan, and Nina Wacholder. 2011. Identifying sarcasm in twitter: A closer look. In *Proceedings of the 49th Annual Meeting of the Association for Computational Linguistics: Human Language Technologies: Short Papers - Volume 2*, pages 581–586, Stroudsburg, PA, USA. Association for Computational Linguistics.

Nitin Jindal and Bing Liu. 2008. Opinion spam and analysis. In *Proceedings of the 2008 International Conference on Web Search and Data Mining*, WSDM '08, pages 219–230, New York, NY, USA. ACM.

Jussi Karlgren and Douglass Cutting. 1994. Recognizing text genres with simple metrics using discriminant analysis. In *Proceedings of the 15th Conference on Computational Linguistics - Volume 2*, pages 1071–1075, Stroudsburg, PA, USA. Association for Computational Linguistics.

Qiaozhu Mei, Xu Ling, Matthew Wondra, Hang Su, and ChengXiang Zhai. 2007. Topic sentiment mixture: Modeling facets and opinions in weblogs. In *Proceedings of the 16th International Conference on World Wide Web*, WWW '07, pages 171–180, New York, NY, USA. ACM.

Michael J. Paul, ChengXiang Zhai, and Roxana Girju. 2010. Summarizing contrastive viewpoints in opinionated text. In *Proceedings of the 2010 Conference on Empirical Methods in Natural Language Processing*, EMNLP '10, pages 66–76, Stroudsburg, PA, USA. Association for Computational Linguistics.

Emily Pitler and Ani Nenkova. 2008. Revisiting readability: A unified framework for predicting text quality. In *Proceedings of the Conference on Empirical Methods in Natural Language Processing*, pages 186–195, Stroudsburg, PA, USA. Association for Computational Linguistics.

Michal Rosen-Zvi, Thomas Griffiths, Mark Steyvers, and Padhraic Smyth. 2004. The author-topic model for authors and documents. In *Proceedings of the 20th Conference on Uncertainty in Artificial Intelligence*, pages 487–494, Arlington, Virginia, United States. AUAI Press.

Self-disclosure topic model for Twitter conversations

JinYeong Bak
Department of Computer Science
KAIST
Daejeon, South Korea
jy.bak@kaist.ac.kr

Chin-Yew Lin
Microsoft Research Asia
Beijing 100080, P.R. China
cyl@microsoft.com

Alice Oh
Department of Computer Science
KAIST
Daejeon, South Korea
alice.oh@kaist.edu

Abstract

Self-disclosure, the act of revealing oneself to others, is an important social behavior that contributes positively to intimacy and social support from others. It is a natural behavior, and social scientists have carried out numerous quantitative analyses of it through manual tagging and survey questionnaires. Recently, the flood of data from online social networks (OSN) offers a practical way to observe and analyze self-disclosure behavior at an unprecedented scale. The challenge with such analysis is that OSN data come with no annotations, and it would be impossible to manually annotate the data for a quantitative analysis of self-disclosure. As a solution, we propose a semi-supervised machine learning approach, using a variant of latent Dirichlet allocation for automatically classifying self-disclosure in a massive dataset of Twitter conversations. For measuring the accuracy of our model, we manually annotate a small subset of our dataset, and we show that our model shows significantly higher accuracy and F-measure than various other methods. With the results our model, we uncover a positive and significant relationship between self-disclosure and online conversation frequency over time.

1 Introduction

Self-disclosure is an important and pervasive social behavior. People disclose personal information about themselves to improve and maintain relationships (Jourard, 1971; Joinson and Paine, 2007). For example, when two people meet for the first time, they disclose their names and interests. One positive outcome of self-disclosure is social support from others (Wills, 1985; Derlega et al., 1993), shown also in online social networks (OSN) such as Twitter (Kim et al., 2012). Receiving social support would then lead the user to be more active on OSN (Steinfield et al., 2008; Trepte and Reinecke, 2013). In this paper, we seek to understand this important social behavior using a large-scale Twitter conversation data, automatically classifying the level of self-disclosure using machine learning and correlating the patterns with subsequent OSN usage.

Twitter conversation data, explained in more detail in section 4.1, enable a significantly larger scale study of naturally-occurring self-disclosure behavior, compared to traditional social science studies. One challenge of such large scale study, though, remains in the lack of labeled ground-truth data of self-disclosure level. That is, naturally-occurring Twitter conversations do not come tagged with the level of self-disclosure in each conversation. To overcome that challenge, we propose a semi-supervised machine learning approach using probabilistic topic modeling. Our self-disclosure topic model (SDTM) assumes that self-disclosure behavior can be modeled using a combination of simple linguistic features (e.g., pronouns) with automatically discovered semantic themes (i.e., topics). For instance, an utterance "I am finally through with this disastrous relationship" uses a first-person pronoun and contains a topic about personal relationships.

In comparison with various other models, SDTM shows the highest accuracy, and the resulting self-disclosure patterns of the users are correlated significantly with their future OSN usage. Our contributions to the research community include the following:

- We present a topic model that explicitly includes the level of self-disclosure in a conversation using linguistic features and the latent semantic topics (Sec. 3).

Proceedings of the Joint Workshop on Social Dynamics and Personal Attributes in Social Media, pages 42–49,
Baltimore, Maryland USA, 27 June 2014.

- We collect a large dataset of Twitter conversations over three years and annotate a small subset with self-disclosure level (Sec. 4).

- We compare the classification accuracy of SDTM with other models and show that it performs the best (Sec. 5).

- We correlate the self-disclosure patterns of users and their subsequent OSN usage to show that there is a positive and significant relationship (Sec. 6).

2 Background

In this section, we review literature on the relevant aspects of self-disclosure.

Self-disclosure (*SD*) level: To quantitatively analyze self-disclosure, researchers categorize self-disclosure language into three levels: `G` (general) for no disclosure, `M` for medium disclosure, and `H` for high disclosure (Vondracek and Vondracek, 1971; Barak and Gluck-Ofri, 2007). Utterances that contain general (non-sensitive) information about the self or someone close (e.g., a family member) are categorized as `M`. Examples are personal events, past history, or future plans. Utterances about age, occupation and hobbies are also included. Utterances that contain sensitive information about the self or someone close are categorized as `H`. Sensitive information includes personal characteristics, problematic behaviors, physical appearance and wishful ideas. Generally, these are thoughts and information that one would generally keep as secrets to himself. All other utterances, those that do not contain information about the self or someone close are categorized as `G`. Examples include gossip about celebrities or factual discourse about current events.

Classifying self-disclosure level: Prior work on quantitatively analyzing self-disclosure has relied on user surveys (Trepte and Reinecke, 2013; Ledbetter et al., 2011) or human annotation (Barak and Gluck-Ofri, 2007). These methods consume much time and effort, so they are not suitable for large-scale studies. In prior work closest to ours, Bak et al. (2012) showed that a topic model can be used to identify self-disclosure, but that work applies a two-step process in which a basic topic model is first applied to find the topics, and then the topics are post-processed for binary classification of self-disclosure. We improve upon this work by applying a single unified model of topics and self-disclosure for high accuracy in classifying the three levels of self-disclosure.

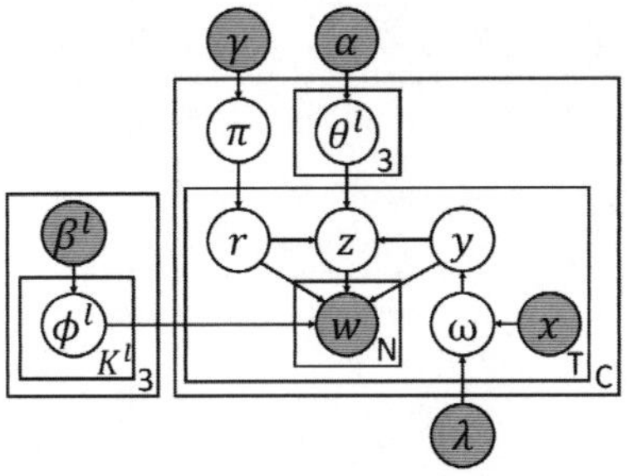

Figure 1: Graphical model of SDTM

Self-disclosure and online social network: According to social psychology, when someone discloses about himself, he will receive social support from those around him (Wills, 1985; Derlega et al., 1993), and this pattern of self-disclosure and social support was verified for Twitter conversation data (Kim et al., 2012). Social support is a major motivation for active usage of social networks services (SNS), and there are findings that show self-disclosure on SNS has a positive longitudinal effect on future SNS use (Trepte and Reinecke, 2013; Ledbetter et al., 2011). While these previous studies focused on small, qualitative studies, we conduct a large-scale, machine learning driven study to approach the question of self-disclosure behavior and SNS use.

3 Self-Disclosure Topic Model

This section describes our model, the self-disclosure topic model (SDTM), for classifying self-disclosure level and discovering topics for each self-disclosure level.

3.1 Model

We make two important assumptions based on our observations of the data. First, first-person pronouns (*I, my, me*) are good indicators for medium level of self-disclosure. For example, phrases such as 'I live' or 'My age is' occur in utterances that reveal personal information. Second, there are topics that occur much more frequently at a particular *SD* level. For instance, topics such as *physical appearance* and *mental health* occur frequently at level `H`, whereas topics such as *birthday* and *hobbies* occur frequently at level `M`.

Figure 1 illustrates the graphical model of SDTM and how these assumptions are embodied

Notation	Description
$G; M; H$	{general; medium; high} SD level
$C; T; N$	Number of conversations; tweets; words
$K^G; K^M; K^H$	Number of topics for {G; M; H}
$c; ct$	Conversation; tweet in conversation c
y_{ct}	SD level of tweet ct, G or M/H
r_{ct}	SD level of tweet ct, M or H
z_{ct}	Topic of tweet ct
w_{ctn}	n^{th} word in tweet ct
$\boldsymbol{\lambda}$	Learned Maximum entropy parameters
$\boldsymbol{x}_{ct}$	First-person pronouns features
$\boldsymbol{\omega}_{ct}$	Distribution over SD level of tweet ct
$\boldsymbol{\pi}_c$	SD level proportion of conversation c
$\boldsymbol{\theta}_c^G; \boldsymbol{\theta}_c^M; \boldsymbol{\theta}_c^H$	Topic proportion of {G; M; H} in conversation c
$\boldsymbol{\phi}^G; \boldsymbol{\phi}^M; \boldsymbol{\phi}^H$	Word distribution of {G; M; H}
$\boldsymbol{\alpha}; \boldsymbol{\gamma}$	Dirichlet prior for θ; π
$\boldsymbol{\beta}^G, \boldsymbol{\beta}^M; \boldsymbol{\beta}^H$	Dirichlet prior for $\phi^G; \phi^M; \phi^H$
n_{cl}	Number of tweets assigned SD level l in conversation c
n_{ck}^l	Number of tweets assigned SD level l and topic k in conversation c
n_{kv}^l	Number of instances of word v assigned SD level l and topic k
m_{ctkv}	Number of instances of word v assigned topic k in tweet ct

Table 1: Summary of notations used in SDTM.

in it. The first assumption about the first-person pronouns is implemented by the observed variable $\boldsymbol{x}_{ct}$ and the parameters $\boldsymbol{\lambda}$ from a maximum entropy classifier for G vs. M/H level. The second assumption is implemented by the three separate word-topic probability vectors for the three levels of SD: $\boldsymbol{\phi}^l$ which has a Bayesian informative prior $\boldsymbol{\beta}^l$ where $l \in \{G, M, H\}$, the three levels of self-disclosure. Table 1 lists the notations used in the model and the generative process, Figure 2 describes the generative process.

3.2 Classifying G vs M/H levels

Classifying the SD level for each tweet is done in two parts, and the first part classifies G vs. M/H levels with first-person pronouns (*I, my, me*). In the graphical model, y is the latent variable that represents this classification, and $\boldsymbol{\omega}$ is the distribution over y. x is the observation of the first-person pronoun in the tweets, and $\boldsymbol{\lambda}$ are the parameters learned from the maximum entropy classifier. With the annotated Twitter conversation dataset (described in Section 4.2), we experimented with several classifiers (Decision tree, Naive Bayes) and chose the maximum entropy classifier because it performed the best, similar to other joint topic models (Zhao et al., 2010; Mukherjee et al., 2013).

1. For each level $l \in \{\mathtt{G}, \mathtt{M}, \mathtt{H}\}$:
   For each topic $k \in \{1, \ldots, K^l\}$:
   Draw $\boldsymbol{\phi}_k^l \sim Dir(\boldsymbol{\beta}^l)$
2. For each conversation $c \in \{1, \ldots, C\}$:
   (a) Draw $\boldsymbol{\theta}_c^G \sim Dir(\boldsymbol{\alpha})$
   (b) Draw $\boldsymbol{\theta}_c^M \sim Dir(\boldsymbol{\alpha})$
   (c) Draw $\boldsymbol{\theta}_c^H \sim Dir(\boldsymbol{\alpha})$
   (d) Draw $\boldsymbol{\pi}_c \sim Dir(\boldsymbol{\gamma})$
   (e) For each message $t \in \{1, \ldots, T\}$:
   i. Observe first-person pronouns features $\boldsymbol{x}_{ct}$
   ii. Draw $\boldsymbol{\omega}_{ct} \sim MaxEnt(\boldsymbol{x}_{ct}, \boldsymbol{\lambda})$
   iii. Draw $y_{ct} \sim Bernoulli(\boldsymbol{\omega}_{ct})$
   iv. If $y_{ct} = 0$ which is G level:
   A. Draw $z_{ct} \sim Mult(\boldsymbol{\theta}_c^G)$
   B. For each word $n \in \{1, \ldots, N\}$:
   Draw word $w_{ctn} \sim Mult(\boldsymbol{\phi}_{z_{ct}}^G)$
   Else which can be M or H level:
   A. Draw $r_{ct} \sim Mult(\boldsymbol{\pi}_c)$
   B. Draw $z_{ct} \sim Mult(\boldsymbol{\theta}_c^{r_{ct}})$
   C. For each word $n \in \{1, \ldots, N\}$:
   Draw word $w_{ctn} \sim Mult(\boldsymbol{\phi}_{z_{ct}}^{r_{ct}})$

Figure 2: Generative process of SDTM.

3.3 Classifying M vs H levels

The second part of the classification, the M and the H level, is driven by informative priors with seed words and seed trigrams.

Utterances with M level include two types: 1) information related with past events and future plans, and 2) general information about self (Barak and Gluck-Ofri, 2007). For the former, we add as seed trigrams 'I have been' and 'I will'. For the latter, we use seven types of information generally accepted to be personally identifiable information (McCallister, 2010), as listed in the left column of Table 2. To find the appropriate trigrams for those, we take Twitter conversation data (described in Section 4.1) and look for trigrams that begin with 'I' and 'my' and occur more than 200 times. We then check each one to see whether it is related with any of the seven types listed in the table. As a result, we find 57 seed trigrams for M level. Table 2 shows several examples.

Type	Trigram
Name	My name is, My last name
Birthday	My birthday is, My birthday party
Location	I live in, I lived in, I live on
Contact	My email address, My phone number
Occupation	My job is, My new job
Education	My high school, My college is
Family	My dad is, My mom is, My family is

Table 2: Example seed trigrams for identifying M level of SD. There are 51 of these used in SDTM.

Utterances with H level express secretive wishes or sensitive information that exposes self or someone close (Barak and Gluck-Ofri, 2007). These are

Category	Keywords
physical appearance	acne, hair, overweight, stomach, chest, hand, scar, thighs, chubby, head, skinny
mental/physical condition	addicted, bulimia, doctor, illness, alcoholic, disease, drugs, pills, anorexic

Table 3: Example words for identifying H level of SD. Categories are hand-labeled.

generally keep as secrests. With this intuition, we crawled 26,523 secret posts from *Six Billion Secrets* [1] site where users post secrets anonymously.

To extract seed words that might express secretive personal information, we compute mutual information (Manning et al., 2008) with the secret posts and 24,610 randomly selected tweets. We select 1,000 words with high mutual information and filter out stop words. Table 3 shows some of these words. To extract seed trigrams of secretive wishes, we again look for trigrams that start with 'I' or 'my', occur more than 200 times, and select trigrams of wishful thinking, such as 'I want to', and 'I wish I'. In total, there are 88 seed words and 8 seed trigrams for H.

3.4 Inference

For posterior inference of SDTM, we use collapsed Gibbs sampling which integrates out latent random variables $\boldsymbol{\omega}, \boldsymbol{\pi}, \boldsymbol{\theta}$, and $\boldsymbol{\phi}$. Then we only need to compute $\boldsymbol{y}, \boldsymbol{r}$ and $\boldsymbol{z}$ for each tweet. We compute full conditional distribution $p(y_{ct} = j', r_{ct} = l', z_{ct} = k' | \boldsymbol{y}_{-ct}, \boldsymbol{r}_{-ct}, \boldsymbol{z}_{-ct}, \boldsymbol{w}, \boldsymbol{x})$ for tweet ct as follows:

$$p(y_{ct} = 0, z_{ct} = k' | \boldsymbol{y}_{-ct}, \boldsymbol{r}_{-ct}, \boldsymbol{z}_{-ct}, \boldsymbol{w}, \boldsymbol{x}) \propto \frac{exp(\boldsymbol{\lambda}_0 \cdot \boldsymbol{x}_{ct})}{\sum_{j=0}^{1} exp(\boldsymbol{\lambda}_j \cdot \boldsymbol{x}_{ct})} \, g(c, t, l', k')$$

$$p(y_{ct} = 1, r_{ct} = l', z_{ct} = k' | \boldsymbol{y}_{-ct}, \boldsymbol{r}_{-ct}, \boldsymbol{z}_{-ct}, \boldsymbol{w}, \boldsymbol{x}) \propto \frac{exp(\boldsymbol{\lambda}_1 \cdot \boldsymbol{x}_{ct})}{\sum_{j=0}^{1} exp(\boldsymbol{\lambda}_j \cdot \boldsymbol{x}_{ct})} (\gamma_{l'} + n_{cl'}^{(-ct)}) \, g(c, t, l', k')$$

where $\boldsymbol{z}_{-ct}, \boldsymbol{r}_{-ct}, \boldsymbol{y}_{-ct}$ are $\boldsymbol{z}, \boldsymbol{r}, \boldsymbol{y}$ without tweet ct, $m_{ctk'(\cdot)}$ is the marginalized sum over word v of $m_{ctk'v}$ and the function $g(c, t, l', k')$ as follows:

$$g(c, t, l', k') = \frac{\Gamma(\sum_{v=1}^{V} \beta_v^{l'} + n_{k'v}^{l'-(ct)})}{\Gamma(\sum_{v=1}^{V} \beta_v^{l'} + n_{k'v}^{l'-(ct)} + m_{ctk'(\cdot)})} \left(\frac{\alpha_{k'} + n_{ck'}^{l'(-ct)}}{\sum_{k=1}^{K} \alpha_k + n_{ck}^{l'}} \right) \prod_{v=1}^{V} \frac{\Gamma(\beta_v^{l'} + n_{k'v}^{l'-(ct)} + m_{ctk'v})}{\Gamma(\beta_v^{l'} + n_{k'v}^{l'-(ct)})}$$

[1] `http://www.sixbillionsecrets.com`

4 Data Collection and Annotation

To answer our research questions, we need a large longitudinal dataset of conversations such that we can analyze the relationship between self-disclosure behavior and conversation frequency over time. We chose to crawl Twitter because it offers a practical and large source of conversations (Ritter et al., 2010). Others have also analyzed Twitter conversations for natural language and social media research (Boyd et al., 2010; Danescu-Niculescu-Mizil et al., 2011), but we collect conversations from the same set of dyads over several months for a unique longitudinal dataset.

4.1 Collecting Twitter conversations

We define a Twitter conversation as a chain of tweets where two users are consecutively replying to each other's tweets using the Twitter reply button. We identify dyads of English-tweeting users with at least twenty conversations and collect their tweets. We use an open source tool for detecting English tweets [2], and to protect users' privacy, we replace Twitter userid, usernames and url in tweets with random strings. This dataset consists of 101,686 users, 61,451 dyads, 1,956,993 conversations and 17,178,638 tweets which were posted between August 2007 to July 2013.

4.2 Annotating self-disclosure level

To measure the accuracy of our model, we randomly sample 101 conversations, each with ten or fewer tweets, and ask three judges, fluent in English, to annotate each tweet with the level of self-disclosure. Judges first read and discussed the definitions and examples of self-disclosure level shown in (Barak and Gluck-Ofri, 2007), then they worked separately on a Web-based platform. Inter-rater agreement using Fleiss kappa (Fleiss, 1971) is 0.67.

5 Classification of Self-Disclosure Level

This section describes experiments and results of SDTM as well as several other methods for classification of self-disclosure level.

We first start with the annotated dataset in section 4.2 in which each tweet is annotated with SD level. We then aggregate all of the tweets of a conversation, and we compute the proportions of tweets in each SD level. When the proportion of

[2] `https://github.com/shuyo/ldig`

tweets at M or H level is equal to or greater than 0.2, we take the level of the larger proportion and assign that level to the conversation. When the proportions of tweets at M or H level are both less than 0.2, we assign G to the SD level.

We compare SDTM with the following methods for classifying tweets for SD level:

- LDA (Blei et al., 2003): A Bayesian topic model. Each conversation is treated as a document. Used in previous work (Bak et al., 2012).
- MedLDA (Zhu et al., 2012): A supervised topic model for document classification. Each conversation is treated as a document and response variable can be mapped to a SD level.
- LIWC (Tausczik and Pennebaker, 2010): Word counts of particular categories. Used in previous work (Houghton and Joinson, 2012).
- Seed words and trigrams (SEED): Occurrence of seed words and trigrams which are described in section 3.3.
- ASUM (Jo and Oh, 2011): A joint model of sentiment and topic using seed words. Each sentiment can be mapped to a SD level. Used in previous work (Bak et al., 2012).
- First-person pronouns (FirstP): Occurrence of first-person pronouns which are described in section 3.2. To identify first-person pronouns, we tagged parts of speech in each tweet with the Twitter POS tagger (Owoputi et al., 2013).

SEED, LIWC, LDA and FirstP cannot be used directly for classification, so we use Maximum entropy model with outputs of each of those models as features. We run MedLDA, ASUM and SDTM 20 times each and compute the average accuracies and F-measure for each level. We set 40 topics for LDA, MedLDA and ASUM, 60; 40; 40 topics for SDTM K^G, K^M and K^H respectively, and set $\alpha = \gamma = 0.1$. To incorporate the seed words and trigrams into ASUM and SDTM, we initialize $\boldsymbol{\beta}^G$, $\boldsymbol{\beta}^M$ and $\boldsymbol{\beta}^H$ differently. We assign a high value of 2.0 for each seed word and trigram for that level, and a low value of 10^{-6} for each word that is a seed word for another level, and a default value of 0.01 for all other words. This approach is same as other topic model works (Jo and Oh, 2011; Kim et al., 2013).

Method	*Acc*	G F_1	M F_1	H F_1	*Avg* F_1
LDA	49.2	0.000	0.650	0.050	0.233
MedLDA	43.3	0.406	0.516	0.093	0.338
LIWC	49.2	0.341	0.607	0.180	0.376
SEED	52.0	0.412	0.600	0.178	0.397
ASUM	56.6	0.320	0.704	0.375	0.466
FirstP	63.2	**0.630**	0.689	0.095	0.472
SDTM	**64.5**	0.611	**0.706**	**0.431**	**0.583**

Table 4: SD level classification accuracies and F-measures using annotated data. *Acc* is accuracy, and G F_1 is F-measure for classifying the G level. *Avg* F_1 is the average value of G F_1, M F_1 and H F_1. SDTM outperforms all other methods compared. The difference between SDTM and FirstP is statistically significant (p-value < 0.05 for accuracy, < 0.0001 for *Avg* F_1).

As Table 4 shows, SDTM performs better than other methods by accuracy and F-measure. LDA and MedLDA generally show the lowest performance, which is not surprising given these models are quite general and not tuned specifically for this type of semi-supervised classification task. LIWC and SEED perform better than LDA, but these have quite low F-measure for G and H levels. ASUM shows better performance for classifying H level than others, but not for classifying the G level. FirstP shows good F-measure for the G level, but the H level F-measure is quite low, even lower than SEED. Finally, SDTM has similar performance in G and M level with FirstP, but it performs better in H level than others. Classifying the H level well is important because as we will discuss later, the H level has the strongest relationship with longitudinal OSN usage (see Section 6.2), so SDTM is overall the best model for classifying self-disclosure levels.

6 Self-Disclosure and Conversation Frequency

In this section, we investigate whether there is a relationship between self-disclosure and conversation frequency over time. (Trepte and Reinecke, 2013) showed that frequent or high-level of self-disclosure in online social networks (OSN) contributes positively to OSN usage, and vice versa. They showed this through an online survey with

Facebook and StudiVZ users. With SDTM, we can automatically classify self-disclosure level of a large number of conversations, so we investigate whether there is a similar relationship between self-disclosure in conversations and subsequent frequency of conversations with the same partner on Twitter. More specifically, we ask the following two questions:

1. If a dyad displays high SD level in their conversations at a particular time period, would they have more frequent conversations subsequently?

2. If a dyad shows high conversation frequency at a particular time period, would they display higher SD in their subsequent conversations?

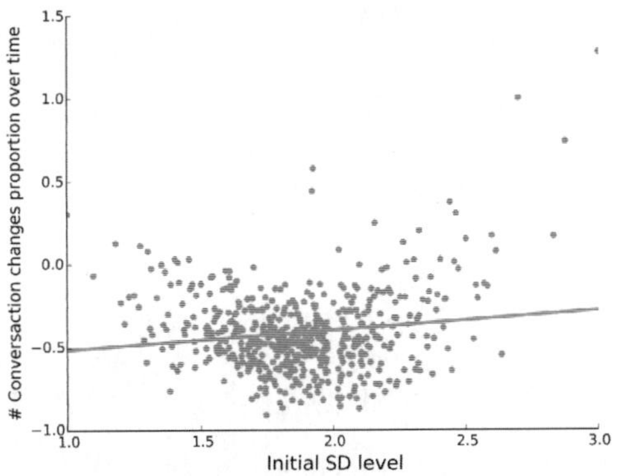

Figure 3: Relationship between initial SD level and conversation frequency changes over time. The solid line is the linear regression line, and the coefficient is 0.118 with $p < 0.001$, which shows a significant positive relationship.

	G level	M level	H level
Coeff (β)	0.094	0.419	0.464
p-value	0.1042	< 0.0001	< 0.0001

Table 6: Relationship between initial SD level proportions and changes in conversation frequency. For M and H levels, there is significant positive relationship ($p < 0.0001$), but for the G level, there is not ($p > 0.1$).

6.1 Experiment Setup

We first run SDTM with all of our Twitter conversation data with 150; 120; 120 topics for SDTM K^G, K^M and K^H respectively. The hyper-parameters are the same as in section 5. To handle a large dataset, we employ a distributed algorithm (Newman et al., 2009).

Table 5 shows some of the topics that were prominent in each SD level by KL-divergence. As expected, G level includes general topics such as food, celebrity, soccer and IT devices, M level includes personal communication and birthday, and finally, H level includes sickness and profanity.

For comparing conversation frequencies over time, we divided the conversations into two sets for each dyad. For the *initial* period, we include conversations from the dyad's first conversation to 60 days later. And for the *subsequent* period, we include conversations during the subsequent 30 days.

We compute proportions of conversation for each SD level for each dyad in the *initial* and *subsequent* periods. Also, we define a new measurement, SD level score for a dyad in the period, which is a weighted sum of each conversation with SD levels mapped to 1, 2, and 3, for the levels G, M, and H, respectively.

6.2 Does self-disclosure lead to more frequent conversations?

We investigate the effect of the level self-disclosure on long-term use of OSN. We run linear regression with the intial SD level score as the independent variable, and the rate of change in conversation frequency between *initial* period and *subsequent* period as the dependent variable.

The result of regression is that the independent variable's coefficient is 0.118 with a low p-value ($p < 0.001$). Figure 3 shows the scatter plot with the regression line, and we can see that the slope of regression line is positive.

We also investigate the importance of each SD level for changes in conversation frequency. We run linear regression with initial proportions of each SD level as the independent variable, and the same dependent variable as above. As table 6 shows, there is no significant relationship between the initial proportion of the G level and the changes in conversation frequency ($p > 0.1$). But for the M and H levels, the initial proportions show positive and significant relationships with the subsequent changes to the conversation frequency ($p < 0.0001$). These results show that M and H levels are correlated with changes to the frequency of conversation.

G level			M level			H level		
101	184	176	36	104	82	113	33	19
chocolate	obama	league	send	twitter	going	ass	better	lips
butter	he's	win	email	follow	party	bitch	sick	kisses
good	romney	game	i'll	tumblr	weekend	fuck	feel	love
cake	vote	season	sent	tweet	day	yo	throat	smiles
peanut	right	team	dm	following	night	shit	cold	softly
milk	president	cup	address	account	dinner	fucking	hope	hand
sugar	people	city	know	fb	birthday	lmao	pain	eyes
cream	good	arsenal	check	followers	tomorrow	shut	good	neck

Table 5: High ranked topics in each level by comparing KL-divergence with other level's topics

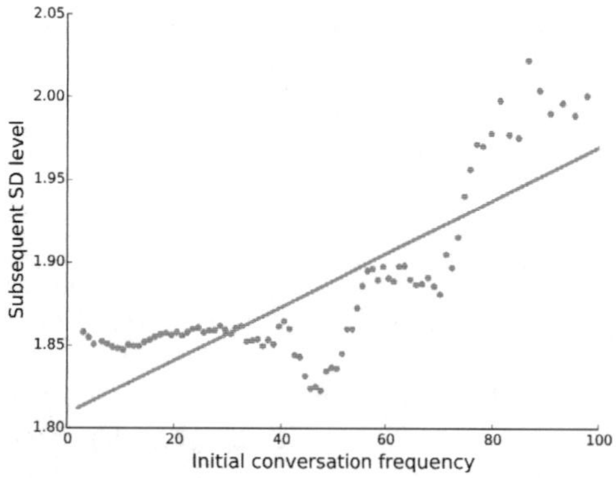

Figure 4: Relationship between initial conversation frequency and subsequent SD level. The solid line is the linear regression line, and the coefficient is 0.0016 with $p < 0.0001$, which shows a significant positive relationship.

6.3 Does high frequency of conversation lead to more self-disclosure?

Now we investigate whether the *initial* conversation frequency is correlated with the SD level in the *subsequent* period. We run linear regression with the initial conversation frequency as the independent variable, and SD level in the subsequent period as the dependent variable.

The regression coefficient is 0.0016 with low p-value ($p < 0.0001$). Figure 4 shows the scatter plot. We can see that the slope of the regression line is positive. This result supports previous results in social psychology (Leung, 2002) that frequency of instant chat program ICQ and session time were correlated to depth of SD in message.

7 Conclusion and Future Work

In this paper, we have presented the self-disclosure topic model (SDTM) for discovering topics and classifying SD levels from Twitter conversation data. We devised a set of effective seed words and trigrams, mined from a dataset of secrets. We also annotated Twitter conversations to make a ground-truth dataset for SD level. With annotated data, we showed that SDTM outperforms previous methods in classification accuracy and F-measure.

We also analyzed the relationship between SD level and conversation frequency over time. We found that there is a positive correlation between initial SD level and subsequent conversation frequency. Also, dyads show higher level of SD if they initially display high conversation frequency. These results support previous results in social psychology research with more robust results from a large-scale dataset, and show importance of looking at SD behavior in OSN.

There are several future directions for this research. First, we can improve our modeling for higher accuracy and better interpretability. For instance, SDTM only considers first-person pronouns and topics. Naturally, there are patterns that can be identified by humans but not captured by pronouns and topics. Second, the number of topics for each level is varied, and so we can explore nonparametric topic models (Teh et al., 2006) which infer the number of topics from the data. Third, we can look at the relationship between self-disclosure behavior and general online social network usage beyond conversations.

Acknowledgments

We thank the anonymous reviewers for helpful comments. Alice Oh was supported by the IT R&D Program of MSIP/KEIT. [10041313, UX-oriented Mobile SW Platform]

References

JinYeong Bak, Suin Kim, and Alice Oh. 2012. Self-disclosure and relationship strength in twitter conversations. In *Proceedings of ACL*.

Azy Barak and Orit Gluck-Ofri. 2007. Degree and reciprocity of self-disclosure in online forums. *CyberPsychology & Behavior*, 10(3):407–417.

David M Blei, Andrew Y Ng, and Michael I Jordan. 2003. Latent dirichlet allocation. *Journal of Machine Learning Research*, 3:993–1022.

Danah Boyd, Scott Golder, and Gilad Lotan. 2010. Tweet, tweet, retweet: Conversational aspects of retweeting on twitter. In *Proceedings of HICSS*.

Cristian Danescu-Niculescu-Mizil, Michael Gamon, and Susan Dumais. 2011. Mark my words!: Linguistic style accommodation in social media. In *Proceedings of WWW*.

Valerian J. Derlega, Sandra Metts, Sandra Petronio, and Stephen T. Margulis. 1993. *Self-Disclosure*, volume 5 of *SAGE Series on Close Relationships*. SAGE Publications, Inc.

Joseph L Fleiss. 1971. Measuring nominal scale agreement among many raters. *Psychological bulletin*, 76(5):378.

David J Houghton and Adam N Joinson. 2012. Linguistic markers of secrets and sensitive self-disclosure in twitter. In *Proceedings of HICSS*.

Yohan Jo and Alice H Oh. 2011. Aspect and sentiment unification model for online review analysis. In *Proceedings of WSDM*.

Adam N Joinson and Carina B Paine. 2007. Self-disclosure, privacy and the internet. *The Oxford handbook of Internet psychology*, pages 237–252.

Sidney M Jourard. 1971. Self-disclosure: An experimental analysis of the transparent self.

Suin Kim, JinYeong Bak, and Alice Haeyun Oh. 2012. Do you feel what i feel? social aspects of emotions in twitter conversations. In *Proceedings of ICWSM*.

Suin Kim, Jianwen Zhang, Zheng Chen, Alice Oh, and Shixia Liu. 2013. A hierarchical aspect-sentiment model for online reviews. In *Proceedings of AAAI*.

Andrew M Ledbetter, Joseph P Mazer, Jocelyn M DeGroot, Kevin R Meyer, Yuping Mao, and Brian Swafford. 2011. Attitudes toward online social connection and self-disclosure as predictors of facebook communication and relational closeness. *Communication Research*, 38(1):27–53.

Louis Leung. 2002. Loneliness, self-disclosure, and icq (" i seek you") use. *CyberPsychology & Behavior*, 5(3):241–251.

Christopher D Manning, Prabhakar Raghavan, and Hinrich Schütze. 2008. *Introduction to information retrieval*, volume 1. Cambridge University Press Cambridge.

Erika McCallister. 2010. *Guide to protecting the confidentiality of personally identifiable information*. DIANE Publishing.

Arjun Mukherjee, Vivek Venkataraman, Bing Liu, and Sharon Meraz. 2013. Public dialogue: Analysis of tolerance in online discussions. In *Proceedings of ACL*.

David Newman, Arthur Asuncion, Padhraic Smyth, and Max Welling. 2009. Distributed algorithms for topic models. *Journal of Machine Learning Research*, 10:1801–1828.

Olutobi Owoputi, Brendan OConnor, Chris Dyer, Kevin Gimpel, Nathan Schneider, and Noah A Smith. 2013. Improved part-of-speech tagging for online conversational text with word clusters. In *Proceedings of HLT-NAACL*.

Alan Ritter, Colin Cherry, and Bill Dolan. 2010. Unsupervised modeling of twitter conversations. In *Proceedings of HLT-NAACL*.

Charles Steinfield, Nicole B Ellison, and Cliff Lampe. 2008. Social capital, self-esteem, and use of online social network sites: A longitudinal analysis. *Journal of Applied Developmental Psychology*, 29(6):434–445.

Yla R Tausczik and James W Pennebaker. 2010. The psychological meaning of words: Liwc and computerized text analysis methods. *Journal of Language and Social Psychology*.

Yee Whye Teh, Michael I Jordan, Matthew J Beal, and David M Blei. 2006. Hierarchical dirichlet processes. *Journal of the american statistical association*, 101(476).

Sabine Trepte and Leonard Reinecke. 2013. The reciprocal effects of social network site use and the disposition for self-disclosure: A longitudinal study. *Computers in Human Behavior*, 29(3):1102 – 1112.

Sarah I Vondracek and Fred W Vondracek. 1971. The manipulation and measurement of self-disclosure in preadolescents. *Merrill-Palmer Quarterly of Behavior and Development*, 17(1):51–58.

Thomas Ashby Wills. 1985. Supportive functions of interpersonal relationships. *Social support and health*, xvii:61–82.

Wayne Xin Zhao, Jing Jiang, Hongfei Yan, and Xiaoming Li. 2010. Jointly modeling aspects and opinions with a maxent-lda hybrid. In *Proceedings of EMNLP*.

Jun Zhu, Amr Ahmed, and Eric P Xing. 2012. Medlda: maximum margin supervised topic models. *Journal of Machine Learning Research*, 13:2237–2278.

Detecting and Evaluating Local Text Reuse in Social Networks

Shaobin Xu*, **David A. Smith***, **Abigail Mullen**†, and **Ryan Cordell**‡
NULab for Texts, Maps, and Networks
College of Computer and Information Science*, Department of History†, Department of English‡
Northeastern University, Boston, MA

Abstract

Texts propagate among participants in many social networks and provide evidence for network structure. We describe intrinsic and extrinsic evaluations for algorithms that detect clusters of reused passages embedded within longer documents in large collections. We explore applications of these approaches to two case studies: the culture of free reprinting in the nineteenth-century United States and the use of similar language in the public statements of U.S. members of Congress.

1 Introduction

While many studies of social networks use surveys and direct observation to catalogue actors (nodes) and their interactions (edges), we often cannot directly observe network links. Instead, we might observe behavior by network participants that provides indirect evidence for social ties.

One revealing form of shared behavior is the reuse of text by different social actors. Methods to uncover invisible links among sources of text methods would have broad applicability because of the very general nature of the problem—sources of text include websites, newspapers, individuals, corporations, political parties, and so on. Further, discerning those hidden links between sources would provide more effective ways of identifying the provenance and diverse sources of information, and to build predictive models of the diffusion of information.

There are substantial challenges, however, in building a methodology to study text reuse, including: scalable detection of reused passages; identification of appropriate statistical models of text mutation; inference methods for characterizing missing nodes that originate or mediate text transmission; link inference conditioned on textual topics; and the development of testbeds through which predictions of the resulting models might be validated against some broader understanding of the processes of transmission.

In this paper, we sketch relevant features of our two testbed collections (§2) and then describe initial progress on developing algorithms for detecting reused passages embedded within the larger text output of social network nodes (§3). We then describe an intrinsic evaluation of the efficiency of these techniques for scaling up text reuse detection (§4). Finally, we perform an extrinsic evaluation of the network links inferred from text reuse by correlating them with side information about the underlying social networks (§5). A preliminary version of the text reuse detection system was presented for a single, smaller corpus in (Anonymous, 2013), but without the extrinsic or much of the intrinsic evaluation and without data on the underlying networks.

2 Case Studies in Text Reuse

The case studies in this paper, which form the basis for our experimental evaluations below, involve two fairly divergent domains: the informational and literary ecology of the nineteenth-century United States and of twenty-first century U.S. legislators.

2.1 Tracking Viral Texts in 19c Newspapers

In *American Literature and the Culture of Reprinting*, McGill (2003) argues that American literary culture in the nineteenth century was shaped by the widespread practice of reprinting stories and poems, usually without authorial permission or even

Proceedings of the Joint Workshop on Social Dynamics and Personal Attributes in Social Media, pages 50–57,
Baltimore, Maryland USA, 27 June 2014.

knowledge, in newspapers, magazines, and books. Without substantial copyright enforcement, texts circulated promiscuously through the print market and were often revised by editors during the process. These "viral" texts—be they news stories, short fiction, or poetry—are much more than historical curiosities. The texts that editors chose to pass on are useful barometers of what was exciting or important to readers during the period, and thus offer significant insight into the priorities and concerns of the culture.

Nineteenth-century U.S. newspapers were usually associated with a particular political party, religious denomination, or social cause (e.g., temperance or abolition). Mapping the specific locations and venues in which varied texts circulated would therefore allow us to answer questions about how reprinting and the public sphere in general were affected by geography, communication and transportation networks, and social, political, and religious affinities. These effects should be particularly observable in the period before the Civil War and the rise of wire services that broadcast content at industrial scales (Figure 1).

To study the reprint culture of this period, we crawled the online newspaper archives of the Library of Congress's *Chronicling America* project (`chroniclingamerica.loc.gov`). Since the Chronicling America project aggregates state-level digitization efforts, there are some significant gaps: e.g., there are no newspapers from Massachusetts, which played a not insubstantial role in the literary culture of the period. While we continue to collect data from other sources in order to improve our network analysis, the current dataset remains a useful, and open, testbed for text reuse detection and analysis of overall trends. For the pre-Civil War period, this corpus contains 1.6 billion words from 41,829 issues of 132 newspapers.

Another difficulty with this collection is that it consists of the OCR'd text of newspaper issues without any marking of article breaks, headlines, or other structure. The local alignment methods described in §3 are designed not only to mitigate this problem, but also to deal with partial reprinting. One newspaper issue, for instance, might reprint chapters 4 and 5 of a Thackeray novel while another issue prints only chapter 5.

Since our goal is to detect texts that spread from one venue to another, we are not interested in texts that were reprinted frequently in the same newspaper, or *series*, to use the cataloguing term. This includes material such as mastheads and manifestos and also the large number of advertisements that recur week after week in the same newspaper.

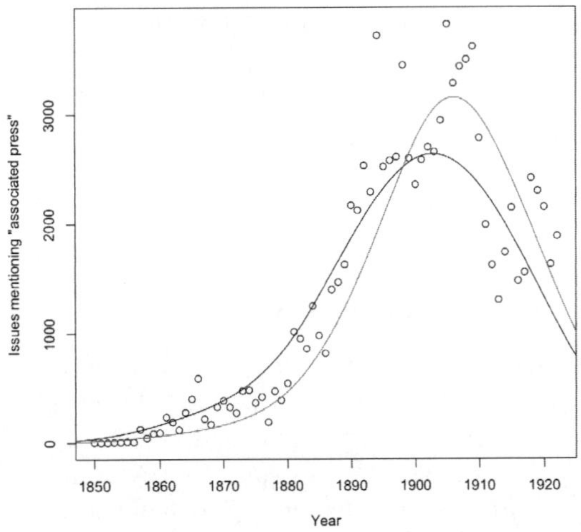

Figure 1: Newspaper issues mentioning "associated press" by year, from the *Chronicling America* corpus. The black regression line fits the raw number of issues; the red line fits counts corrected for the number of times the Associated Press is mentioned in each issue.

2.2 Statements by Members of Congress

Members of the U.S. Congress are of course even more responsive to political debates and incentives than nineteenth-century newspapers. Representatives and senators are also a very well-studied social network. Following Margolin et al. (2013), we analyzed a dataset of more than 400,000 public statements made by members of the 112th Senate and House between January 2011 and August 2012. The statements were downloaded from the Vote Smart Project website (`votesmart.com`). According to Vote Smart, the Members' public statements include any press releases, statements, newspaper articles, interviews, blog entries, newsletters, legislative committee websites, campaign websites and cable news show websites (Meet the Press, This Week, etc.) that contain direct quotes from the Member. Since we are primarily interested in the connections *between* Members, we will, as we see below, want to filter out reuse among different statements by the same member. That information could be interesting for other reasons—for instance, tracking slight changes in the phrasing of talking points or substantive positions.

We supplemented these texts with categorical data chambers and parties and with continuous representations of ideology using the first dimension of the DW-NOMINATE scores (Carroll et al., 2009).

3 Text Reuse Detection

As noted above, we are interested in detecting passages of text reuse (poems or stories; political talking points) that comprise a small fraction of the containing documents (newspaper issues; political speeches). Using the terminology of biological sequence alignment, we are interested in *local alignments* between documents. In text reuse detection research, two primary methods are n-gram shingling and locality-sensitive hashing (LSH) (Henzinger, 2006). The need for local alignments makes LSH less practical without performing a large number of sliding-window matches.

In contrast to work on near-duplicate document detection and to work on "meme tracking" that takes text between quotation marks as the unit of reuse (Leskovec et al., 2009; Suen et al., 2013), here the boundaries of the reused passages are not known. Also in contrast to work on the contemporary news cycle and blogosphere, we are interested both in texts that are reprinted within a few days and after many years. We thus cannot exclude potentially matching documents for being far removed in time. Text reuse that occurs only among documents from the same "source" (run of newspapers; Member of Congress) should be excluded. Similarly, Henzinger (2006) notes that many of the errors in near-duplicate webpage detection arose from false matches among documents from the same website that shared boilerplate navigational elements.

3.1 Efficient N-gram Indexing

The first step is to build for each n-gram feature an inverted index of the documents where it appears. As in other duplicate detection and text reuse applications, we are only interested in the n-grams shared by two or more documents. The index, therefore, does not need to contain entries for the n-grams that occur only once. We use the two-pass space-efficient algorithm described in Huston et al. (2011), which, empirically, is very efficient on large collections. In a first pass, n-grams are hashed into a fixed number of bins. On the second pass, n-grams that hash to bins with one occupant can be discarded; other postings are passed through. Due to hash collisions, there may still be a small number of singleton n-grams that reach this stage. These singletons are filtered out as the index is written.

In building an index of n-grams, an index of (n-1)-grams can also provide a useful filter. No 5-gram, for example, can occur twice unless its constituent 4-grams occur at least twice. We do not use this optimization in our experiments; in practice, n-gram indexing is less expensive than the later steps.

3.2 Extracting and Ranking Candidate Pairs

Once we have an inverted index of the documents that contain each (skip) n-gram, we use it to generate and rank document pairs that are candidates for containing reprinted texts. Each entry, or *posting list*, in the index may be viewed as a set of pairs (d_i, p_i) that record the document identifier and position in that document of that n-gram.

Once we have a posting list of documents containing each distinct n-gram, we output all pairs of documents in each list. We suppress repeated n-grams that appear in different issues of the same newspaper. These repetitions often occur in editorial boilerplate or advertisements, which, while interesting, are outside the scope of this project. We also suppress n-grams that generate more than $\binom{u}{2}$ pairs, where u is a parameter.[1] These frequent n-grams are likely to be common fixed phrases. Filtering terms with high document frequency has led to significant speed increases with small loss in accuracy in other document similarity work (Elsayed et al., 2008). We then sort the list of repeated n-grams by document pair, which allows us to assign a score to each pair based on the number of overlapping n-grams and the distinctiveness of those n-grams. Table 1 shows the parameters for trading off recall and precision at this stage.

3.3 Computing Local Alignments

The initial pass returns a large ranked list of candidate document pairs, but it ignores the order of the n-grams as they occur in each document. We therefore employ local alignment techniques to find compact passages with the highest probability of matching. The goal of this alignment is

[1] The filter is parameterized this way because it is applied after removing document pairs in the same series.

n	n-gram order
w	maximum width of skip n-grams
g	minimum gap of skip n-grams
u	maximum distinct series in the posting list

Table 1: Parameters for text reuse detection

to increase the precision of the detected document pairs while maintaining high recall. Due to the high rate of OCR errors, many n-grams in matching articles will contain slight differences.

Unlike some partial duplicate detection techniques based on global alignment (Yalniz et al., 2011), we cannot expect all or even most of the articles in two newspaper issues, or the text in two books with a shared quotation, to align. Rather, as in some work on biological subsequence alignment (Gusfield, 1997), we are looking for regions of high overlap embedded within sequences that are otherwise unrelated. We therefore employ the Smith-Waterman dynamic programming algorithm with an affine gap penalty. This use of model-based alignment distinguishes this approach for other work, for detecting shorter quotations, that greedily expands areas of n-gram overlap (Kolak and Schilit, 2008; Horton et al., 2010). We do, however, prune the dynamic programming search by forcing the alignment to go through position pairs that contain a matching n-gram from the previous step, as long as the two n-grams are unique in their respective texts. Even the exact Smith-Waterman algorithm, however, is an approximation to the problem we aim to solve. If, for instance, two separate articles from one newspaper issue were reprinted in another newspaper issue in the opposite order—or separated by a long span of unrelated matter—the local alignment algorithm would simply output the better-aligned article pair and ignore the other. Anecdotally, we only observed this phenomenon once in the newspaper collection, where two different parodies of the same poem were reprinted in the same issue. In any case, our approach can easily align different passages in the same document to passages in two other documents.

The dynamic program proceeds as follows. In this paper, two documents would be treated as sequences of text X and Y whose individual characters are indexed as X_i and Y_j. Let $W(X_i, Y_j)$ be the score of aligning character X_i to character Y_j. Higher scores are better. We use a scoring function where only exact character matches get a positive score and any other pair gets a negative score. We also account for additional text appearing on either X or Y. Let W_g be the score, which is negative, of starting a "gap", where one sequence includes text not in the other. Let W_c be the cost for continuing a gap for one more character. This "affine gap" model assigns a lower cost to continuing a gap than to starting one, which has the effect of making the gaps more contiguous. We use an assignment of weights fairly standard in genetic sequences where matching characters score 2, mismatched characters score -1, beginning a gap costs -5, and continuing a gap costs -0.5. We leave for future work the optimization of these weights for the task of capturing shared policy ideas.

As with other dynamic programming algorithms such as Levenshtein distance, the Smith-Waterman algorithm operates by filling in a "chart" of partial results. The chart in this case is a set of cells indexed by the characters in X and Y, and we initialize it as follows:

$$\begin{aligned} H(0,0) &= 0 \\ H(i,0) &= E(i,0) = W_g + i \cdot W_c \\ H(0,j) &= F(0,j) = W_g + j \cdot W_c \end{aligned}$$

The algorithm is then defined by the following recurrence relations:

$$H(i,j) = \max \begin{cases} 0 \\ E(i,j) \\ F(i,j) \\ H(i-1,j-1) + W(X_i, Y_j) \end{cases}$$

$$E(i,j) = \max \begin{cases} E(i,j-1) + W_c \\ H(i,j-1) + W_g + W_c \end{cases}$$

$$F(i,j) = \max \begin{cases} F(i-1,j) + W_c \\ H(i-1,j) + W_g + W_c \end{cases}$$

The main entry in each cell $H(i,j)$ represents the score of the best alignment that terminates at position i and j in each sequence. The intermediate quantities E and F are used for evaluating gaps. Due to taking a max with 0, $H(i,j)$ cannot be negative. This is what allows Smith-Waterman to ignore text before and after the locally aligned substrings of each input.

After completing the chart, we then find the optimum alignment by tracing back from the cell with the highest cumulative value $H(i,j)$ until a cell with a value of 0 is reached. These two cells represent the bounds of the sequence, and the overall SW alignment score reflects the extent to which the characters in the sequences align and the overall length of the sequence.

In our implementation, we include one further speedup: since in a previous step we identified n-grams that are shared between the two documents, we assume that any alignment of those documents must include those n-grams as matches. In some cases, this anchoring of the alignment might lead to suboptimal SW alignment scores.

4 Intrinsic Evaluation

To evaluate the precision and recall of text reuse detection, we create a pseudo-relevant set of document pairs by pooling the results of several runs with different parameter settings. For each document pair found in the union of these runs, we observe the length, in matching characters, of the longest local alignment. (Using matching character length allows us to abstract somewhat from the precise cost matrix.) We can then observe how many aligned passages each method retrieves that are at least 50,000 character matches in length, at least 20,000 character matches in length, and so on. The candidate pairs are sorted by the number of overlapping n-grams; we measure the pseudo-recall at several length cutoffs. For each position in a ranked list of document pairs, we then measure the precision: what proportion of documents retrieved are in fact 50k, 20k, etc., in length? Since we wish to rank documents by the length of the aligned passages they contain, this is a reasonable metric. One summary of these various values is the *average precision*: the mean of the precision at every rank position that contains an actually relevant document pair. One of the few earlier evaluations of local text reuse, by Seo and Croft (2008), compared fingerprinting methods to a trigram baseline. Since their corpus contained short individual news articles, the extent of the reused passages was evaluated qualitatively rather than by alignment.

Figure 2 shows the average precision of different parameter settings on the newspaper collection, ranked by the number of pairs each returns. If the pairwise document step returns a large number of pairs, we will have to perform a large number of more costly Smith-Waterman alignments. On this collection, a good tradeoff between space and speed is achieved by skip bigram features. In the best case, we look at bigrams where there is a gap of at least 95, and not more than 105, words between the first and second terms (n=2 u=100 w=105 g=95).

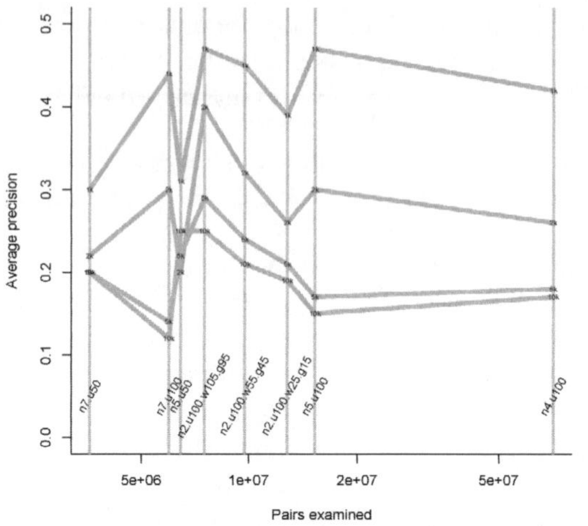

Figure 2: Average precision for aligned passages of different minimum length in characters. Vertical red lines indicate the performance of different parameter settings (see Table 1).

While average precision is a good summary of the quality of the ranked list at any one point, many applications will simply be concerned with the total recall after some fixed amount of processing. Figure 3 also summarizes these recall results by the absolute number of document pairs examined. From these results, it is clear the several good settings perform well at retrieving all reprinted passages of at least 5000 characters. Even using the pseudo-recall metric, however, even the best operating points fail in the end to retrieve about 10% of the reprints detected by some other setting for all documents of at least 1000 characters.

5 Extrinsic Evaluation

While political scientists, historians, and literary scholars will, we hope, find these techniques useful and perform close reading and manual analysis on texts of interest, we would like to validate our results without a costly annotation campaign. In this paper, we explore the correlation of patterns of text reuse with what is already known from other

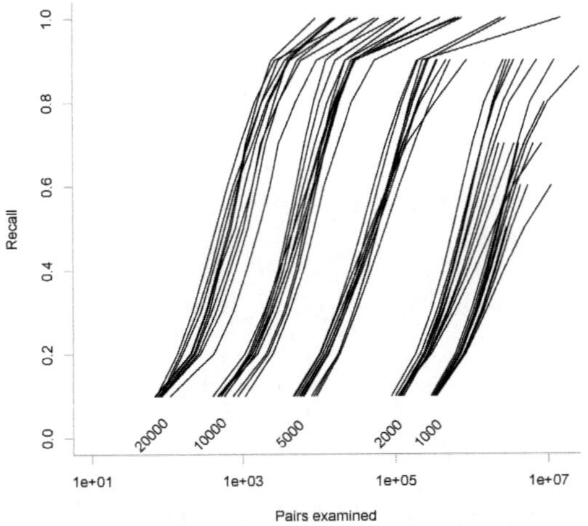

Figure 3: (Pseudo-)Recall for aligned passages of different minimum lengths in characters.

sources about the connections among Members of Congress, newspaper editors, and so on. This idea was inspired by Margolin et al. (2013), who used these techniques to test rhetorical theories of "semantic organizing processes" on the congressional statements corpus.

The approach is quite simple: measure the correlation between some metric of text reuse between actors in a social network and other features of the network links between those actors. The metric of text reuse might be simply the number of exact n-grams shared by the language of two authors (Margolin et al., 2013); alternately, it might be the absolute or relative length of all the aligned passages shared by two authors or the tree distance between them in a phylogenetic reconstruction. To measure the correlation of a text reuse metric with a single network, we can simply use Pearson's correlation; for more networks, we can use multivariate regression. Due to, for instance, autocorrelation among edges arising from a particular node, we cannot proceed as if the weight of each edge in the text reuse network can be compared independently to the weight of the corresponding edges in other networks. We therefore use nonparametric permutation tests using the quadratic assignment procedure (QAP) to resample several networks with the same structure but different labels and weights. The QAP achieves this by reordering the rows and columns of one network's adjacency matrix according to the same permutation. The permuted network then has the same structure—e.g., degree distribution—but should no longer exhibit the same correlations with the other network(s). We can run QAP to generate confidence intervals for both single (Krackhardt, 1987) and multiple correlations (Dekker et al., 2007).

5.1 Congressional Statements

We model the connection between the log magnitude of reused text and the strength of ties among Members according to whether they are in the same chamber and how similar they are on the first dimension of the DW-nominate ideological scale (Carroll et al., 2009). On the left side of Table 2 are shown the results for correlating reused passages of certain minimum lengths (10, 16, 32 words) with these underlying features. On the right are shown the similar results of (Margolin et al., 2013) that simply used the exact size of the n-gram overlap between Members' statements for increasing values of n. The alignment analysis proposed in this paper achieves similar results when passages and n-grams are short. Our analysis, however, achieves higher single and multiple correlations among networks are the passages grow longer. This is unsurprising since the probability of an exact 32-gram match is much smaller than that of a 32-word-long alignment that might contain a few differences. In particular, the much higher coefficients for DW-nominate at longer aligned lengths suggests that ideological influence still dominates over similarities induced by the procedural environment of each congressional chamber.

5.2 Network Connections of 19c Reprints

For the antebellum newspaper corpus, we are also interested in how political affinity correlates with reprinting similar texts. We have also added variables for social causes such as temperance, women's rights, and abolition that—while certainly not orthogonal to political commitments—might sometimes operate independently. In addition, we also added a "shared state" variable to account for shared political and social environments of more limited scope. Figure 4 shows a particularly strong example of a geographic effect: the statement of the radical abolitionist John Brown after being condemned to death for attacking a federal arsenal and attempting to raise a slave rebellion was very unlikely to be published in the

	aligned passages of $\geq n$ words			n-grams of length		
	10	16	32	8	16	32
	First-order Pearson correlations					
DW-nominate	0.26***	0.25***	0.23***	0.26***	0.22***	0.16***
same chamber	0.05*	0.08**	0.13***	-0.05***	0.21***	0.10***
	Regression coefficients					
DW-nominate	0.72***	0.75***	0.74***	1.31***	2.67***	0.36
same chamber	0.15**	0.27***	0.42***	0.20	3.14***	0.81***
R-squared	.069	.070	.073	.068	.073	.010

Table 2: Correlations between log length of aligned text and other author networks in public statements by Members of Congress. $*p < .05, **p < .01, ***p < .001$

South.

Using information from the Chronicling America cataloguing and from other newspaper histories, we coded each of the 132 newspapers in the corpus with these political and social affinities. We then counted the number of reprinted passages shared by each pair of newspapers. There is not a deterministic relationship between the number of *pairs* of newspapers sharing an affinity and the number of *reprints* shared by those papers. While our admittedly partial corpus only contains a single pair of avowedly abolitionist papers—a radical position at the time—those two papers shared articles 306 times, compared for instance to the 71 stories shared among the 6 pairs of "nativist" papers.

Table 3 shows that geographic proximity had by far the strongest correlation with (log) reprinting counts. Interestingly, the only political affinity to show as strong a correlation was the Republican party, which in this period had just been organized and, one might suppose, was trying to control its "message". The Republicans were more geographically concentrated in any case, compared to the sectionally more diffuse Democrats. Another counterexample is the Whigs, the party from which the new Republican party drew many of its members, which also has a slight negative effect on reprinting. The only other large coefficients are in the complete model for smaller movements such as nativism and abolition. It is interesting to speculate about whether the speed or faithfulness of reprinting—as opposed to the volume—might be correlated with more of these variables.

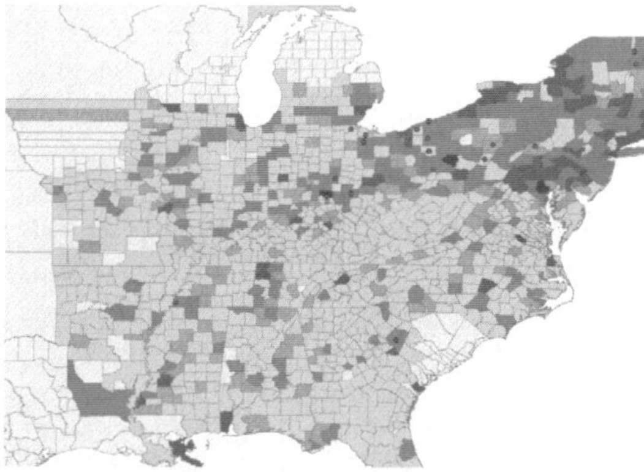

Figure 4: Reprints of John Brown's 1859 speech at his sentencing. Counties are shaded with historical population data, where available. Even taking population differences into account, few newspapers in the South printed the abolitionist's statement.

6 Conclusions

We have presented techniques for detecting reused passages embedded within the larger discourses produced by actors in social networks. Some of this shared content is as brief as partisan talking points or lines of poetry; other reprints can encompass extensive legislative boilerplate or chapters of novels. The longer passages are easier to detect, with prefect pseudo-recall without exhaustive scanning of the corpus. Precision-recall tradeoffs will vary with the density of text reuse and the noise introduced by optical character recognition and other features of data collection. We then showed the feasibility of using network regression to measure the correlations between connections inferred from text reuse and networks derived from outside information.

References

Royce Carroll, Jeff Lewis, James Lo, Nolan McCarty, Keith Poole, and Howard Rosenthal. 2009. Measur-

newspaper affinity	pairs of papers	reprints	regression w/pairs ≥ 1	≥ 10	≥ 100
Republican	1176	134,302	0.74***	0.73*	0.72***
Whig	1176	91,139	-0.35	-0.34	-0.35
Democrat	1081	62,609	-0.08	-0.09	-0.07
same state	672	103,057	1.12***	1.11***	1.13***
anti-secession	435	22,009	-0.58*	-0.58	-0.60
anti-slavery	231	12,742	-0.65	-0.64	-0.60
pro-slavery	120	11,040	-0.35	-0.35	-0.27
Free-State	15	1,194	0.80	0.80	
Constitutional Union	15	1,070	-0.21	-0.21	
pro-secession	15	529	0.11	0.11	
Free Soil	10	1,936	-0.42	-0.42	
Copperhead	10	797	1.53	1.54	
temperance	6	560	0.65		
independent	6	186	-0.22		
nativist	6	71	-1.93*		
women's rights	3	721	1.91		
abolitionist	1	306	3.49**		
Know-Nothing	1	25	1.33		
Mormon	1	3	-1.13		
R-squared	–	–	.065	.063	.062

Table 3: Correlations between shared reprints between 19c newspapers and political and other affinities. While many Whig papers became Republican, they do not completely overlap in our dataset; the identical number of pairs is coincidental.

ing bias and uncertainty in DW-NOMINATE ideal point estimates via the parametric bootstrap. *Political Analysis*, 17(3).

David Dekker, David Krackhardt, and Tom Snijders. 2007. Sensitivity of MRQAP tests to collinearity and autocorrelation conditions. *Psychometrika*, 72(4):563–581.

Tamer Elsayed, Jimmy Lin, and Douglas W. Oard. 2008. Pairwise document similarity in large collections with MapReduce. In *ACL Short Papers*.

Dan Gusfield. 1997. *Algorithms on Strings, Trees, and Sequences*. Cambridge University Press.

Monika Henzinger. 2006. Finding near-duplicate web pages: A large-scale evaluation of algorithms. In *SIGIR*.

Russell Horton, Mark Olsen, and Glenn Roe. 2010. Something borrowed: Sequence alignment and the identification of similar passages in large text collections. *Digital Studies / Le champ numérique*, 2(1).

Samuel Huston, Alistair Moffat, and W. Bruce Croft. 2011. Efficient indexing of repeated n-grams. In *WSDM*.

Okan Kolak and Bill N. Schilit. 2008. Generating links by mining quotations. In *Hypertext*.

David Krackhardt. 1987. QAP partialling as a test of spuriousness. *Social Networks*, 9(2):171–186.

Jure Leskovec, Lars Backstrom, and Jon Kleinberg. 2009. Meme-tracking and the dynamics of the news cycle. In *KDD*.

Drew Margolin, Yu-Ru Lin, and David Lazer. 2013. Why so similar?: Identifying semantic organizing processes in large textual corpora. *SSRN*.

Meredith L. McGill. 2003. *American Literature and the Culture of Reprinting, 1834–1853*. U. Penn. Press.

Jangwon Seo and W. Bruce Croft. 2008. Local text reuse detection. In *SIGIR*.

Caroline Suen, Sandy Huang, Chantat Eksombatchai, Rok Sosič, and Jure Leskovec. 2013. NIFTY: A system for large scale information flow tracking and clustering. In *WWW*.

Ismet Zeki Yalniz, Ethem F. Can, and R. Manmatha. 2011. Partial duplicate detection for large book collections. In *CIKM*.

Generating Subjective Responses to Opinionated Articles in Social Media: An Agenda-Driven Architecture and a Turing-Like Test

Tomer Cagan
School of Computer Science
The Interdisciplinary Center
Herzeliya, Israel
cagan.tomer@idc.ac.il

Stefan L. Frank
Centre for Language Studies
Radboud University
Nijmegen, The Netherlands
s.frank@let.ru.nl

Reut Tsarfaty
Mathematics and Computer Science
Weizmann Institute of Science
Rehovot, Israel
tsarfaty@weizmann.ac.il

Abstract

Natural language traffic in social media (blogs, microblogs, talkbacks) enjoys vast monitoring and *analysis* efforts. However, the question whether computer systems can *generate* such content in order to effectively interact with humans has been only sparsely attended to. This paper presents an architecture for generating subjective responses to opinionated articles based on users' agenda, documents' topics, sentiments and a knowledge graph. We present an empirical evaluation method for quantifying the human-likeness and relevance of the generated responses. We show that responses generated using world knowledge in the input are regarded as more human-like than those that rely on topic, sentiment and agenda only, whereas the use of world knowledge does not affect perceived relevance.

1 Introduction

Digital media, user-generated content and social networks enable effective human interaction; so much so that much of our day-to-day interaction is conducted online (Viswanath et al., 2009). Interaction in social media fundamentally changes the way businesses and consumers behave (Qualman, 2012), can be instrumental to the success of individuals and businesses (Haenlein and Kaplan, 2009), and even affects the stability of political regimes (Howard et al., 2011; Lamer, 2012). These facts force organizations (businesses, governments, and non-profit organizations) to be constantly involved in the monitoring of, and the interaction with, human agents in digital environments (Langheinrich and Karjoth, 2011).

Automatic analysis of user-generated online content benefits from extensive research and commercial opportunities. In natural language processing, there is ample research on the analysis of subjectivity and sentiment of content in social media. The development of tools for sentiment analysis (Davidov et al., 2010), mood aggregation (Agichtein et al., 2008), opinion mining (Mishne, 2006), and many more, now enjoys wide interest and exposure, as is also evident by the many workshops and dedicated tracks at ACL venues.[1] Methods are also developed for the analysis of political texts (O'Connor et al., 2010; O'Connor et al., 2013) and for text-driven forecasting based on these data (Yano et al., 2009). A related strand of research uses computational methods to find out what kind of published utterances are influential, and how they affect linguistic communities (Danescu-Niculescu-Mizil et al., 2009). Such work complements, and contributes to, studies from sociology and sociolinguistics that aim to delineate the process of generating meaningful responses (e.g., Amabile (1981)).

In contrast to these analysis efforts, the topic of *generating* responses to content in social media is only sparsely explored. Commercially, there is movement towards online response automation (Owyang, 2012; Mah, 2012).[2] Research on user interfaces is trying to move away from script-based interaction towards the development of chat bots that attempt natural human-like interaction (Mori et al., 2003; Feng et al., 2006). However, these chat bots are typically designed to provide an automated one-size-fits-all type of interaction.

A study by Ritter et al. (2011) addresses the generation of responses to natural language tweets in a data-driven setup. It applies a machine-translation approach to response generation, where moods and sentiments already ex-

[1] E.g., the ACL series LASM `http://tinyurl.com/ludyrkz`; WASSA `http://tinyurl.com/kjjdhax`.

[2] There is a general debate on the efficiency of automated tools (Nall, 2013) and whether such tools are desirable in social media (McConnell (2012); responses to Owyang (2012)).

Proceedings of the Joint Workshop on Social Dynamics and Personal Attributes in Social Media, pages 58–67,
Baltimore, Maryland USA, 27 June 2014.

pressed in the past are replicated or reused. A recent study by Hasegawa et al. (2013) modifies Ritter's approach to produce responses that elicit an emotion from the addressee. Yet, these responses do not target particular topics and are not driven by a user agenda.

The present paper addresses the problem of generating novel, subjective, responses to online opinionated articles. We formally define the document-to-response mapping problem and suggest an end-to-end system to solve it. Our system integrates a range of NLP and NLG technologies (including topic models, sentiment analysis, and the integration of a knowledge graph) to design a flexible generation mechanism that allows us to vary the information in the input to the generation procedure. We then use a Turing-inspired test to study the different factors that contribute to the perceived human-likeness and relevance of the generated responses, and show how the perception of responses depends on external knowledge and the expressed sentiment.

The remainder of this paper is organized as follows. The next section presents our proposal: Section 2.1 describes our approach, Section 2.2 formalizes the proposal, and Section 2.3 presents our end-to-end architecture. This is followed by our evaluation method and empirical results in Section 3. We discuss related and future work in Section 4, and in Section 5 we conclude.

2 The Proposal: Generating Subjective Responses

2.1 Our Approach

Natural language is, above all, a communicative device that we employ to achieve certain goals. In social media, the driving force behind generating responses is a responder's disposition towards some topic. This topic could be a political campaign or a candidate, a product, or some abstract idea, which the responder has a motive to promote. Let us call this goal our user's *agenda*.

User response generation, like any other natural language utterance generation, is triggered by a certain event that is related to the communicative goal. In a social media setting, this event is often a new online *document*. The document and the agenda thus form the input to our generation system. Each document and each agenda contain (possibly many) topics, each of which is associated with a (positive or negative) sentiment. Document sentiments are attributed to the author, whereas agenda sentiments are attributed to the user (henceforth: the responder).

For each non-empty intersection of the topics in the document and in the agenda, our response-generation system aims to generate utterances that are fluent, human-like, and effectively engage readers. The generation is based on three assumptions, roughly reflecting the Gricean maxims of cooperative interaction (Grice, 1967). Online user responses should then be:

- *Economic* (Maxim of Quantity): Responses are brief and concise;
- *Relevant* (Maxim of Relation): Responses directly address the documents' content.
- *Opinionated* (Maxim of Quality): Responses express responders beliefs, sentiments, or dispositions towards the topic(s).

2.2 The Formal Model

Let D be a set of documents and let A be a set of user agendas as we define shortly. Let S be a set of English sentences over a finite vocabulary $S = \Sigma^*$. Our system implements a function that maps each $\langle document, agenda \rangle$ pair to a natural language response sentence $s \in S$.

$$f_{\text{response}} : D \times A \rightarrow S$$

Response generation takes place in two phases, roughly corresponding to macro and micro planning in Reiter and Dale (1997):

- Macro Planning (below, the *analysis* phase): What are we going to talk about?
- Micro Planning (below, the *generation* phase): How are we going to say it?

The analysis function $p : D \rightarrow C$ maps a document to a subjective representation of its content.[3] The generation function $g : C \times A \rightarrow S$ intersects the content elements in the document and in the user agenda, and generates a response based on the content of the intersection. All in all, our system implements a composition of the analysis and the generation functions:

$$f_{\text{response}}(d, a) = g(p(d), a) = s$$

[3] A content element may conceivably encompass a topic, its sentiment, its objectivity, its evidentiality, its perceived truthfulness, and so on. In this paper we focus on topic and sentiment, and leave the rest for future research.

Each content element $c \in C$ or an agenda item $a \in A$ is composed of a topic t associated with a sentiment value $sentiment_t \in [-n..n]$ that signifies the (negative or positive) disposition of the document's author (if $c \in C$) or the user's agenda (if $a \in A$) towards the topic. We assume here that a topic is simply a bag of words from our vocabulary Σ. Thus, we have the following:

$$A, C \subseteq \mathcal{P}(\Sigma) \times [-n..n]$$

Our generation component accepts the result of the intersection as input and relies on a template-based grammar and a set of functions for generating referring expressions in order to construct the output. To make the responses *economic*, we limit the content of a response to one statement about the document or its author, followed by a statement on the relevant topic. To make the response *relevant*, the templates that generate the response make use of topics in the intersection of the document and the agenda. To make the response *opinionated*, the sentiment of the response depends on the (mis)match between the sentiment values for the topic in the document and in the agenda. Concretely, the response is positive if the sentiments for the topic in the document and agenda are the same (both positive or both negative) and it is negative otherwise.

We suggest two variants of the generation function g. The basic variant implements the baseline function defined above:

$$g_{\text{base}}(c, a) = s$$

$$c \in C, a \in A, s \in \Sigma^*$$

For the other variant we define a knowledge base (KB) as a directed graph in which words $w \in \Sigma$ from the topic models correspond to nodes in the graph, and relations $r \in R$ between the words are predicates that hold in the real world. Our second generation function now becomes:

$$g_{\text{kb}}(c, a, \mathit{KB}) = s$$

$$\mathit{KB} \subseteq \{(w_i, r, w_j) | w_i, w_j \in \Sigma, r \in R\}$$

with $c \in C, a \in A, s \in \Sigma^*$ as defined in g_{base} above.

2.3 The Architecture

The system architecture from a bird's eye view is presented in Figure 1. In a nutshell, a document enters the analysis phase, where topic inference and sentiment scoring take place, resulting in ⟨topic, sentiment⟩-pairs. During the subsequent generation phase, these are intersected with the ⟨topic, sentiment⟩-pairs in the user agenda. This intersection, possibly augmented with a knowledge graph, forms the input for a template-based generation component.

Analysis phase For the task of inferring the topics of the document we use topic modeling: a probabilistic generative modeling technique that allows for the discovery of abstract topics over a large body of documents (Papadimitriou et al., 1998; Hofmann, 1999; Blei et al., 2003). Specifically, we use topic modeling based on *Latent Dirichlet Allocation* (LDA) (Blei et al., 2003; Blei, 2012). Given a new document and a trained model, the inference method provides a weighted mix of topics for that document, where each topic is represented as a vector containing keywords associated with probabilities. For training the topic model and inferring the topics in new documents we use *Gensim* (Rehurek and Sojka, 2010), a fast and easy-to-use implementation of LDA.

Next, we wish to infer the sentiment that is expressed in the text with relation to the topic(s) identified in the document. We use the semantic/lexical method as implemented in Kathuria (2012). We rely on a WSD sentiment classifier that uses the SentiWordNet (Baccianella et al., 2010) database and calculates the positivity and negativity scores of a document based on the positivity and negativity of individual words. The result of the sentiment analysis is a pair of values, indicating the positive and negative sentiments of the document-based scores for individual words. We use the larger of these two values as the sentiment value for the whole document.[4]

Generation phase Our generation function first intersects the set of topics in the document and the set of topics in the agenda in order to discover relevant topics to which the system would generate responses. A response may in principle integrate content from a range of topics in the topic model distribution, but, for the sake of generating concise responses, in the current implementation we focus on the single most prevalent, topic. We pick the highest scoring word of the highest scoring topic, and intersect it with topics in the agenda. The system generates a response based on the identified

[4]Clearly, this is a simplifying assumption. We discuss this assumption further in Section 4.

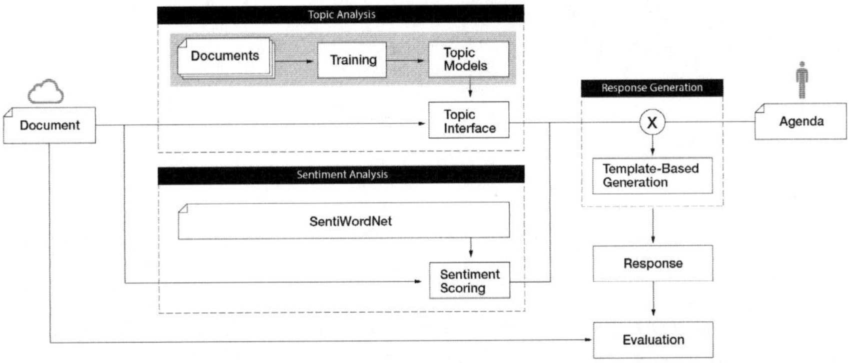

Figure 1: The system architecture from a bird's eye view. Components on gray background are executed offline.

topic, the sentiment for the topic in the document, and the sentiment for that topic in the user agenda.

The generation component relies on a template-based approach similar to Reiter and Dale (1997) and Van Deemter et al. (2005). Templates are essentially subtrees with leaves that are placeholders for other templates or for functions generating referring expressions (Theune et al., 2001). These functions receive (relevant parts of) the input and emit the sequence of fine-grained part-of-speech (POS) tags that realizes the relevant referring expression. The POS tags in the resulting sequences are ultimately place holders for words from a lexicon Σ. In order to generate a variety of expression forms — nouns, adjectives and verbs — these items are selected randomly from a fine-grained lexicon we defined. The sentiment (positive or negative) is expressed in a similar fashion via templates and randomly selected lexical entries for the POS slots, after calculating the overall sentiment for the intersection as stated above. Our generation implementation is based on SimpleNLG (Gatt and Reiter, 2009) which is a surface realizer API that allows us to create the desired templates and functions, and aggregates content into coherent sentences. The templates and functions that we defined are depicted in Figure 2.

In addition, we handcrafted a simple knowledge graph (termed here KB) containing the words in a set of pre-defined user agendas. Table 1 shows a snippet of the constructed knowledge graph. The knowledge graph can be used to expand the response in the following fashion: The topic of the response is a node in the KB. We randomly select one of its outgoing edges for creating a related statement that has the target node of this relation as its subject. The related sentence generation uses the same template-based mechanism as before. In principle, this process may be repeated any number of times and express larger parts of the KB. Here we only add one single knowledge-base relation per response, to keep the responses concise.

Source	Relation	Target
Apple	CompetesWith	Samsung
Apple	CompetesWith	Google
Apple	Creates	iOS

Table 1: A knowledge graph snippet.

3 Evaluation

We set out to evaluate how computer-generated responses compare to human responses in their perceived *human-likeness* and *relevance*. More in particular, we compare different system variants in order to investigate what makes responses seem more human-like or relevant.

3.1 Materials

Our empirical evaluation is restricted to topics related to mobile telephones, specifically Apple's iPhone and devices based on the Android operating system. We collected 300 articles from leading technology sites in the domain to train the topic models on, settling on 10 topics models. Next, we generated a set of user agendas referring to the same 10 topics. Each agenda is represented by a single keyword from a topic model distribution and a sentiment value $sentiment_t \in \{-8, -4, 0, 4, 8\}$. Finally, we selected 10 new articles from similar sites and generated a pool of

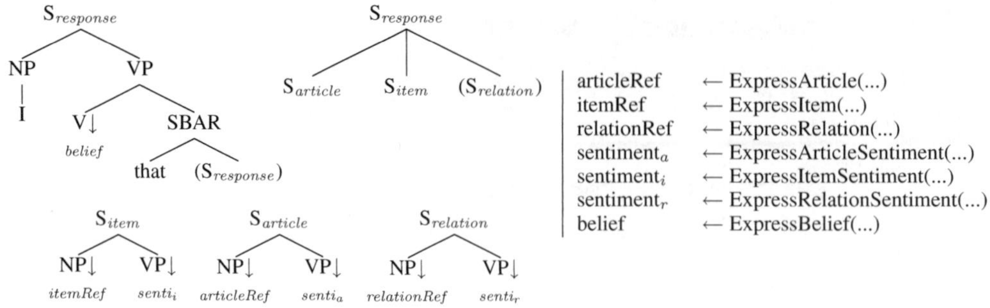

Figure 2: Template-based response generation. The templates are on the left. The Express* functions on the right uses regular expressions over the arguments and vocabulary items from a closed lexicon.

1000 responses for each, comprising 100 unique responses for each combination of $sentiment_t$ and system variant (i.e., with or without a knowledge base). Table 2 presents an example response for each such combination. In addition, we randomly collected 5 to 10 real, short or medium-length, online human responses for each article.

3.2 Surveys

We collected evaluation data via two online surveys on Amazon Mechanical Turk (`www.mturk.com`). In Survey 1, participants judged whether responses to articles were written by human or computer, akin to (a simplified version of) the Turing test (Turing, 1950). In Survey 2, responses were rated on their relevance to the article, in effect testing whether they abide by the Gricean Maxim of Relation. This is comparable to the study by Ritter et al. (2011) where people judged which of two responses was 'best'.

Each survey comprises 10 randomly ordered trials, corresponding to the 10 selected articles. First, the participant was presented with a snippet from the article. When clicking a button, the text was removed and its presentation duration recorded. Next, a multiple-choice question asked about the snippet's topic. Data on a trial was discarded from analysis if the participant answered incorrectly or if the snippet was presented for less than 10 msec per character; we took these to be cases where the snippet was not properly read. Next, the participant was shown a randomly ordered list of responses to the article.

In Survey 1, four responses were presented for each article: three randomly selected from the pool of human responses to that article and one generated by our system. The task was to categorize each response on a 7-point scale with labels 'Certainly human/computer', 'Probably human/computer', 'Maybe human/computer' and 'Unsure'. In Survey 2, five responses were presented: three human responses and two computer-generated. The task was to rate the responses' relevance on a 7-point scale labeled 'Completely (not) relevant', 'Mostly (not) relevant', 'Somewhat (not) relevant', and 'Unsure'. As a control condition, one of the human responses and one of the computer responses were actually taken from another article than the one just presented. In both surveys, the computer-generated responses presented to each participant were balanced across sentiment levels and generation functions (g_{base} and g_{kb}). After completing the 10 trials, participants provided basic demographic information, including native language. Data from non-native English speakers was discarded. Surveys 1 and 2 were completed by 62 and 60 native speakers, respectively.

3.3 Analysis and Results

Survey 1: Computer-Likeness Rating. Table 3 shows the mean 'computer-likeness'-ratings from 1 ('Certainly human') to 7 ('Certainly computer') for each response category. Clearly, the human responses are rated as more human-like than the computer-generated ones: our model did not generally mislead the participants. This may be due to the template-based response structure: over the course of the survey, human raters are likely to notice this structure and infer that such responses are computer-generated. To investigate whether such learning indeed occurs, a linear mixed-effects model was fitted, with predictor variables IS_COMP (+1:computer-generated, −1:human responses), POS (position of the trial in the survey, 0 to 9), and the interaction between the two. Table 4

Sent.	KB	Response
-8	No	Android is horrendous so I think that the writer is completely correct!!!
	Yes	Apple is horrendous so I feel that the author is not really right!!! iOS is horrendous as well.
-4	No	I think that the writer is mistaken because apple actually is unexceptional.
	Yes	I think that the author is wrong because Nokia is mediocre. Apple on the other hand is pretty good ...
0	No	The text is accurate. Apple is okay.
	Yes	Galaxy is okay so I think that the content is accurate. All-in-all samsung makes fantastic gadgets.
4	No	Android is pretty good so I feel that the author is right.
	Yes	Nokia is nice. The article is precise. Samsung on the other hand is fabulous...
8	No	Galaxy is great!!! The text is completely precise.
	Yes	Galaxy is awesome!!! The author is not completely correct. In fact I think that samsung makes awesome products.

Table 2: Responses generated by the system with or without a knowledge-base (KB), with different sentiment levels.

Response Type	Mean and CI
Human	3.33 ± 0.08
Computer (all)	4.49 ± 0.15
Computer ($-$KB)	4.66 ± 0.20
Computer ($+$KB)	4.32 ± 0.22

Table 3: Mean and 95% confidence interval of computer-likeness rating per response category. $\pm$KB indicates whether g_{base} or g_{kb} was used.

Factor	b	t	$P(b < 0)$
(intercept)	3.590		
IS_COMP	0.193	2.11	0.015
POS	0.069	4.76	0.000
IS_COMP × POS	0.085	6.27	0.000

Table 4: Computer-likeness rating regression results, comparing human to computer responses.

presents, for each factor in the regression analysis, the coefficient b and its t-statistic. The coefficient equals the increase in computer-likeness rating for each unit increase in the predictor variable. The t-statistic is indicative of how much variance in the ratings is accounted for by the predictor. We also obtained a probability distribution over each coefficient by Markov Chain Monte Carlo sampling using the R package `lme4` version 0.99 (Bates, 2005). From each coefficient's distribution, we estimate the posterior probability that b is negative, which quantifies the reliability of the effect.

The positive b value for POS shows that responses drift towards the 'computer'-end of the scale. More importantly, a positive interaction with IS_COMP indicates that the difference between human and computer responses becomes more noticeable as the survey progresses — the participants did learn to identify computer-generated responses. However, the positive coefficient for IS_COMP means that even at the very first trial, computer responses are considered to be more computer-like than human responses.

Factors Affecting Human-Likeness. Our finding that the identifiability of computer-generated responses cannot be fully attributed to their repetitiveness, raises the question: What makes a such a response more human-like? The results provide several insights into this matter.

First, the mean scores in Table 3 suggest that including a knowledge base increases the responses' human-likeness. To further investigate this, we performed a separate regression analysis, using only the data on computer-generated responses. This analysis also included predictors KB ($+1$: knowledge base included, -1: otherwise), SENT ($sentiment_t$, from -8 to $+8$), absolute value of SENT, and the interaction between KB and POS. As can be seen in Table 5, there is no reliable interaction between KB and POS: the effect of including the KB on the human-likeness of responses remained constant over the course of the survey.

Furthermore, we see evidence that responses with a more positive sentiment are considered more computer-like. The (only weakly reliable) negative effect of the absolute value of sentiment suggests that more extreme sentiments are considered more human-like. Apparently, people count on computer responses to be mildly positive, whereas human responses are expected to be more extreme, and extremely negative in particular.

Survey 2: Relevance Rating. The mean relevance scores in Table 6 reveal that a response is rated as more relevant to a snippet if it was actually a response to that snippet, rather than to a different snippet. This reinforces our design choice

Factor	b	t	$P(b < 0)$
(intercept)	4.022		
KB	−0.240	−2.13	0.987
POS	0.144	5.82	0.000
SENT	0.035	2.98	0.002
abs(SENT)	−0.041	−1.97	0.967
KB × POS	0.023	1.03	0.121

Table 5: Computer-likeness rating regression results, comparing systems with and without KB.

Response Type	Source	Mean and CI
Human	this	4.85 ± 0.11
	other	3.56 ± 0.18
Computer (all)	this	4.52 ± 0.16
	other	2.52 ± 0.15
Computer (−KB)	this	4.53 ± 0.23
	other	2.46 ± 0.21
Computer (+KB)	this	4.51 ± 0.23
	other	2.58 ± 0.22

Table 6: Mean and 95% confidence interval of relevance rating per response category. 'Source' indicates whether the response is from the presented text snippet or a random other snippet. ±KB indicates whether g_{base} or g_{kb} was used.

Factor	b	t	$P(b < 0)$
(intercept)	3.861		
IS_COMP	−0.339	−7.10	1.000
SOURCE	0.824	16.80	0.000
IS_COMP × PRES	0.179	5.03	0.000

Table 7: Relevance ratings regression results, comparing human to computer responses.

Factor	b	t	$P(b < 0)$
(intercept)	3.603		
KB	0.026	0.49	0.322
SOURCE	1.003	15.90	0.000
SENT	0.023	1.94	0.029
abs(SENT)	−0.017	−0.93	0.819
KB × SOURCE	−0.032	−0.61	0.731

Table 8: Relevance ratings regression results, comparing systems with and without KB.

to include input items referring specifically to the topic and sentiment of the author. However, human responses are considered more relevant than the computer-generated ones. This is confirmed by a reliably negative regression coefficient for IS_COMP (see regression results in Table 7).

The analysis included the binary factor SOURCE (+1 if the response came from the presented snippet, −1 if it came from a random article). We see a positive interaction between SOURCE and IS_COMP, indicating that presenting a response from a random article is more detrimental to relevance of computer-generated responses than that of the human responses. This is not surprising, as the computer-generated responses (unlike the human responses) always includes the article's topic.

When analyzing only data on computer-generated responses, and including predictors for agenda sentiment and for presence of the knowledge base, we see that including the KB does not affect response relevance (see Table 8). Also, there is no interaction between KB and SOURCE, that is, the effect of presenting a response from a different article does not differ between the models with and without the knowledge base. Possibly, responses are considered as more relevant if they have more positive sentiment, but the evidence for this is fairly weak.

4 Related and Future Work

In contrast to the vast amount of research on sentiment and topic analysis, as well as generation tasks in which the input is artificial or pre-defined, our system implements a full end-to-end cycle from natural language analysis to natural language generation with applications in social media and automated interaction in real-world settings.

The only two other studies on response generation in social media we know of are Ritter et al. (2011) and Hasegawa et al. (2013). Ritter's and Hasegawa's approaches differ from ours in their objective and their approach to generation. Specifically, Ritter's approach is based on machine translation, creating responses by directly re-using previous content. Their data-driven approach generates relevant, but not opinionated responses. In addition, both Ritter's and Hasegawa's systems respond to tweets, while our system analyzes and responds to complete articles. Hasegawa's approach is closer to ours in that it generates responses that are intended to elicit a specific emotion from the addressee. However, it still differs considerably in settings (dialogues versus online posting) and in the goal itself (eliciting emotion versus expressing opinion). Thus, we see these studies as complementary to ours in the realm of response generation in social media.

A natural contact point of our work with existing work in social media analysis is the investigation of how a change in the implementation of individual components (e.g., topic inference or sentiment scoring) would affect the result of the overall generation. In particular, it would be interesting to test whether a novel mechanism for joint inference of topic/sentiment distributions could lead to improvement in the human-likeness of the generated responses.

The syntactic and semantic means of expression that we use are based on bare bone templates and fine-grained POS tags (Theune et al., 2001). These may potentially be expanded with different ways to express subject/object relations, relations between phrases, polarity of sentences, and so on. Additional approaches to generation can factor in such aspects, e.g., the template-based methods in Becker (2002) and Narayan et al. (2011), or grammar based methods, as in DeVault et al. (2008). Using more sophisticated generation methods with a rich grammatical backbone may combat the sensitivity to computer-generated response patterns as acquired by our human raters over time.

Furthermore, our result concerning the human-likeness of g_{kb} clearly demonstrates that semantic knowledge must be brought in to support better, and more human-like, response generation. Large-scale knowledge graphs such as Freebase support many semantic tasks (Jacobs, 1985), and can be used for providing richer context for automatically generating human-like responses.

From a theoretical viewpoint, the system will clearly benefit from rigorous analysis of human interaction in online media. Responses to user-generated content on the Internet share some linguistic characteristics in structure, length and manner of expression. Studying these features theoretically and then examining them empirically using a Turing-like evaluation as presented here can take us a big step in the direction of better generation, and also better understanding of the processes underlying human response generation.

This latter understanding may be complemented with insights into the causes, motivations and intricacies of human interaction in such environments, as studied by sociologists and psychologists. In particular, our preliminary interaction with colleagues from communication studies suggests that the present endeavor nicely complements that of "persuasive computing" (Fogg, 1998; Fogg, 2002), and we hope that this collaboration will lead to valuable synergies.

Finally, bridging the gap between the technical and the theoretical, it would be fascinating to test the responses in the context for which they are generated – social media. Generated texts may be posted as a response to the original article, or shared with a link of the original article, followed by measuring the responses to, and shares of, that response. Such real-world evaluation could indicate that generated responses are indeed believable and engaging, and may better simulate a Turing-like test in which machine-generated responses cannot be distinguished from human responses.

5 Conclusion

We presented a system for generating responses that are directly tied to responders' agendas and document content. To the best of our knowledge, this is the first system to generate subjective responses directly reflecting users' agendas. Our response generation architecture provides an easy-to-use and easy-to-extend solution encompassing a range of NLP and NLG techniques. We evaluated both the human-likeness and the relevance of the generated content, thereby empirically quantifying the efficacy of computer-generated responses compared head-to-head against human responses.

Generating concise, relevant, and opinionated responses that are also human-like is hard — it requires the integration of text-understanding and sentiment analysis, and it is also contingent on the expression of the agents' prior knowledge, reasons and motives. We suggest our architecture and evaluation method as a baseline for future research on generated content that would effectively pass a Turing-like test, and successfully convince humans of the authenticity of generated responses.[5]

Acknowledgments

We thank Yoav Francis for his contribution in the early stages of this research. We further thank our anonymous reviewers for their insightful comments on an earlier draft.

[5]Our code, training data, experimental data (computer and human responses) and analysis scripts are publicly available via `www.tsarfaty.com/nlg-sd/`.

References

Eugene Agichtein, Carlos Castillo, Debora Donato, Aristides Gionis, and Gilad Mishne. 2008. Finding high-quality content in social media. In *Proceedings of the international conference on Web search and web data mining*, pages 183–194. ACM.

Teresa M. Amabile. 1981. *Brilliant but Cruel: Perceptions of Negative Evaluators*. Washington, DC: ERIC Clearinghouse.

Stefano Baccianella, Andrea Esuli, and Fabrizio Sebastiani. 2010. SentiWordNet 3.0: An enhanced lexical resource for sentiment analysis and opinion mining. In *Proceedings of the Seventh International Conference on Language Resources and Evaluation (LREC'10)*, Valletta, Malta. European Language Resources Association (ELRA).

Douglas M. Bates. 2005. Fitting linear mixed models in R. *R News*, 5:27–30.

Tilman Becker. 2002. Practical, template-based natural language generation with TAG. In *Proceedings of the 6th International Workshop on Tree Adjoining Grammars and Related Frameworks (TAG+6)*.

David M. Blei, Andrew Y. Ng, and Michael I. Jordan. 2003. Latent Dirichlet Allocation. *J. Mach. Learn. Res.*, 3:993–1022.

David M. Blei. 2012. Probabilistic topic models. *Commun. ACM*, 55(4):77–84.

Cristian Danescu-Niculescu-Mizil, Gueorgi Kossinets, Jon Kleinberg, and Lillian Lee. 2009. How opinions are received by online communities: A case study on amazon.com helpfulness votes. In *Proceedings of the 18th International Conference on World Wide Web*, WWW '09, pages 141–150, New York, NY, USA. ACM.

Dmitry Davidov, Oren Tsur, and Ari Rappoport. 2010. Enhanced sentiment learning using Twitter hashtags and smileys. In *Proceedings of the 23rd International Conference on Computational Linguistics*, pages 241–249, Stroudsburg, PA, USA. Association for Computational Linguistics.

David DeVault, David Traum, and Ron Artstein. 2008. Practical grammar-based NLG from examples. In *Proceedings of the Fifth International Natural Language Generation Conference*, INLG '08, pages 77–85, Stroudsburg, PA, USA. Association for Computational Linguistics.

Donghui Feng, Erin Shaw, Jihie Kim, and Eduard Hovy. 2006. An intelligent discussion-bot for answering student queries in threaded discussions. In *Proceedings of Intelligent User Interface (IUI-2006)*, pages 171–177.

B. J. Fogg. 1998. Persuasive computers: Perspectives and research directions. In *Proceedings of the SIGCHI Conference on Human Factors in Computing Systems*, CHI '98, pages 225–232, New York, NY, USA. ACM Press/Addison-Wesley Publishing Co.

B. J. Fogg. 2002. Persuasive technology: Using computers to change what we think and do. *Ubiquity*, December.

Albert Gatt and Ehud Reiter. 2009. SimpleNLG: A realisation engine for practical applications. In *Proceedings of the 12th European Workshop on Natural Language Generation*, ENLG '09, pages 90–93, Stroudsburg, PA, USA. Association for Computational Linguistics.

H. P. Grice. 1967. Logic and conversation. In H. P. Grice, editor, *Studies in the ways of words*, pages 22–40. Harvard University Press.

Michael Haenlein and Andreas M. Kaplan. 2009. Flagship brand stores within virtual worlds: The impact of virtual store exposure on real-life attitude toward the brand and purchase intent. *Recherche et Applications en Marketing (English Edition)*, 24(3):57–79.

Takayuki Hasegawa, Nobuhiro Kaji, Naoki Yoshinaga, and Masashi Toyoda. 2013. Predicting and eliciting addressee's emotion in online dialogue. In *Proceedings of the 51st Annual Meeting of the Association for Computational Linguistics (Volume 1: Long Papers)*, pages 964–972, Sofia, Bulgaria, August. Association for Computational Linguistics.

Thomas Hofmann. 1999. Probabilistic Latent Semantic Indexing. In *Proceedings of the 22nd Annual International ACM SIGIR Conference on Research and Development in Information Retrieval*, SIGIR '99, pages 50–57, New York, NY, USA. ACM.

Philip N. Howard, Aiden Duffy, Deen Freelon, Muzammil Hussain, Will Mari, and Marwa Mazaid. 2011. Opening closed regimes: What was the role of social media during the Arab spring? *Project on Information Technology and Political Islam.*

Paul S Jacobs. 1985. A knowledge-based approach to language production. Technical report, University of California at Berkeley, Berkeley, CA, USA.

Pulkit Kathuria. 2012. Sentiment Classification using WSD, Maximum Entropy and Naive Bayes Classifiers. *https://github.com/kevincobain2000/sentiment_classifier*. Visited March 2014.

Wiebke Lamer. 2012. Twitter and tyrants: New media and its effects on sovereignty in the Middle East. *Arab Media and Society*.

Marc Langheinrich and Günter Karjoth. 2011. Social networking and the risk to companies and institutions. *Information Security Technical Report. Special Issue: Identity Reconstruction and Theft*, pages 51–56.

Paul Mah. 2012. Tools to automate your customer service response on social media. *http://www.itbusinessedge.com/blogs/smb-tech/tools-to-automate-your-customer-service-response-on-social-media.html*. Visited August 2013.

Chris McConnell. 2012. When brands automate Twitter and Facebook responses I'll revolt. *http://dailytekk.com/2012/06/07/brands-automating-social-media/*. Visited August 2013.

Gilad Mishne. 2006. Multiple ranking strategies for opinion retrieval in blogs. In *Proceedings of the 15th Text Retrieval Conference*.

Kyoshi Mori, Adam Jatowt, and Mitsuru Ishizuka. 2003. Enhancing conversational flexibility in multimodal interactions with embodied lifelike agent. In *Proceedings of the 8th International Conference on Intelligent User Interfaces*, IUI '03, pages 270–272, New York, NY, USA. ACM.

Mickey Nall. 2013. You can't automate social media engagement, argues PRSA's Mickey Nall. *http://www.prmoment.com/1359/you-cant-automate-social-media-engagement-argues-prsas-mickey-nall.aspx*. Visited August 2013.

Karthik Sankaran Narayan, Charles Lee Isbell Jr., and David L. Roberts. 2011. Dextor: Reduced effort authoring for template-based natural language generation. In Vadim Bulitko and Mark O. Riedl, editors, *Proceedings of the Seventh Artificial Intelligence and Interactive Digital Entertainment Conference*. The AAAI Press.

Brendan O'Connor, Ramnath Balasubramanyan, Bryan R. Routledge, and Noah A. Smith. 2010. From tweets to polls: Linking text sentiment to public opinion time series. In William W. Cohen and Samuel Gosling, editors, *ICWSM*. The AAAI Press.

Brendan O'Connor, Brandon M. Stewart, and Noah A. Smith. 2013. Learning to extract international relations from political context. In *Proceedings of the 51st Annual Meeting of the Association for Computational Linguistics (Volume 1: Long Papers)*, pages 1094–1104. The Association for Computer Linguistics.

Jeremiah Owyang. 2012. Brands Start Automating Social Media Responses on Facebook and Twitter. *http://techcrunch.com/2012/06/07/brands-start-automating-social-media-responses-on-facebook-and-twitter/*. Visited August 2013.

Christos H. Papadimitriou, Hisao Tamaki, Prabhakar Raghavan, and Santosh Vempala. 1998. Latent Semantic Indexing: A probabilistic analysis. In *Proceedings of the Seventeenth ACM SIGACT-SIGMOD-SIGART Symposium on Principles of Database Systems*, PODS '98, pages 159–168, New York, NY, USA. ACM.

Erik Qualman. 2012. *Socialnomics: How social media transforms the way we live and do business*. John Wiley & Sons, Hoboken, NJ, USA, 2nd edition.

Radim Rehurek and Petr Sojka. 2010. Software framework for topic modelling with large corpora. In *Proceedings of the LREC 2010 Workshop on New Challenges for NLP Frameworks*, pages 45–50, Valletta, Malta, May. ELRA.

Ehud Reiter and Robert Dale. 1997. Building applied natural language generation systems. *Nat. Lang. Eng.*, 3(1):57–87.

Alan Ritter, Colin Cherry, and William B. Dolan. 2011. Data-driven response generation in social media. In *Proceedings of the Conference on Empirical Methods in Natural Language Processing*, EMNLP '11, pages 583–593, Stroudsburg, PA, USA. Association for Computational Linguistics.

M. Theune, E. Klabbers, J. R. De Pijper, E. Krahmer, and J. Odijk. 2001. From data to speech: A general approach. *Nat. Lang. Eng.*, 7(1):47–86.

Alan M. Turing. 1950. Computing machinery and intelligence. *Mind*, LIX:433–460.

Kees Van Deemter, Emiel Krahmer, and Mariët Theune. 2005. Real versus template-based natural language generation: A false opposition? *Comput. Linguist.*, 31(1):15–24.

Bimal Viswanath, Alan Mislove, Meeyoung Cha, and Krishna P. Gummadi. 2009. On the evolution of user interaction in Facebook. In *Proceedings of the 2nd ACM Workshop on Online Social Networks*, WOSN '09, pages 37–42, New York, NY, USA. ACM.

Tae Yano, William W. Cohen, and Noah A. Smith. 2009. Predicting response to political blog posts with topic models. In *Proceedings of Human Language Technologies: The 2009 Annual Conference of the North American Chapter of the Association for Computational Linguistics*, NAACL '09, pages 477–485, Stroudsburg, PA, USA. Association for Computational Linguistics.

A Semi-Automated Method of Network Text Analysis Applied to 150 Original Screenplays

Starling David Hunter III
Carnegie Mellon University
Tepper School of Business
starling@andrew.cmu.edu

Abstract

In this paper I apply a novel method of network text analysis to a sample of 150 original screenplays. That sample is divided evenly between unproduced, original screenplays (n = 75) and those that were nominated for Best Original Screenplay by either the Academy of Motion Picture Arts & Sciences or by major film critics associations (n = 75). As predicted, I find that the text networks derived from unproduced screenplays are significantly less complex, i.e. they contain fewer concepts (nodes) and statements (links). Unexpectedly, I find that those same networks are more cohesive, i.e. they exhibit higher density and coreness.

1 Introduction

Diesner & Carley (2005, p. 83) employ the term *network text analysis* (NTA) to describe a wide variety of "computer supported solutions" that enable analysts to "extract networks of concepts" from texts and to discern the "meaning" represented or encoded therein. The key underlying assumption of such methods or solutions, they assert, is that the "language and knowledge" embodied in a text may be "modeled" as a network "of words *and the relations between them* " (ibid, emphasis added). A second important assumption is that the position of concepts within a text network provides insight into the meaning or prominent themes of the text as a whole.

Broadly considered, creating networks from texts has two basic steps: (1) the assignment of words and phrases to conceptual categories and (2) the assignment of links to pairs of those categories. Approaches to NTA differ with regard to how these steps are performed, as well as to the level of automation or computer support, the linguistic unit of analysis (e.g. noun or verbs), and the degree and basis of concept generalization. In the social sciences, several studies in the last two decades have linked the structural properties of text networks to measures of individual, group/team, and organizational performance (Nadkarni & Narayaran, 2005). The quantitative empirical literature on this topic can be divided into two groups or streams—educational psychology (EP) and managerial and organizational cognition (MOC). The former typically links structural properties of text networks abstracted from documents like exams and case analyses to academic performance and learning outcomes. The latter abstracts text networks from reports generated by firm's managers, e.g. letters to shareholders and 10-K filings, and links those properties directly or indirectly to firm performance.

Across both streams, the structural properties of networks that have been examined fall into three broad categories—measures of *complexity* or size, measures of *cohesion* or connectedness, and measures of *centrality* or concentration. Another point of consensus concerns the underlying relationships from which the text networks are constructed. Most of the quantitative and empirical studies have relied upon logical relationships among concepts in documents for that purpose. These relationships include, but are not limited to, dependence, chronology, similarity, functionality, causality, and composition (Popping, 2003, pp. 94-5). The second and less commonly used type of relationship involves the co-occurrence of concepts within a user-defined window (e.g. Carley, 1997). Notably, grammatical and lexical relationships have received no attention in the empirical literature. However, Hunter (in press) recently described a "novel", semi-automated method of network text analysis whereby multimorphemic compounds (e.g. abbreviations, acronyms, blend words, clipped words, and compound words) in a text are linked via shared etymological roots. He applied that method to sample of seven recent winners of the Academy Award for Best Original Screenplay and found that the most centrally-positioned words in five of the seven networks corresponded very closely to the themes contained in the films' synopses

Proceedings of the Joint Workshop on Social Dynamics and Personal Attributes in Social Media, pages 68–76,
Baltimore, Maryland USA, 27 June 2014.

found on Wikipedia, IMDb and Rotten Tomatoes.

This study represents the first application of Hunter's method to a sample of screenplays of sufficient size to permit multivariate statistical analysis. The specific aim of the study is to examine the relationship between text networks' properties and performance outcomes. To that end, I herein develop and test two falsifiable hypotheses concerning that relationship on a sample of 150 contemporary screenplays—half winners and nominees of major awards and the other half unproduced screenplays obtained from two online screenplay portals. Consistent with the prior literature I find that the more favorably rated screenplays—i.e. the award winners and nominees—have significantly larger text networks than the unproduced ones. Unexpectedly, I find that text networks of these screenplays exhibit significantly lower cohesiveness, i.e. lower density and coreness.

The remainder of this paper is organized as follows. In section 2, *Theory & Hypotheses*, I summarize the relevant social science literature on text network properties and performance and formulate two hypotheses concerning that relationship. In the third section, *Data & Methods*, I describe the data set and the method for constructing the text networks for each screenplay in the sample. In the fourth section, *Results & Discussion*, I report the level of statistical support found for each hypothesis and discuss the implication of the results for current and future research in this area.

2 Theory & Hypotheses

Figure 1, below, is adapted from Carley (1997) and it is typical of many network representations of texts. The network itself was constructed from the following two sentences: "Organizations use information systems to handle data. Information is processed by organizations who are interested in locating behavioral trends."

Several things about the network are noteworthy. First, observe that there are seven *concepts* depicted as nodes in the network, each of which appears only once. They are "organizations", "information systems", "process", "information", "interested", "locating", and "trends." Second, see that there are also seven *statements*, i.e. pairs of concepts: (1) "information systems" and "process" (2) "information systems" and "organizations" (3) "process" and 'information" (4) "process" and "organizations" (5) "interested" and "organizations" (6) "interested" and "locating" and (7) "locating" and "trends." Third, note that the *map* itself is comprised of the network formed by all seven *statements*. Typically, the analyst must read some or all of the *statements* in a *map* in order to extract the meaning of the text as a whole. In this regard, it is then notable that the seven *concepts* are implicated in varying numbers of *statements*. Specifically, the *concepts* labeled "organization" and "process" are found in three *statements* while all other *concepts* are found in either two or one.

Figure1: A Simple Text Network (adapted from Carley, 1997)

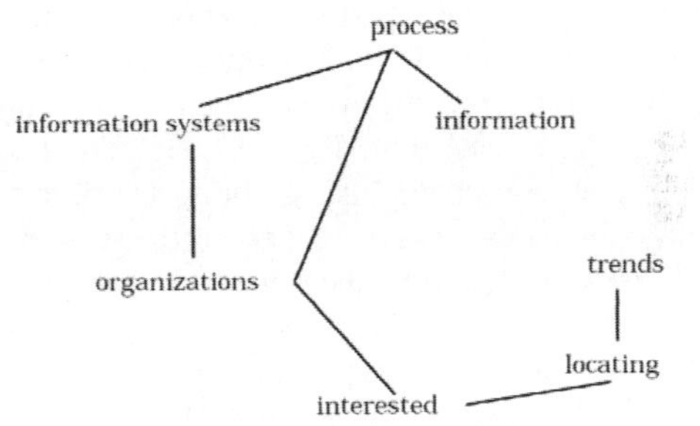

In the social science literature, the most widely-investigated structural property of text networks are the number of concepts and the number of links between pairs of concepts. For example, Calori, Johnson & Sarnin (1994) studied the moderating effects of "environmental complexity", i.e. the scope of the organization as measured by the number of distinct businesses and geographic segments, on the relationship between the "cognitive complexity of the chief executive" and firm performance. One of their measures of cognitive complexity was the number of concepts abstracted from interviews with each CEO about their firm's environment. They hypothesized that cognitive maps of CEOs of more diverse firms had more "comprehensive", i.e. larger, cognitive maps than CEOs of more focused firms. This hypothesis was NOT supported. However, they also hypothesized that cognitive maps of CEOs in firms with greater international geographic scope would contain more concepts. This hypothesis was supported.

Nadkarni (2003, p. 336) employed the term "comprehensiveness" to refer to the "number of concepts in a mental model." In a study of students exposed to three different instructional methods, he hypothesized and found (1) significant differences in the comprehensiveness of the mental models of students of student across methods and (2) greater comprehensiveness in said models among students with low-learning maturity who were exposed to a "hybrid" method of instruction, i.e. a mix of lecture-discussion and experiential learning.

Nadkarni & Narayaran (2005) examined the relationship of two measures of "complexity"—the number of concepts and the number of statements—on learning outcomes. Specifically, they reported a positive relationship between the number of concepts and links found in "text-based causal maps" abstracted from students' written case analyses and their course grades.

Carley (1997) compared the mental models of eight project teams, each with 4-6 members, enrolled in an information systems project course at a private university. Each team was required to "analyze a client's need and then design and build an information system to meet that need within one semester." Five of these teams were eventually deemed successful and three were not. At three points during the semester, each team was required to provide responses to two open-ended questions—"What is an information system?" and "What leads to information system success or failure?" Their answers were coded and used as data. On average, the "cognitive maps" of the members of successful groups had significantly more concepts and more statements (links) compared to maps by members of non-successful groups. In light of the aforementioned studies, the first hypothesis (H1) is that *network complexity, measured as the number of concepts and/or links, is positively related to performance.*

As a class, measures of network *cohesion* indicate the degree to which the nodes in a network are connected to one another. Common measures of cohesion include, but are not limited to, density, fragmentation, connectedness, average path distance, and diameter (Borgatti, Everett, and Freeman, 2002). But while many such measures exist, very few empirical studies have directly examined the linkage between the cohesion in text networks and measures of performance. One such study is Nadkarni & Narayaran's (2005) aforementioned analysis of text-based causal maps abstracted from business case studies. They hypothesized and found network density—measured as the ratio of the number of links to the number of *possible* links—to be positively related to three measures of academic performance—test grades, case analysis grades, and class participation scores.

A second such study is Bodin's (2012) investigation of "university physics student's epistemic framing when solving and visualizing a physics problem using a particle-spring model system" (p. 1). In that study, concept networks were developed from two sets of interview transcripts where students described the task and (physics) problem they were about to solve, as well as their planned strategies for solving the problem. An analysis of networks drawn prior to and right after completion of the assignment revealed a 24% increase in the number of concepts, a 71% increase in the number of links, and 12% increase in network density. While all of these quantities were in the predicted direction, no statistical significance was indicated. Still, the existing empirical evidence suggests network density is positively related to performance. And because various network cohesion measures are closely related conceptually—and can be strongly correlated, as well (Borgatti, Everett, &Johnson, 2014)—then it is more appropriate to phrase the second hypothesis (H2) in more general terms, i.e. *that network cohesion is positively related to performance.*

3 Methods & Data

As indicated in the preceding section, the empirical literature has been focused on two kinds of texts—student assignments and firm reporting—and two kinds of performance—grades and financial performance. But there is nothing inherent in these network text analytic methods that limits investigation to the texts mentioned above. Nor has any of the research reviewed indicated otherwise. That said, a number of specific rationales motivated the selection of screenplays, in general, and original screenplays in particular. First, screenplays are highly structured texts, both logically and temporally, with the three-act structure in screenwriting being a prime example (Field, 1998). Second, there exists a large, widely-read, and broadly-disseminated body of knowledge concerning the theory and best practice of screenwriting (e.g. Snyder, 2005; McKee, 2010; Field, 2007). Third, screenplays are carefully evaluated by many interested parties on numerous dimensions, not the least of which are commercial success and artistic merit (Simonton, 2005; Pardoe & Simonton 2008). Finally, the performance of their authors is discrete and quite unambiguous: more than 15,000 screenplays are registered in the US each year with the Writer's Guild of America but fewer than 700 get "green-lighted" and are subsequently produced (Eliashberg, Elberse, & Enders, 2006). Further, those screenplays that do get "green-lighted" either garner awards or critical acclaim or they do not (Simonton, 2004, 2005).

Somewhat surprisingly, textual analyses of screenplays are relatively rare when compared to analyses of other literary forms such as novels, plays, and poetry. The only studies of which I am aware that links textual variables of screenplays to performance are those by Elishaberg, Hui, & Zhang (2007, 2014) whose kernel-based approach to the study of 300 movies released between 1995 and 2010 significantly predicted Return on investment, i.e. box office revenues as a percentage of budget. The present study represents the first attempt to link textual measures of screenplays to a non-financial-related performance measure.

Screenplays contained in the sample were obtained from a variety of sources. The oldest and most prestigious awards in American cinema are the Academy Awards, aka the "Oscars" (Osborne, 1989) and several studies have been done explaining their artistic and commercial importance (e.g., Krauss, Nan, Simon, et al, 2008; Lee, 2009; Simonton, 2004). Academy Award nominated and winning screenplays are routinely studied by aspiring screenwriters (New York Film Academy, 2014) and widely available online either for free (Simply Scripts, 2014) or purchase (Script Fly, 2014). Winners and nominees of other awards are often available online, as are the screenplays of films which garner no particular artistic acclaim. There are, as well, numerous online forums, websites, and blogs devoted to their discussion and analysis. Moreover, the screenplays for award-nominated, award-winning, and critically-acclaimed films are usually made available by their producers or studios during the award season, but not all of them remain so. In this study, the "produced" or high-performing sample of screenplays are of two kinds. The first consists of nominees and winners of the Academy Award for Best Original Screenplay. Five screenplays are nominated each year making for a potential sample of 40 screenplays. However, two screenplays by Woody Allen—*Blue Jasmine* and *Midnight in Paris*—were not available. Another five nominees whose films were all or partially in foreign-languages were also excluded—*Pan's Labyrinth* (Spanish), *Amour* (French), *A Separation* (Farsi), *Babel* (Arabic, English, Spanish, and Japanese), and *Letters from Iwo Jima* (Japanese). Thus there were 32 remaining Academy Award nominated screenplays for films released in the years 2006-2013.

Another fifty-two (52) screenplays were nominated in the years 2006-13 for Best Original Screenplay by the 32 regional members of the American Film Critics Association, e.g. the New York, Washington D.C., and San Francisco Film Critics Circles. Several of these were not commercially or otherwise available. These include *Upstream Color*, *The Tree of Life*, *Frances Ha*, *World's End*, *Sound of My Voice*, *United 93*, and *Stranger than Fiction*. *Toy Story 3* was excluded because, while an original screenplay, it was part of a film franchise. The South African film *Black Book* was excluded, as well, because it was not in English. The remaining 43 screenplays were obtained. Thus there was a total of 75 screenplays contained in the produced and thus "high-performing" category.

Another 75 unproduced screenplays were randomly selected from two online screenplay databases—*Simply Scripts* and *Trigger Street Labs*. The former hosts pages within its site titled "Unproduced Scripts" where screenwriters are invited to upload their screenplays. Trigger Street Labs is a portal maintained by actor Kevin Spacey's Trigger Street Productions. It allows writers to post original short stories, short films, and screenplays. Thirty-eight (38) screenplays posted between January 1, 2006 and December 31st, 2013 and between 100 and 140 pages were randomly selected from both sites. One was then selected at random and eliminated, making the total number of unproduced screenplays seventy-five (75).

Diesner (2012) outlines four steps for the creation of a text network—(1) Selection (2) Abstraction (3) Relation and (4) Extraction. The first step involves identification of those words that will be subjected to subsequent analysis and the elimination of those that will not. Following Hunter (in press), this stage involved retention of all multi-morphemic compounds comprised of two or more free (unbound) morphemes. These included, but were not limited to, closed and hyphenated compound words, clipped words, blend words or portmanteau, and all acronyms, anacronyms, abbreviations, and initialisms.

Also included were selected instances of conversion, certain prefixes and suffixes, plus selected multi-word compounds and infixes, Examples are shown in Table 1 below. And though it may seem otherwise, this is no random grouping. Rather, they comprise a well-defined, interrelated set that is extensively-studied in the field of morphology. Specifically, they all belong to the branch of morphology known as word-formation, the study of creation of new or "novel" words principally through changes in their form (Wisniewski, 2007).

Because no existing text mining software selects these groups words from a text, the process for identifying them was only semi-automated with the help of a software program called Automap 3.0.10 (Carley, 2001-2013).

Table 1: Examples of 12 Types of Novel Words in the Sample

Type	Examples
Compounding *>Closed Compounds*	briefcase, cowboy, deadline, handcuffs, inmate
Compounding *>Copulative compounds*	attorney-client, actor/model
Compounding *> Open Compounds*	post office, fire alarm
Compounding *>Hyphenated Compounds*	open-minded, panic-stricken, tree-lined
Compounding *> Multi-word Compounds*	Over-the-top, jack-in-the-box, sister-in-law
Derivation *> Affixation> Prefix*	understand, overdrive, overhand, underhanded
Derivation *> Affixation> Suffix*	awesome, hardware, software, clockwise
Derivation *> Affixation> Infix*	*Un*bloody*believable*, *fan*blooming*tastic*
Derivation *> non-Affixation> Abbreviations, Acronyms*	DMV, MTV, FBI, VCR, Yuppie, radar, scuba, laser
Derivation> *non-Affixation> Blend Words*	medevac, motel, guess-timate, camcorder, helipad
Derivation> *non-Affixation> Clipped Words*	Internet, hi-fi, email, slo-mo, vid-com
Derivation> *non-Affixation> Conversion*	eyeball; photoshop

The process was as follows. First the screenplay was converted to a text file and uploaded to Automap. After removing single letters, extra spaces, and spurious characters, two routines were run within Automap—*Identify Possible Acronyms* and *Concept List.* The former routine identified and extracted all words that were capitalized. Several of these turned out to acronyms or abbreviations. The latter routine used was *Concept List (Per Text)* which generated a list of all unique words for each text. Excluded from consideration were all proper nouns (Green Zone, Hollywood), place and organization names (South Pole, Scotland Yard, Burger King), product names (Land Rover), holidays (New Year's Eve, Christmas Eve), as well as any other word or phrase connoting a specific person, place, or thing through capitalization. Also eliminated were all instances of screenplay and film jargon, e.g. ECU (extreme close-up), off-screen, VO (voice-over) and POV (point of view), as well as multi-word exclamations and interjections such as good night, goodbye, OMG (oh my God), etc.

The second of the four steps of constructing a text network involves abstraction of the selected multi-morphemic compounds to higher-order concepts. In this study, each of the free (unbound) morphemes in each compound was assigned to its etymological root, typically the Indo-European, Latin, or Greek (Watkins, 2011).

By definition, from every etymological root descends or originates at least one word, otherwise it is not a root. That relationship is genitive, i.e. a relational case typically expressing source, possession, or partition. It is hierarchical and directed—from the root (parent) to word (descendent). Thus, in the third step of network construction, two or more etymological roots were linked or related when words (free morphemes) descending from them co-occurred within the same word, as the following examples demonstrates.

Consider a text that contains the following nine words: the closed compound words *manpower*, *sunlight, southwestern*, and *gentlemen*; the open compounds *vesper rose,* and *native tongue*; the hyphenated compound *solar-powered self-possessed*; and the proper noun *Secretary General.* As shown in Table 2, below, these words are all multi-morphemic compounds, each element of which descends from two different etymological roots.

Table 2: Selected Indo-European Roots and their Derivatives (Watkins, 2011)

Roots (definition)	Selected Derivatives
wes-pero- (evening)	West, Visigoth, vesper
wrod- (rose)	rose, julep, rhodium
dnghu- (tongue)	tongue, language, linguist
leuk- (light, brightness)	light, lux, illumination, lunar, luster, illustrate, lucid,
man-1 (man)	man, mannequin, mensch
poti (powerful; lord)	possess, power, possible, potent, and pasha
saewel (the sun)	sun, south, solar, solstice
gene- (to give birth)	gender, general, gene, genius, engine, genuine, gentle, pregnant, nation, native.
s(w)e- (self)	self, suicide, secede, secret, secure, sever, sure, sober, sole, idiom, and idiot.

Figure 2: A Text Network Based on Etymological Relationships among Selected Multi-morphemic Compounds Contained in Table 1

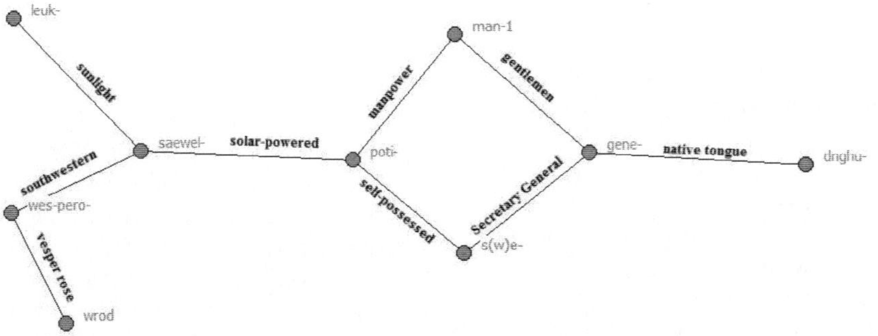

Recall that a *statement* in NTA is comprised of two concepts and the relationship that links them. In Figure 2, above, each of these words appears on the link between the two etymological roots—the concepts—that co-occur within the word. Put another way, the relationship is the co-occurrence of two different etymological roots in the same multi-morphemic compound or multi-word expression—co-occurrence in what is essentially a window of one word. For example, the etymological roots **gene-** (to give birth; beget) and **man-1** (man) are linked by their co-occurrence in the compound word *gentleman*. Taken together, that word and those two roots comprise a statement. And as shown below, it is possible to construct an entire map or network from these interconnected statements. Specifically, that network is comprised of eight concepts—namely, the Indo-European roots ***dnghu-***, ***gene-***, ***man1***, ***s(w)e-***, ***poti-***, ***saewel-***, ***leuk***, ***wrod-*** and ***wes-pero***—and the nine multi-morphemic compounds—*native tongue*, *gentleman*, *Secretary General*, *self-possessed*, *manpower*, *solar power*, *sunlight*, *vesper rose*, and *southwestern*.

A similar approach was used to constructing text networks for each of the 150 screenplays in the sample. Specifically, after matching all of the above classes of multi-morphemic compounds to their corresponding etymological roots, all pairs of roots for each screenplay were converted into a symmetrical matrix which was then uploaded into version 6.487 of the UCINet software program (Borgatti, Everett, and Freeman, 2002). Text networks were then generated using version 2.118 of the NetDraw software program embedded in UCINet. Figure 3, below, is depicted main component of the text network for the screenplay of *Zero Dark Thirty*. which was nominated for Best Original Screenplay in 2012. The main component is the largest group of mutually-reachable nodes in a network. Note that the node labels are etymological roots, typically Indo-European (Watkins, 2011) In the case of words with non-Indo-European roots, the base form of the component of the multi-morphemic compound is used.

The fourth stage involves the extraction of meaning from the completed text network. But since the investigation of meaning is not a part of this analysis, it is excluded from further consideration. See Hunter (in press) for a detailed discussion and examples. Table 3, below, summarizes some basic statistics and network metrics for the 150 screenplays in the sample.

Table 3 Summary Statistics (n =150)

Variable	Mean	Range
Words (000's)	20.9	9.3 - 36.2
Genre = Comedy Only	0.17	0 - 1
Concepts/Nodes	176	84 - 320
Statements/Pairs of Nodes	173	72 337
Density	1.2%	0.66 - 2.50%
Core-Periphery	1.7%	0.40 - 3.10%
Normalized Degree	0.32	0.14 - 1.06
Network Centralization	1.7%	0.83 - 4.43%

4 Results & Discussion

Recall that the first hypothesis (H1) proposed that network complexity was positively related to performance. Following the prior literature, complexity was measured as both the number of concepts in a network, i.e. the number of unique etymological roots, and as the number of statements, i.e. the number of pairs of concepts.. Because these values were very highly correlated ($\rho = 0.98$, $p < 0.0001$) their respective z-scores were averaged to obtain a single value for complexity. Table 4a, below, presents the results of a multinomial regression of screenplay genre, word count, and network complexity on screenplay type. The positive coefficients on complexity indicate that, as predicted, text networks of screenplays of winners and nominees of Academy Awards ($\beta = 0.574$, $p < 0.0001$) and critics' awards ($\beta = 0.359$, $p < 0.01$) have significantly greater complexity than text networks of unproduced screenplays. The Nagelkerke, Cox & Snell, and McFadden pseudo-R2 values were 30.6%, 26.7%, and 15.0%, respectively. Thus, H1 is strongly supported.

Table 4a: Multinomial Regression of Genre, Word Count, and Network Complexity on Type of Screenplay

Category	Variable	Estimate
Critic's Awards	Genre = Comedy	-3.775
	SQRT(Words/1000)	-0.114
	Complexity	**0.359****
Academy Awards	Genre = Comedy	-0.315*
	SQRT(Words/1000)	0.011
	Complexity	**0.574******

The second hypothesis (H2) predicted that network cohesion would be positively related to performance. In this study cohesion was measured by density and coreness (the degree to which the network is characterized by a tightly interconnected core and a much less tightly connected periphery).

Because these two values were highly correlated ($\rho = 0.55$, $p < 0.001$), the z-scores for each measure were averaged to obtain a single value for cohesion. Table 4b presents the results of a multinomial regression of screenplay genre, word count, and network cohesion on screenplay type. The negative and significant value of the coefficients indicates that cohesion is negatively associated with performance, the exact opposite of what was predicted.

Specifically, cohesion of text networks derived from screenplays in the Academy ($\beta = -0.870$, $p < 0.0001$) and critics award ($\beta = -0.413$, $p < 0.001$) categories is significantly lower than that for unproduced screenplays. That means they typically have both lower density and/or a less core-periphery type structure. The Nagelkerke, Cox & Snell, and McFadden pseudo-R^2 values were 36.8%, 32.1%, and 18.7%, respectively.

Taken together, the results suggest that text networks derived from original screenplays selected by the Academy and by film critics have very different structural properties than text networks derived from unproduced screenplays. In short, the former are larger, yet held together by proportionately fewer linkages.

Table 4b: Multinomial Regression of Genre, Word Count, and Network Cohesion on Type of Screenplay

Category	Variable	β
Critic's Awards	Genre = Comedy	-3.809
	SQRT(Words/1000)	-0.139
	Cohesion	**-0.413*****
Academy Awards	Comedy	-0.395**
	SQRT(Words/1000)	-0.078
	Cohesion	**-0.870******

The reason for this disparity may well have to do with the size of the networks under examination. In both the educational psychology and the managerial and organizational cognition literatures, the typical size of the networks is about 1/6 that of those examined here. Recall that as a network grows, the number of *possible* connections grows exponentially. As such, density becomes smaller at an exponential rate. In this study, the text networks derived from both sets of screenplays had concept to statement ratios of close to unity. Thus, given that the award winners and nominees had much larger text networks, it follows logically that those networks were also much less dense.

Figure 3: Main Component of the Text Network of *Zero Dark Thirty*

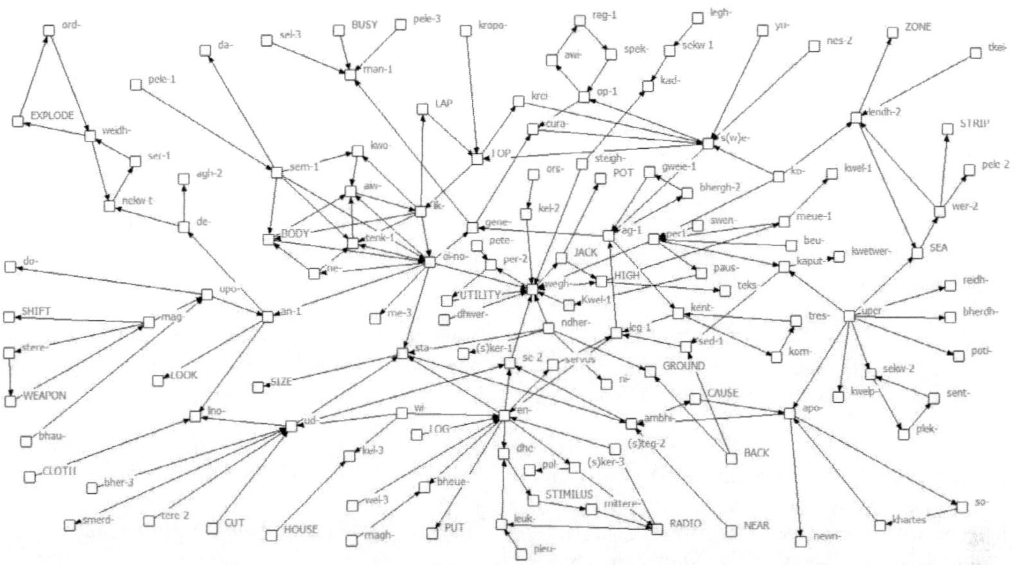

In closing, it is important to recognize three important limitations of the current study. Firstly, the sample size is relatively small—only half the size of that found in the only other study of screenplays that includes textual analysis, i.e. Eliashberg, Hui, & Zhang (2014). The sample is also not ideally constructed. Rather than comparing award winners to unproduced screenplays, a better sample would include entries from a screenplay competition and the study design would attempt to select finalists and winners from that sample. Winners of top competitions are very frequently optioned and eventually produced. Alternatively, another approach would be to increase sample size and to include screenplays which garnered no critical or artistic awards. Even though many such screenplays can be located, finding a representative sample of them is difficult because they are not uniformly available. Still, if that hurdle can be overcome, the sample could be used to study box-office revenues, potentially improving upon the current understanding of screenplays' contribution to a film's financial success.

A third limitation of this study concerns the labor-intensive nature of the coding. At present, the process outlined above is only semi-automated. Unless and until advanced computational methods of text analysis can be developed and applied, sample sizes will remain small and the coding prone to human error.

Finally, recall that the fourth stage of network text analysis involves the extraction of meaning from the network itself. Typically, this involves a study of the most central nodes (concepts), as well as the statements (links) associated with them. For example, in the case of Zero Dark Thirty the most influential node or concept, as measured by network constraint, is the Indo-European root ***wegh-*** which means "way" and from which descends such words as way and weight. One of the multi-morphemic compounds associated with that concept in the Figure 3, above, is "hijacker" which is a clipped word, the full form being "highwayjacker" (Online Etymological Dictionary, 2014). Other multi-morphemic compounds associated with highly influential nodes in the network include SEAL, CIA, WMD, QRF (Quick Reaction Force), and NSA. As noted by Hunter (in press), other award-winning and critically-acclaimed screenplays exhibit the same pattern, i.e. words associated with influential nodes are also closely related to key themes of the story. Anecdotally, the unproduced screenplays give less evidence of this tendency. Future research might examine whether this difference is systematic. To that end, all data involved in this study—the text of all 150 screenplays and all of the network coding—will be made freely available to interested and qualified researchers upon request.

References

Bodin, M. (2012). Mapping university students' epistemic framing of computational physics using network analysis. *Physical Review Special Topics-Physics Education Research*, *8*(1), 1-14.

Borgatti, S. P., Everett, M. G., & Freeman, L. C. (2002). Ucinet for Windows: Software for social network analysis.

Calori, R., Johnson, G., & Sarnin, P. (1994). CEOs' cognitive maps and the scope of the organization. *Strategic Management Journal*, *15*(6), 437-457.

Carley, K. M. (1997). Extracting team mental models through textual analysis.*Journal of Organizational Behavior*, *18*(1), 533-558.

Carley, K.M. (2001-13), Automap 3.0.10. Center for Computational Analysis of Social and Organizational Systems (CASOS), Institute for Software Research International (ISRI), School of Computer Science, Carnegie Mellon University, Pittsburgh, PA.

Diesner, Jana, (2012). Uncovering and Managing the Impact of Methodological Choices for the Computational Construction of Socio-Technical Networks from Texts. *Dissertations.* Paper 194.

Eliashberg, Jehoshua, Anita Elberse, and Mark AAM Leenders (2006). The motion picture industry: Critical issues in practice, current research, and new research directions. *Marketing Science* 25(6), 638-661.

Eliashberg, J., Hui, S. K., & Zhang, Z. J. (2007). From story line to box office: A new approach for green-lighting movie scripts. *Management Science*, *53*(6), 881-893.

Eliashberg, J., Hui, S. K., & Zhang, Z. J. (2014, forthcoming). Assessing Box Office Performance Using Movie Scripts: A Kernel-based Approach. *IEEE Transactions on Knowledge and Data Engineering*.

Field, S. (2007). *Screenplay: The foundations of screenwriting*. Random House LLC.

Hunter, S. (2014, forthcoming). A Novel Method of Network Text Analysis. Open Journal of Modern Linguistics.

Krauss, J., Nann, S., Simon, D., Gloor, P. A., & Fischbach, K. (2008). Predicting Movie Success and Academy Awards through Sentiment and Social Network Analysis. *Proceedings of the 16th European Conference on Information Systems*, 2026-2037.

Lee, F. L. (2009). Cultural discount of cinematic achievement: the academy awards and US movies' East Asian box office. *Journal of Cultural Economics*, *33*(4), 239-263.

McKee, R. (2010). Story: Substance, Structure, Style and the Principles of Screenwriting, Harper Collins, New York.

Nadkarni, S. (2003). Instructional methods and mental models of students: An empirical investigation. *Academy of Management Learning & Education*, *2*(4), 335-351.

Nadkarni, S., & Narayanan, V. K. (2005). Validity of the structural properties of text-based causal maps: An empirical assessment. *Organizational Research Methods*, *8*(1), 9-40.

Nadkarni, S., & Narayanan, V. K. (2007). Strategic schemas, strategic flexibility, and firm performance: the moderating role of industry clockspeed. *Strategic management journal*, *28*(3), 243-270.

New York Film Academy: Bachelor of Fine Arts in Screenwriting. (2014). Retrieved from http://www.nyfa.edu/bfa/screenwriting.php

Osborne, R., & Davis, B. (1989). *60 years of the Oscar: the official history of the Academy Awards*. New York: Abbeville Press.

Pardoe, I., & Simonton, D. K. (2008). Applying discrete choice models to predict Academy Award winners. *Journal of the Royal Statistical Society: Series A (Statistics in Society)*, *171*(2), 375-394.

Popping, R. (2003). Knowledge graphs and network text analysis. *Social Science Information* 42(1):91-106.

Script Fly. (2014). Retrieved from http://scriptfly.com

Simply Scripts. (2014). Retrieved from http://simplyscripts.com

Simonton, D. K. (2004). Film awards as indicators of cinematic creativity and achievement: A quantitative comparison of the Oscars and six alternatives. *Creativity Research Journal*, *16*(2-3), 163-172.

Simonton, D. K. (2005). Film as art versus film as business: Differential correlates of screenplay characteristics. *Empirical Studies of the Arts*, *23*(2), 93-117.

Snyder, B. (2005). *Save the Cat*. Michael Wiese Productions.

Watkins, C. (2011), The American Heritage Dictionary of Indo-European Roots, 3rd Edition, Houghton Mifflin Harcourt, Boston MA.

Wisniewski, K. (2007). Word formation. http://www.tlumaczenia-angielski.info/linguistics/word-formation.htm

Power of Confidence: How Poll Scores Impact Topic Dynamics in Political Debates

Vinodkumar Prabhakaran
Dept. of Computer Science
Columbia University
New York, NY
vinod@cs.columbia.edu

Ashima Arora
Dept. of Computer Science
Columbia University
New York, NY
aa3470@columbia.edu

Owen Rambow
CCLS
Columbia University
New York, NY
rambow@ccls.columbia.edu

Abstract

In this paper, we investigate how topic dynamics during the course of an interaction correlate with the power differences between its participants. We perform this study on the US presidential debates and show that a candidate's power, modeled after their poll scores, affects how often he/she attempts to shift topics and whether he/she succeeds. We ensure the validity of topic shifts by confirming, through a simple but effective method, that the turns that shift topics provide substantive topical content to the interaction.

1 Introduction

Analyzing political speech has gathered great interest within the NLP community. Researchers have analyzed political text to identify markers of persuasion (Guerini et al., 2008), predict voting patterns (Thomas et al., 2006; Gerrish and Blei, 2011), and detect ideological positions (Sim et al., 2013). Studies have also looked into how personal attributes of political personalities such as charisma, confidence and power affect how they interact (Rosenberg and Hirschberg, 2009; Prabhakaran et al., 2013b). Our work belongs to this genre of studies. We analyze how a presidential candidate's power, modeled after his/her relative poll standings, affect the dynamics of topic shifts during the course of a presidential debate.

2 Motivation

In early work on correlating personal attributes to political speech, Rosenberg and Hirschberg (2009) analyzed speech transcripts in the context of 2004 Democratic presidential primary elections, to identify prosodic and lexico-syntactic cues that signal charisma of political personalities. More recently, Prabhakaran et al. (2013a) introduced the notion of power an election candidate has at a certain point in the election campaign, modeled after the confidence that stems from their recent poll standings. They analyzed the 2012 Republican presidential primary debates and found that the candidate's power at the time of a debate impacts the structure of interactions (e.g., frequency of turns and interruption patterns). They followed up their study with an automatic ranker to identify leading candidates based on the interaction within a debate (Prabhakaran et al., 2013b).

One of the interesting findings by Prabhakaran et al. (2013a) was that candidates' power correlates with the distribution of topics they speak about in the debates. They found that when candidates have more power, they speak significantly more about certain topics (e.g., *economy*) and less about certain other topics (e.g., *energy*). However, these findings relate to the specific election cycle they analyzed and will not carry over to all political debates in general. A topical dimension with broader relevance is how topics change during the course of an interaction (e.g., who introduces more topics, who attempts to shift topics etc.). For instance, Nguyen et al. (2013) found that topic shifts within an interaction are correlated with the role a participant plays in it (e.g., being a moderator). They also analyzed US presidential debates, but with the objective of validating a topic segmentation method they proposed earlier (Nguyen et al., 2012). They do not study the topic shifting tendencies among the candidates in relation to their power differences.

In this paper, we bring these two ideas together. We analyze the 2012 Republican presidential debates, modeling the power of a candidate based on poll scores as proposed by Prabhakaran et al. (2013a) and investigate various features that capture the topical dynamics in the debates. We show that the power affects how often candidates at-

Proceedings of the Joint Workshop on Social Dynamics and Personal Attributes in Social Media, pages 77–82,
Baltimore, Maryland USA, 27 June 2014.

Turn #	Speaker	Turn Text	Substantive?
223	PAWLENTY (C)	I support a constitutional amendment to define marriage between a man and woman. I was the co-author of the state – a law in Minnesota to define it and now we have courts jumping over this.	[S]
224	KING (M)	OK. Let's just go through this.	[NS]
225	PAUL (C)	The federal government shouldn't be involved. I wouldn't support an amendment. [...] I don't think government should give us a license to get married. It should be in the church.	[S]
226	KING (M)	Governor Romney, constitutional amendment or state decision?	[NS]
227	ROMNEY (C)	Constitutional.	[NS]
228	KING (M)	Mr. Speaker?	[NS]
229	GINGRICH (C)	Well, I helped author the Defense of Marriage Act which the Obama administration should be frankly protecting in court. [...]	[S]
		[...]	
235	CAIN (C)	If I had my druthers, I never would have overturned "don't ask/don't tell" in the first place. [...] Our men and women have too many other things to be concerned about rather than have to deal with that as a distraction.	[S]
		[...]	
240	KING (M)	Leave it in place, [...] or overturn it?	[S]
241	ROMNEY (C)	Well, one, we ought to be talking about the economy and jobs. But given the fact you're insistent, the – the answer is, I believe that "don't ask/don't tell" should have been kept in place until conflict was over.	[S]

Table 1: Excerpt from Goffstown, NH debate (06/13/11), discussing marriage equality and the "Don't Ask/Don't Tell" policy **[S]**/ **[NS]** denote substantiveness of turns

tempt to shift topics and whether they succeed in it or not. In order to correctly model topic shifts, we ensure that the shifts happen in turns that contribute substantial topical content to the interaction. We introduce the notion of a "non-substantial turn", and use a simple, but effective method to automatically identify non-substantial turns. This allows us to identify different topic segments within the interaction, while permitting (and capturing) interruptions within those segments. We will compare the segments that we obtain with those by Nguyen et al. (2012) in future work.

3 Domain and Data

We use the same corpus as Prabhakaran et al. (2013b). The corpus contains manual transcripts of 20 debates held between May 2011 and February 2012 as part of the 2012 Republican presidential primaries. The transcripts are obtained from The American Presidency Project.[1] Each turn is clearly demarcated in the transcripts and their speakers are identified. The turns in the corpus are preprocessed using the Stanford CoreNLP package to perform basic NLP steps such as tokenization, sentence segmentation, parts-of-speech tagging and lemmatization. We show an excerpt from one of the debates in Table 1. This segment of the debate discusses marriage equality followed by the overturning of the "Don't Ask/Don't Tell" policy prohibiting openly gay, lesbian, or bisexual persons from US military service.

Prabhakaran et al. (2013b) added each candidate's power at the time of each debate to the corpus, computed based on their relative standing in recent public polls. We refer the reader to (Prabhakaran et al., 2013b) for the detailed description of how the relative standings in national and state-level polls from various sources are aggregated to obtain candidates' power. The poll numbers capture how successful candidates are in convincing the electorate of their candidature, which in turn affects their confidence within the debates. These debates serve as a rich domain to explore manifestations of power since they are a medium through which candidates pursue and maintain power over other candidates.

4 Modeling Topics

Prabhakaran et al. (2013a) model topics in the debates using Latent Dirichlet Allocation (LDA), assigning topic probabilities to each turn. The number of topics was set to be 15 and the topic that was assigned the highest probability for a turn was cho-

[1] http://www.presidency.ucsb.edu/debates.php

sen as its topic. Assigning topics to each turn in this manner, however, is problematic. Not all turns by themselves contribute to the conversational topics in an interaction. A large number of turns, especially by the moderator, manage the conversation rather than contribute content to it. These include turns redirecting questions to specific candidates (e.g., turns 224, 226 and 228 in Table 1) as well as moderator interruptions (e.g., "Quickly.", "We have to save time"). Furthermore, some other turns address a topic only when considered together with preceding turns, but not when read in isolation. These include turns that are short one-word answers (e.g., turn 227) and turns that are uninterpretable without resolving anaphora (e.g., "That's right"). While these turns are substantive to human readers, topic modeling approaches such as LDA cannot assign them topics correctly because of their terseness.

We define the turns that do not, in isolation, contribute substantially to the conversational topics as **non-substantive** turns. In order to obtain a gold standard for non-substantivity, two of the authors manually annotated each turn in one entire debate (dated 06/13/11) as either *substantive (S)* or *non-substantive (NS)*. The annotators were instructed not to consider the identity of the speaker or the context of the turn (preceding/following turns) in making their assessment. We obtained a high inter-annotator agreement (observed agreement = 89.3%; Kappa = .76). We took the assessments by one of the annotators as the gold standard, in which 108 (31.5%) of the 343 turns were identified as *non-substantive*. We show the *S* vs. *NS* assessments for each turn in column 4 of Table 1.

Figure 1a shows the line graph of topic probabilities assigned by LDA to the sequence of turns in Table 1. As the graph shows, non-substantive turns are assigned spurious topic probabilities by LDA. For example, turn 224 by KING ("OK. Lets just go through this.") was assigned small probabilities for all topics; the highest of which was *economy* (probability of 0.12). This error is problematic when modeling topic shifts, since this turn and the next one by PAUL would have been incorrectly identified as shifts in topic from their corresponding previous turns. Instead, if we assume that the non-substantive turns follow the same topic probabilities as the most recent substantive turn, we obtain the line graph shown in Figure 1b. This topic assignment captures the topic dynam-

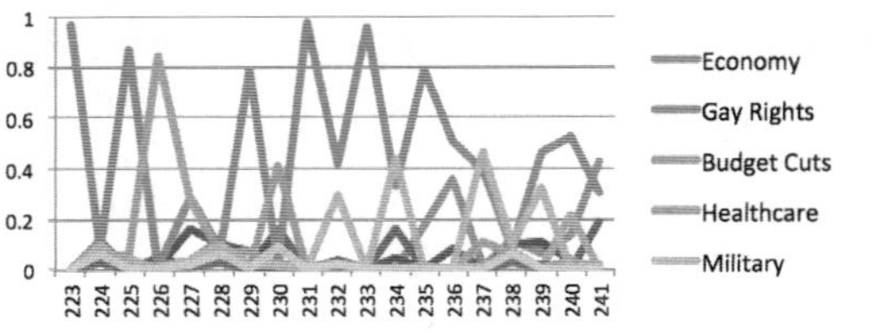

(a) Topic Probabilities assigned by LDA

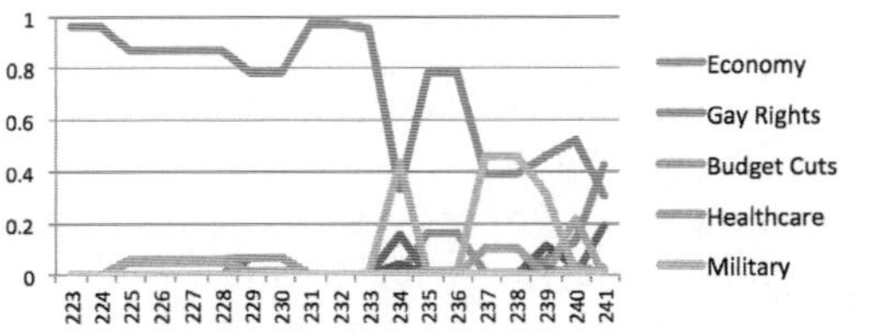

(b) Topic Probabilities after ignoring non-substantive turns

Figure 1: Line graphs of topic probabilities for turns in Table 1 (legend shows only the top 5 topics in this segment)

ics in the segment more accurately. It identifies *Gay Rights* as the predominant topic until turn 234 followed by a mix of *Gay Rights* and *Military* as topics while discussing the "Don't Ask/Don't Tell' policy. It also captures the attempt by ROMNEY in turn 242 to shift the topic to *Economy*.

4.1 Identifying Non-substantive Turns

In order to automatically detect non-substantive turns, we investigate a few alternatives. A simple observation is that many of the *NS* turns such as redirections of questions or short responses have only a few words. We tried a word count threshold based method (**WC_Thresh**) where we assign a turn to be *NS* if the number of tokens (words) in the turn is less than a threshold. Another intuition is that for a non-substantive turn, it would be hard for the LDA to assign topics and hence all topics will get almost equal probabilities assigned. In order to capture this, we used a method based on a standard deviation threshold (**SD_Thresh**), where we assign a turn to be *NS* if the standard deviation of that turn's topic probabilities is below a threshold. We also used a combination system where we tag a turn to be *NS* if either system tags it to be. We tuned for the value of the thresholds and the best performances obtained for each case are shown in Table 2. We obtained the best results for the WC_Thresh method with a threshold of 28 words, while for SD_Thresh the optimal threshold is .13 (almost twice the mean).

Method	Accuracy (%)	F-measure
WC_Thresh	82.6	73.7
SD_Thresh	76.2	64.7
WC_Thresh + SD_Thresh	76.8	70.4

Table 2: Accuracy and F-measure of different methods to identify non-substantive turns

4.2 Topic Assignments

We first ran the LDA at a turn-level for all debates, keeping the number of topics to be 15, and selected the best model after 2000 iterations. Then, we ran the WC_Thresh method described above to detect *NS* turns. For all *NS* turns, we replace the topic probabilities assigned by LDA with the last substantive turn's topic probabilities. Note that an *S* turn coming after one or more *NS* turns could still be of the same topic as the last *S* turn, i.e., non-substantivity of a turn is agnostic to whether the topic changes after that or not. A topic shift (or attempt) happens only when LDA assigns a different topic to a substantive turn.

5 Topical Dimensions

We now describe various features we use to capture the topical dynamics within each debate, with respect to each candidate. When we compute a feature value, we use the topic probabilities assigned to each turn as described in the previous section. For some features we only use the topic with the highest probability, while for some others, we use the probabilities assigned to all topics. We consider features along four dimensions which we describe in detail below.

5.1 Topic Shift Patterns

We build various features to capture how often a candidate stays on the topic being discussed. We say a candidate attempted to shift the topic in a turn if the topic assigned to that turn differs from the topic of the previous (substantive) turn. We use a feature to count the number of times a candidate attempts to shift topics within a debate (**TS_Attempt#**) and a version of that feature normalized over the total number of turns (**TS_Attempt#^{N}**). We also use a variation of these features which considers only the instances of topic shift attempts by the candidates when responding to a question from the moderator (**TS_AttemptAfterMod#** and **TS_AttemptAfterMod#^{N}**). We also compute a softer notion of topic shift where we measure the average Euclidean distance between topic probabilities of each of the candidate turns and turns prior to them (**EuclideanDist**). This feature in essence captures whether the candidate stayed on topic, even if he/she did not completely switch topics in a turn.

5.2 Topic Shift Sustenance Patterns

We use a feature to capture the average number of turns for which topic shifts by a candidate was sustained (**TS_SustTurns**). However, as discussed in Section 4, the turns vary greatly in terms of length. A more sensible measure is the time period for which a topic shift was sustained. We approximate the time by the number of word tokens and compute the average number of tokens in the turns that topic shifts by a candidate were sustained (**TS_SustTime**).

5.3 Topic Shift Success Patterns

We define a topic shift to be successful if it was sustained for at least three turns. We compute three features — total number of successful topic shifts by a candidate (**TS_Success#**), that number normalized over the total number of turns by the candidate (**TS_Success#^{N}**), and the success rate of candidate's topic shifts (**TS_SuccessRate**)

5.4 Topic Introduction Patterns

We also looked at cases where a candidate introduces a new topic, i.e., shifts to a topic which is entirely new for the debate. We use the number of topics introduced by a candidate as a feature (**TS_Intro#**). We also use features to capture how important those topics were, measured in terms of the number of turns about those topics in the en tire debate (**TS_IntroImpTurns**) and the time spent on those topics in the entire debate (**TS_IntroImpTime**).

6 Analysis and Results

We performed a correlation analysis on the features described in the previous section with respect to each candidate against the power he/she had at the time of the debate (based on recent poll scores). Figure 2 shows the Pearson's product correlation between each topical feature and candidate's power. Dark bars denote statistically significant ($p < 0.05$) features.

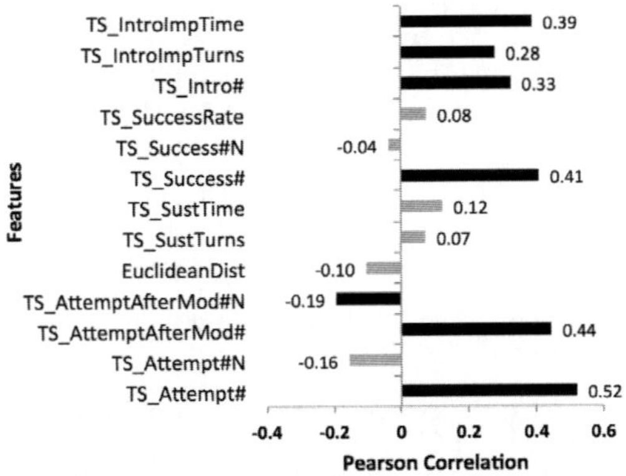

Figure 2: Pearson Correlations for Topical Features

We obtained significant strong positive correlation for TS_Attempt# and TS_AttemptAfterMod#. However, the normalized measure TS_Attempt#^{N} did not have any significant correlation, suggesting that the correlation obtained for TS_Attempt# is mostly due to the fact that candidates with more power have more turns, a finding that is already established by Prabhakaran et al. (2013b). However, interestingly, we obtained a weak, but statistically significant, negative correlation for TS_AttemptAfterMod#^{N} which suggests that more powerful candidates tend to stay on topic when responding to moderators. We did not obtain any correlation for EuclideanDist.

We did not obtain any significant correlations between candidate's power and their topic shift sustenance features. We obtained significant correlation for topic shift success (TS_Success#), modeled based on the sustenance of topic shifts, suggesting that powerful candidates have a higher number of successful topic shifts. However, TS_SuccessRate or TS_Success#^{N} did not obtain any significant correlation. We also found that powerful candidates are more likely to introduce new topics (TS_Intro#) and that the topics they introduce tend to be important (TS_IntroImpTurns and TS_IntroImpTime).

7 Related Work

Studies in sociolinguistics (e.g., (Ng et al., 1993; Ng et al., 1995)) have explored how dialog structure in interactions relates to power and influence. Reid and Ng (2000) identified that factors such as frequency of contribution, proportion of turns, and number of successful interruptions are important indicators of influence. Within the dialog community, researchers have studied notions of control and initiative in dialogs (Walker and Whittaker, 1990; Jordan and Di Eugenio, 1997). Walker and Whittaker (1990) define "control of communication" in terms of whether the discourse participants are providing new, unsolicited information in their utterances. Their notion of control differs from our notion of power; however, the way we model topic shifts is closely related to their utterance level control assignment. Within the NLP community, researchers have studied power and influence in various genres of interactions, such as organizational email threads (Bramsen et al., 2011; Gilbert, 2012; Prabhakaran and Rambow, 2013), online discussion forums (Danescu-Niculescu-Mizil et al., 2012; Biran et al., 2012) and online chat dialogs (Strzalkowski et al., 2012). The correlates analyzed in these studies range from word/phrase patterns, to derivatives of such patterns such as linguistic coordination, to deeper dialogic features such as argumentation and dialog acts. Our work differs from these studies in that we study the correlates of power in topic dynamics. Furthermore, we analyze spoken interactions.

8 Conclusion

We studied the topical dynamics in the 2012 US presidential debates and investigated their correlation with the power differences between candidates. We showed that a candidate's power, modeled after their poll scores, has significant correlation with how often he/she introduces new topics, attempts to shift topics, and whether they succeed in doing so. In order to ensure the validity of our topic shifts we devised a simple yet effective way to eliminate turns which do not provide substantial topical content to the interaction. Furthermore, this allowed us to identify different topic segments within the interaction. In future work, we will explore how our way of identifying segments compares to other approaches on topic segmentation in interactions (e.g., (Nguyen et al., 2012)).

Acknowledgments

This paper is based upon work supported by the DARPA DEFT Program. The views expressed are those of the authors and do not reflect the official policy or position of the Department of Defense or the U.S. Government. We also thank Debanjan Ghosh and several anonymous reviewers for their constructive feedback.

References

Or Biran, Sara Rosenthal, Jacob Andreas, Kathleen McKeown, and Owen Rambow. 2012. Detecting influencers in written online conversations. In *Proceedings of the Second Workshop on Language in Social Media*, pages 37–45, Montréal, Canada, June. Association for Computational Linguistics.

Philip Bramsen, Martha Escobar-Molano, Ami Patel, and Rafael Alonso. 2011. Extracting social power relationships from natural language. In *Proceedings of the 49th Annual Meeting of the Association for Computational Linguistics: Human Language Technologies*, pages 773–782, Portland, Oregon, USA, June. Association for Computational Linguistics.

Cristian Danescu-Niculescu-Mizil, Lillian Lee, Bo Pang, and Jon Kleinberg. 2012. Echoes of power: language effects and power differences in social interaction. In *Proceedings of the 21st international conference on World Wide Web*, WWW '12, New York, NY, USA. ACM.

Sean Gerrish and David Blei. 2011. Predicting legislative roll calls from text. In Lise Getoor and Tobias Scheffer, editors, *Proceedings of the 28th International Conference on Machine Learning*, ICML '11, pages 489–496, New York, NY, USA, June. ACM.

Eric Gilbert. 2012. Phrases that signal workplace hierarchy. In *Proceedings of the ACM 2012 conference on Computer Supported Cooperative Work*, CSCW '12, pages 1037–1046, New York, NY, USA. ACM.

Marco Guerini, Carlo Strapparava, and Oliviero Stock. 2008. Corps: A corpus of tagged political speeches for persuasive communication processing. *Journal of Information Technology & Politics*, 5(1):19–32.

Pamela W. Jordan and Barbara Di Eugenio. 1997. Control and initiative in collaborative problem solving dialogues. In *Working Notes of the AAAI Spring Symposium on Computational Models for Mixed Initiative*, pages 81–84.

Sik Hung Ng, Dean Bell, and Mark Brooke. 1993. Gaining turns and achieving high in influence ranking in small conversational groups. *British Journal of Social Psychology*, pages 32, 265–275.

Sik Hung Ng, Mark Brooke, and Michael Dunne. 1995. Interruption and in influence in discussion groups. *Journal of Language and Social Psychology*, pages 14(4),369–381.

Viet-An Nguyen, Jordan Boyd-Graber, and Philip Resnik. 2012. Sits: A hierarchical nonparametric model using speaker identity for topic segmentation in multiparty conversations. In *Proceedings of the 50th Annual Meeting of the Association for Computational Linguistics (Volume 1: Long Papers)*, pages 78–87, Jeju Island, Korea, July. Association for Computational Linguistics.

Viet-An Nguyen, Jordan Boyd-Graber, Philip Resnik, Deborah A. Cai, Jennifer E. Midberry, and Yuanxin Wang. 2013. Modeling topic control to detect influence in conversations using nonparametric topic models. *Machine Learning*, pages 1–41.

Vinodkumar Prabhakaran and Owen Rambow. 2013. Written dialog and social power: Manifestations of different types of power in dialog behavior. In *Proceedings of the IJCNLP*, pages 216–224, Nagoya, Japan, October. Asian Federation of Natural Language Processing.

Vinodkumar Prabhakaran, Ajita John, and Dorée D. Seligmann. 2013a. Power dynamics in spoken interactions: a case study on 2012 republican primary debates. In *Proceedings of the 22nd international conference on World Wide Web companion*, pages 99–100. International World Wide Web Conferences Steering Committee.

Vinodkumar Prabhakaran, Ajita John, and Dorée D. Seligmann. 2013b. Who had the upper hand? ranking participants of interactions based on their relative power. In *Proceedings of the IJCNLP*, pages 365–373, Nagoya, Japan, October. Asian Federation of Natural Language Processing.

Scott A. Reid and Sik Hung Ng. 2000. Conversation as a resource for in influence: evidence for prototypical arguments and social identification processes. *European Journal of Social Psych.*, pages 30, 83–100.

Andrew Rosenberg and Julia Hirschberg. 2009. Charisma perception from text and speech. *Speech Communication*, 51(7):640–655.

Yanchuan Sim, Brice D. L. Acree, Justin H. Gross, and Noah A. Smith. 2013. Measuring ideological proportions in political speeches. In *Proceedings of the 2013 Conference on EMNLP*, pages 91–101, Seattle, Washington, USA, October. Association for Computational Linguistics.

Tomek Strzalkowski, Samira Shaikh, Ting Liu, George Aaron Broadwell, Jenny Stromer-Galley, Sarah Taylor, Umit Boz, Veena Ravishankar, and Xiaoai Ren. 2012. Modeling leadership and influence in multi-party online discourse. In *Proceedings of COLING*, pages 2535–2552, Mumbai, India, December. The COLING 2012 Organizing Committee.

Matt Thomas, Bo Pang, and Lillian Lee. 2006. Get out the vote: Determining support or opposition from congressional floor-debate transcripts. In *Proceedings of the 2006 Conference on Empirical Methods in Natural Language Processing*, pages 327–335, Sydney, Australia, July. Association for Computational Linguistics.

Marilyn Walker and Steve Whittaker. 1990. Mixed initiative in dialogue: An investigation into discourse segmentation. In *Proceedings of the 28th annual meeting on Association for Computational Linguistics*, pages 70–78. Association for Computational Linguistics.

As Long as You Name My Name Right: Social Circles and Social Sentiment in the Hollywood Hearings

Oren Tsur[†§] orentsur@seas.harvard.edu

Dan Calacci[†] dcalacci@ccs.neu.edu

David Lazer[†⋆] d.lazer@neu.edu

[†]Lazer Laboratory, Northeastern University

[§]School of Engeneering and Applied Sciences, Harvard University

[⋆]Harvard Kennedy School, Harvard University

Abstract

The Hollywood Blacklist was based on a series of interviews conducted by the House Committee on Un-American Activities (HUAC), trying to identify members of the communist party. We use various NLP algorithms in order to automatically analyze a large corpus of interview transcripts and construct a network of the industry members and their "naming" relations. We further use algorithms for Sentiment Analysis in order to add a psychological dimension to the edges in the network. In particular, we test how different types of connections are manifested by different sentiment types and attitude of the interviewees. Analysis of the language used in the hearings can shed new light on the motivation and role of network members.

1 Introduction

A growing body of computational research is focused on how language is used and how it shapes/is shaped by a community of speakers. Computational works in the nexus of language and the social arena deal with various topics such as language accommodation (Danescu-Niculescu-Mizil and Lee, 2011; Danescu-Niculescu-Mizil et al., 2011), demographic language variation (Eisenstein et al., 2010; O'Connor et al., 2010), the factors that facilitate the spread of information in Q&A forums and social networks (Adamic et al., 2008; Bian et al., 2009; Romero et al., 2011) or the correlation between words and social actions (Adali et al., 2012).

All of these works analyze the language and the social dynamics in online communities, mainly due to the increasing popularity of online social networks and greater availability of such data.

However, large scale socio-linguistic analysis should not be restricted to online communities and can be applied in many social and political settings beyond the online world. Two examples are the study of power structures in arguments before the U.S. Supreme Court (Danescu-Niculescu-Mizil et al., 2012) and the evolution of specific words and phrases over time as reflected in Google Books (Goldberg and Orwant, 2013).

In this paper we propose using network science and linguistic analysis in order to understand the social dynamics in the entertainment industry during one of its most controversial periods – the 'red scare' and the witch hunt for Communists in Hollywood during 1950's.

Historical background The *Hollywood hearings* (often confused with Senator McCarthy's hearings and allegations) were a series of interviews conducted by the House Committee on Un-American Activities (HUAC) in the years 1947–1956. The purpose of the committee was to conduct "hearings regarding the communist infiltration of the motion picture industry" (from the HUAC Annual Report). The committee subpoenaed witnesses such as Ayn Rand (writer), Arthur Miller (writer), Walt Disney (producer), future U.S. president Ronald Reagan (Screen Actors Guild), Elia Kazan (writer, actor, director) and Albert Maltz (Screen Writers Guild). Some of the witnesses were 'friendly' while some others were uncooperative[1], refusing to "name names" or self incriminate[2]. Those who were *named* and/or were uncooperative were often jailed or effectively lost their job.

Arguably, many friendly witnesses felt they were complying with their patriotic duty. Many

[1]A note about terminology: by using the terms *friendly* and *uncooperative* there is no implied moral judgment – these are the terms used in the literature.

[2]It should be noted that being a member of the Communist party was not illegal, however, some individuals avoided self "incrimination" either in an effort to protect their job or as an ideological declaration in favor of privacy protection as a civil right protected by the constitution.

Proceedings of the Joint Workshop on Social Dynamics and Personal Attributes in Social Media, pages 83–87, Baltimore, Maryland USA, 27 June 2014.

others were threatened or simply manipulated to name names, and some later admitted to cooperating for other reasons such as protecting their work or out of personal vendettas and professional jealousies. It is also suspected that some naming occurred due to increasing professional tension between some producers and the Screen Writers Guild or (Navasky, 2003).

Motivation In this work we analyze a collection of HUAC hearings. We wish to answer the following questions:

1. Do sentiment and other linguistic categories correlate with naming relations?
2. Can we gain any insight on the social dynamics between the people in the network?
3. Does linguistic and network analysis support any of the social theories about dynamics at Hollywood during that time?

In order to answer the questions above we build a social graph of members of the entertainment industry based on the hearings and add sentiment labels on the graph edges. Layering linguistic features on a the social graph may provide us with new insights related to the questions at hand. In this short paper we describe the research framework, the various challenges posed by the data and present some initial promising results.

2 Data

In this work we used two types of datasets: Hearing Transcripts and Annual Reports. Snippets from hearings can be found in Figures 1(a) and 1(b), Figure 1(c) shows a snippet from an annual report. The transcripts data is based on 47 interviews conducted by the HUAC in the years 1951–2. Each interview is either a long statement (1(a)) or a sequence of questions by the committee members and answers by a witness (1(b)). In total, our hearings corpus consists of 2831 dialogue acts and half a million words.

3 Named Entity Recognition and Anaphora Resolution

The snippets in Figure 1 illustrates some of the challenges in processing HUAC data. The first challenge is introduced by the low quality of the available documents. Due to the low quality of

For the approximately 19 months of my membership, I was assigned to a "unit" composed of those party members who were, like myself, members of the Group Theatre acting company. These were—

Lewis Leverett, co-leader of the unit

J Edward Bromberg, co-leader of the unit, deceased.

Phoebe Brand (later Mrs Morris Carnovsky) I was instrumental in bringing her into the party.

Morris Carnovsky

Tony Kraber, along with Wellman (see below), he recruited me into the party

Paula Miller (later Mrs Lee Strasberg) We are friends today I believe that, as she has told me, she quit the Communists long ago She is far too sensible and balanced a woman, and she is married to too fine and intelligent a man, to have remained among them

Clifford Odets · He has assured me that he got out about the same time I did.

Art Smith.

(a) A snippet from the testimony of Elia Kazan, (actor, writer and director, 3 times Academy Awards winner), 4.10.1952.

Mr. Tavenner. When you first became a member of the Communist Party, did you meet an individual by the name of Stanley Lawrence?

Mr. Ashe. I met Mr. Lawrence later. Mr. Lawrence came along in about 1935. He was misrepresented to the Communist Party as being an expert in underground work and that he was a liaison man in, I believe, Hungary or Austria for important Communist members there. Later independent investigation of mine revealed that he had been a Los Angeles taxicab driver. Just a little deceit on the part of the Communist Party leadership.

Mr. Tavenner. That was a device used by the leadership of the Communist Party to build up Stanley Lawrence?

Mr. Ashe. They undertook to use him to educate the party leadership in Los Angeles County on underground work and things of that

(b) A snippet from the testimony of Harold Ashe's (journalist) testimony 9.17-19.1951.

ANNUAL REPORT, COMMITTEE ON UN-AMERICAN ACTIVITIES 29

	Identified by
Alexander, Hy (Harmon) Radio writer (Appeared Oct. 6, 1952; refused to affirm or deny Communist Party membership.)	Carin Kinzel, May 5, 1953 (testifying in New York). Silvia Richards, Mar. 25, 1953. Dwight Hauser, Mar. 30, 1953. Also identified by two former Communists in 1952.
Alexander, Mrs Hy (*See* Georgia Backus.)	
Allen (Allan), Louis (Lewis) Playwright.	Silvia Richards, Mar. 25, 1953. Leopold Atlas, Mar. 12, 1953. Pauline S. Townsend, Mar. 12, 1953.
Allen (Allan), Mrs. Louis (Lewis)	Silvia Richards, Mar. 25, 1953.
Alpert, Hymie Clothier.	Edith Macia, Mar. 28, 1953.

(c) A snippet from 1951 annual report.

Figure 1: Snippets from HUAC hearings and an annual report.

the documents the OCR output is noisy, containing misidentified characters, wrong alignment of sentences and missing words. These problems introduce complications in tasks like named entity recognition and properly parsing sentences.

Beyond the low graphic quality of the documents, the hearings present the researcher with the typical array of NLP challenges. For example, the hearing excerpt in 1(b) contains four dialogue acts that need to be separated and processed. The committee member (*Mr. Tavenner*) mentions the name *Stanley Lawrence*, later referred to by the witness (*Mr. Ashe*) as *Mr. Lawrence* and *he* thus coreference resolution is required before the graph construction and the sentiment analysis phases.

As a preprocessing stage we performed named entity recognition (NER), disambiguation and unification. For the NER task we used the Stanford NER (Finkel et al., 2005) and for disambiguation and unification we used a number of heuristics based on edit distance and name distribution.

We used the Stanford Deterministic Coreference Resolution System (Lee et al., 2011) to resolve anaphoric references.

4 Naming Graph vs. Mentions Graph

In building the network graph of the members of the entertainment industry we distinguish between *mentioning* and *naming* in our data. While many names may be mentioned in a testimony (either by a committee member or by the witness, see example in Figures 1(a) and 1(b)), not all names are practically *'named'* (=identified) as Communists. We thus use the hearings dataset in order to build a social graph of *mentions* (MG) and the annual reports are used to build a *naming* graph (NG). The NG is used as a "gold standard" in the analysis of the sentiment labels in the MG. Graph statistics are presented in Table 1.

While the hearings are commonly perceived as an "orgy of informing" (Navasky, 2003), the difference in network structure of the graphs portrays a more complex picture. The striking difference in the average *out* degree suggests that while many names were mentioned in the testimonies (either in a direct question or in an answer) – majority of the witnesses avoided mass-explicit naming[3]. The variance in outdegree suggests that most witnesses did not cooperate at all or gave only a name or two, while only a small number of witnesses gave a long list of names. These results are visually captured in the intersection graph (Figure 2) and were also manually verified.

The difference between the MG and the NG graph in the number of nodes with out-going edges (214 vs. 66) suggests that the HUAC used other informers that were not subpoenaed to testify in a hearing[4].

In the remainder of this paper we analyze the the distribution of the usage of various psychological categories based on the role the witnesses play.

5 Sentiment Analysis and Psychological Categories

5.1 Sentiment Analysis

We performed the sentiment analysis in two different settings: lexical and statistical. In the lexical setting we combine (Ding et al., 2008) and the LIWC lexicon (Tausczik and Pennebaker, 2010). In the statistical setting we use NaSent (Socher et al., 2013).

The motivation to use both methods is twofold: first – while statistical models are generally more robust, accurate and sensitive to context, they require parsing of the processed sentences. Parsing our data is often problematic due to the noise introduced by the OCR algorithm due to the poor quality of the documents (see Figure 1). We expected the lexicon-based method to be more tolerant to noisy or ill-structured sentences. We opted for the LIWC since it offers an array of sentiment and psychological categories that might be relevant in the analysis of such data.

	MG	NG	Intersection
Num of nodes	1353	631	122
Num of edges	2434	842	113
Nodes / Edges	0.55	0.467	1
Avg. out degree	36.87	3.93	8.7
Avg. in degree	1.82	1.83	1.04
Var(outdegree)	3902.62	120.75	415.59
Var(indegree)	4.0	2.51	1.04
Nodes with out going edges	66	214	13
Nodes with incoming edges	1341	459	109
Reciprocity	0.016	0.012	0

Table 1: Network features of the Mentions graph, the Naming graph and the intersection of the graphs.

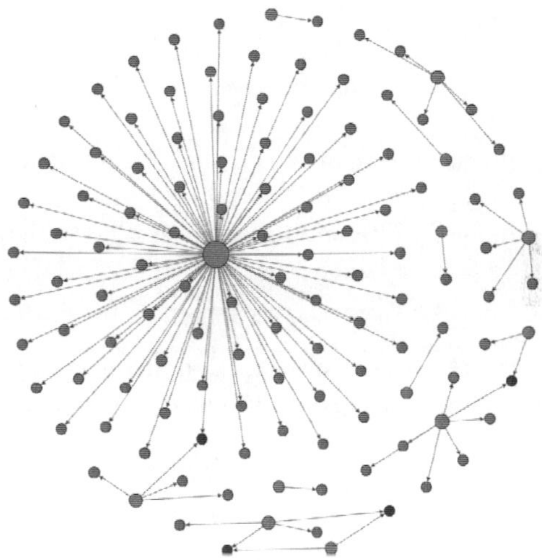

Figure 2: Naming graph based on the intersection of the mentions and the naming data. Larger node size indicates a bigger out degree; Color indicates the in degree (darker nodes were named more times).

[3]Ayn Rand and Ronald Reagan, two of the most 'friendly' witnesses (appeared in front of the HUAC in 1947), did not name anyone.

[4]There might be some hearings and testimonies that are classified or still not publicly accessible.

	Stanford	LIWC
Pos	75	292
Neg	254	37

Table 2: Confusion matrix for Stanford and LIWC sentiment algorithms.

Aggregated Sentiment A name may be mentioned a number of times in a single hearing, each time with a different sentiment type or polarity. The aggregated sentiment weight of a witness i toward a mentioned name j is computed as follows:

$$sentiment(i,j) = \max_{c \in CAT} \frac{\sum_{k \in U_{ij}} score(u_{ij}^k, c)}{|U_{ij}|} \quad (1)$$

Where CAT is the set of categories used by LIWC or Stanford Sentiment and U_{ij} is the set of all utterances (dialogue acts) in which witness i mentions the name j. The $score()$ function is defined slightly different for each setting. In the LIWC setting we define $score$ as:

$$score(u_{ij}^k, c) = \frac{|\{w \in u_{ij}^k | w \in c\}|}{|u_{ij}^k|} \quad (2)$$

In the statistical setting, Stanford Sentiment returns a sentiment category and a weight, we therefore use:

$$score(u_{ij}^k, c) = \begin{cases} w_c, & if\ sentiment\ found \\ 0, & if\ c\ was\ not\ returned \end{cases} \quad (3)$$

Unfortunately, both approaches to sentiment analysis were not as useful as expected. Most graph edges did not have any sentiment label, either due to the limited sentiment lexicon of the LIWC or due to the noise induced in the OCR process, preventing the Stanford Sentiment engine from parsing many of the sentences. Interestingly, the two approaches did not agree on most sentences (or dialogue acts). The sentiment confusion matrix is presented in Table 2, illustrating the challenge posed by the data.

5.2 Psychological Categories

The LIWC lexicon contains more than just positive/negative categories. Table 3 presents a sample of LIWC categories and associated tokens. Figure 3 presents the frequencysave in which each psychological category is used by friendly and uncooperative witnesses. While the *Pronoun* category is equally used by both parties, the uncooperative witnesses tend to use the *I*, *Self* and *You* categories while the friendly witnesses tend to use the *Other* and *Social*. A somewhat surprising result is that the *Tentat* category is used more by friendly witnesses – presumably reflecting their discomfort with their position as informers.

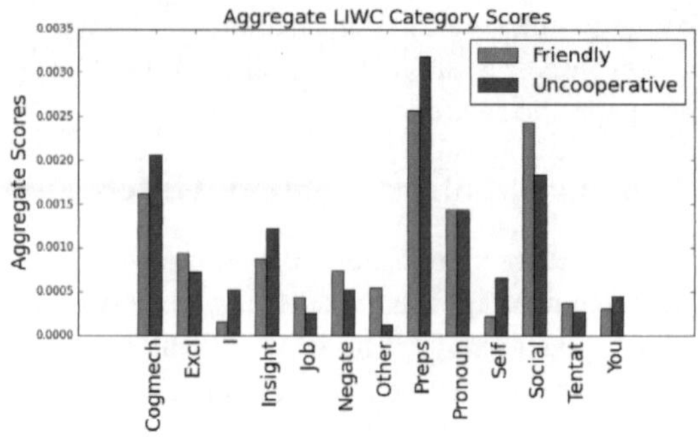

Figure 3: Frequencies of selected LIWC categories in friendly vs. uncooperative testimonies.

Category	Typical Words
Cogmech	abandon, accept, avoid, admit, know, question
Excl	although, besides, but, except
I	I, I'd, I'll, I'm, I've, me, mine, my, myself
Insight	accept, acknowledge, conclude, know, rational
job	work, position, benefit, duty
Negate	no, nope, nothing, neither, never, isn't , can't
Other	he, him, herself, them
Preps	about, against, along, from, outside, since
Pronouns	I, anybody, anyone, something, they, you
Self	I, mine, ours, myself, us
Social	acquaintance, admit, party, comrade, confess, friend, human
Tentat	ambiguous, tentative, undecided, depend, hesitant, guess
You	thou, thoust, thy, y'all, ya, ye, you, you'd

Table 3: LIWC categories and examples of typical words

6 Conclusion and Future Work

In this short paper we take a computational approach in analyzing a collection of HUAC hearings. We combine Natural Language Processing and Network Science techniques in order to gain a better understanding of the social dynamics within the entertainment industry in its darkest time. While sentiment analysis did not prove as useful as expected, analysis of network structures and the language usage in an array of psychological dimensions reveals differences between friendly and uncooperative witnesses.

Future work should include a better preprocessing of the data, which is also expected to improve the sentiment analysis. In future work we will analyze the language use in a finer granularity of witness categories, such as the ideological informer, the naive informer and the vindictive informer. We also hope to expand the hearings corpora to include testimonies from more years.

References

Sibel Adali, Fred Sisenda, and Malik Magdon-Ismail. 2012. Actions speak as loud as words: Predicting relationships from social behavior data. In *Proceedings of the 21st international conference on World Wide Web*, pages 689–698. ACM.

Lada A Adamic, Jun Zhang, Eytan Bakshy, and Mark S Ackerman. 2008. Knowledge sharing and yahoo answers: everyone knows something. In *Proceedings of the 17th international conference on World Wide Web*, pages 665–674. ACM.

Jiang Bian, Yandong Liu, Ding Zhou, Eugene Agichtein, and Hongyuan Zha. 2009. Learning to recognize reliable users and content in social media with coupled mutual reinforcement. In *Proceedings of the 18th international conference on World Wide Web*, pages 51–60. ACM.

Cristian Danescu-Niculescu-Mizil and Lillian Lee. 2011. Chameleons in imagined conversations: A new approach to understanding coordination of linguistic style in dialogs. In *Proceedings of the Workshop on Cognitive Modeling and Computational Linguistics, ACL 2011*.

Cristian Danescu-Niculescu-Mizil, Michael Gamon, and Susan Dumais. 2011. Mark my words! Linguistic style accommodation in social media. In *Proceedings of WWW*, pages 745–754.

Cristian Danescu-Niculescu-Mizil, Lillian Lee, Bo Pang, and Jon Kleinberg. 2012. Echoes of power: Language effects and power differences in social interaction. In *Proceedings of WWW*, pages 699–708.

Xiaowen Ding, Bing Liu, and Philip S. Yu. 2008. A holistic lexicon-based approach to opinion mining. In *Proceedings of the 2008 International Conference on Web Search and Data Mining*, WSDM '08, pages 231–240, New York, NY, USA. ACM.

Jacob Eisenstein, Brendan O'Connor, Noah A Smith, and Eric P Xing. 2010. A latent variable model for geographic lexical variation. In *Proceedings of the 2010 Conference on Empirical Methods in Natural Language Processing*, pages 1277–1287. Association for Computational Linguistics.

Jenny Rose Finkel, Trond Grenager, and Christopher Manning. 2005. Incorporating non-local information into information extraction systems by gibbs sampling. In *Proceedings of the 43rd Annual Meeting on Association for Computational Linguistics*, pages 363–370. Association for Computational Linguistics.

Yoav Goldberg and Jon Orwant. 2013. Syntactic-ngrams over time from a very large corpus of english books. In *Second Joint Conference on Lexical and Computational Semantics*.

Heeyoung Lee, Yves Peirsman, Angel Chang, Nathanael Chambers, Mihai Surdeanu, and Dan Jurafsky. 2011. Stanford's multi-pass sieve coreference resolution system at the conll-2011 shared task. In *Proceedings of the Fifteenth Conference on Computational Natural Language Learning: Shared Task*, pages 28–34. Association for Computational Linguistics.

Victor S Navasky. 2003. *Naming Names: With a New Afterword by the Author*. Macmillan.

Brendan O'Connor, Jacob Eisenstein, Eric P Xing, and Noah A Smith. 2010. A mixture model of demographic lexical variation. In *Proceedings of NIPS workshop on machine learning in computational social science*, pages 1–7.

Daniel M Romero, Brendan Meeder, and Jon Kleinberg. 2011. Differences in the mechanics of information diffusion across topics: idioms, political hashtags, and complex contagion on twitter. In *Proceedings of the 20th international conference on World wide web*, pages 695–704. ACM.

Richard Socher, Alex Perelygin, Jean Wu, Jason Chuang, Christopher D. Manning, Andrew Y. Ng, and Christopher Potts. 2013. Recursive deep models for semantic compositionality over a sentiment treebank. In *Proceedings of the 2013 Conference on Empirical Methods in Natural Language Processing*, pages 1631–1642, Stroudsburg, PA, October. Association for Computational Linguistics.

Yla R. Tausczik and James W. Pennebaker. 2010. The Psychological Meaning of Words: LIWC and Computerized Text Analysis Methods. *Journal of Language and Social Psychology*, 29(1):24–54, March.

Towards Tracking Political Sentiment through Microblog Data

Yu Wang
Emory University
yu.wang@emory.edu

Tom Clark
Emory University
tclark7@emory.edu

Jeffrey Staton
Emory University
jkstato@emory.edu

Eugene Agichtein
Emory University
eugene@mathcs.emory.edu

Abstract

People express and amplify political opinions in Microblogs such as Twitter, especially when major political decisions are made. Twitter provides a useful vehicle for capturing and tracking popular opinion on burning issues of the day. In this paper, we focus on tracking the changes in political sentiment related to the U.S. Supreme Court (SCOTUS) and its decisions, focusing on the key dimensions on support, emotional intensity, and polarity. Measuring changes in these sentiment dimensions could be useful for social and political scientists, policy makers, and the public. This preliminary work adapts existing sentiment analysis techniques to these new dimensions and the specifics of the corpus (Twitter). We illustrate the promise of our work with an important case study of tracking sentiment change building up to, and immediately following one recent landmark Supreme Court decision. This example illustrates how our work could help answer fundamental research questions in political science about the nature of Supreme Court power and its capacity to influence public discourse.

1 Background and Motivation

Political opinions are a popular topic in Microblogs. On June 26th, 2013, when the U.S. Supreme Court announced the decision on the unconstitutionality of the "Defense of Marriage Act" (DOMA), there were millions of Tweets about the users' opinions of the decision. In their Tweets, people not only voice their opinions about the issues at stake, expressing different dimensions of sentiment, such as support or opposition to the decision, or anger or happiness. Thus, simply applying traditional sentiment analysis scales such as "positive" vs. "negative" classification would not be sufficient to understand the public reaction to political decisions.

Research on mass opinion and the Supreme Court is valuable as it could shed light on the fundamental and related normative concerns about the role of constitutional review in American governance, which emerge in a political system possessing democratic institutions at cross-purposes. One line of thought, beginning with Dahl (Dahl, 1957), suggests that the Supreme Court of the United States has a unique capacity among major institutions of American government to leverage its legitimacy in order to change mass opinion regarding salient policies. If the Dahl's hypothesis is correct, then the Supreme Court's same-sex marriage decisions should have resulted in a measurable change in opinion. A primary finding about implication of Dahl's hypothesis is that the Court is polarizing, creating more supportive opinions of the policies it reviews among those who supported the policy before the decision and more negative opinions among those who opposed the policy prior to the decision (Franklin and Kosaki, 1989) (Johnson and Martin, 1998).

We consider Twitter as important example of social expression of opinion. Recent studies of content on Twitter have revealed that 85% of Twitter content is related to spreading and commenting on headline news (Kwak et al., 2010); when users talk about commercial brands in their Tweets, about 20% of them have personal sentiment involved (Jansen et al., 2009). These statistical evidences imply that Twitter has became a portal for public to express opinions. In the context of politics, Twitter content, together with Twitter users'

Proceedings of the Joint Workshop on Social Dynamics and Personal Attributes in Social Media, pages 88–93,
Baltimore, Maryland USA, 27 June 2014.

information, such as user's profile and social network, have shown reasonable power of detecting user's political leaning (Conover et al., 2011) and predicting elections (Tumasjan et al., 2010). Although promising, the effectiveness of using Twitter content to measure public political opinions remains unclear. Several studies show limited correlation between sentiment on Twitter and political polls in elections (Mejova et al., 2013) (O'Connor et al., 2010). Our study mainly focuses on investigating sentiment on Twitter about U.S. Supreme Court decisions.

We propose more fine-grained dimensions for political sentiment analysis, such as supportiveness, emotional intensity and polarity, allowing political science researchers, policy makers, and the public to better comprehend the public reaction to major political issues of the day. As we describe below, these different dimensions of discourse on Twitter allows examination of the multiple ways in which discourse changes when the Supreme Court makes a decision on a given issue of public policy. Our dimensions also open the door to new avenues of theorizing about the nature of public discourse on policy debates.

Although general sentiment analysis has made significant advances over the last decade (Pang et al., 2002) (Pang and Lee, 2008) (Liu, 2012) (Wilson et al., 2009), and with the focus on certain aspects, such as intensity (Wilson et al., 2004), irony detection (Carvalho et al., 2009) and sarcasm detection (Davidov et al., 2010), analyzing Microblog content such as Twitter remains a challenging research topic (Reyes et al., 2012) (Vanin et al., 2013) (Agarwal et al., 2011). Unlike previous work, we introduce and focus on sentiment dimensions particularly important for political analysis of Microblog text, and extend and adapt classification techniques accordingly. To make the data and sentiment analysis results accessible for researchers in other domain, we build a website to visualize the sentiment dynamics over time and let users download the data. Users could also define their own topics of interest and perform deeper analysis with keyword filtering and geolocation filtering.

We present a case study in which our results might be used to answer core questions in political science about the nature of Supreme Court influence on public opinion. Political scientists have long been concerned with whether and how Supreme Court decisions affect public opinion and discourse about political topics (Hoekstra, 2003) (Johnson and Martin, 1998) (Gibson et al., 2003). Survey research on the subject has been limited in two ways. Survey analysis, including panel designs, rely on estimates near but never on the date of particular decisions. In addition, all survey-based research relies on estimates derived from an instrument designed to elicit sentiment – survey responses, useful as they are, do not reflect well how public opinion is naturally expressed. Our analysis allows for the examination of public opinion as it is naturally expressed and in a way that is precisely connected to the timing of decisions.

Next, we state the problem more formally, and outline our approach and implementation.

2 Problem Statement and Approach

2.1 Political Sentiment Classification

We propose three refinements to sentiment analysis to quantify political opinions. Specifically, we pose the following dimensions as particularly important for politics:

- Support: Whether a Tweet is ***Opposed***, ***Neutral***, or ***Supportive*** regarding the topic.
- Emotional Intensity: Whether a Tweet is emotionally ***Intense*** or ***Dispassionate***.
- Sentiment Polarity: Whether a Tweet's tone is ***Angry***, ***Neutral***, or ***Pleased***.

2.2 Approach

In this work, each of the proposed measures is treated as a supervised classification problem. We use multi-class classification algorithms to model Support and Sentiment Polarity, and binary classification for Emotional Intensity and Sarcasm. Section 3.2 describes the labels used to train the supervised classification models. Notice some classes are more interesting than the others. For example, the trends or ratio of opposed vs. supportive Microblogs are more informative than the factual ones. Particularly, we pay more attention to the classes of *opposed*, *supportive*, *intense*, *angry*, and *pleased*.

2.3 Classifier Feature Groups

To classify the Microblog message into the classes of interest, we develop 6 groups of features:
Popularity: Number of times the message has been

posted or favored by users. As for a Tweet, this feature means number of Retweets and favorites.
Capitalization and Punctuation.
N-gram of text: Unigram, bigram, and trigram of the message text.
Sentiment score: The maximum, minimum, average and sum of sentiment score of terms and each Part-of-Speech tags in the message text.
Counter factuality and temporal compression dictionary: This feature counts the number of times such words appear in the message text.
Political dictionary: Number of times a political-related word appears in the message text.
We compute sentiment scores based on SentiWordNet[1], a sentiment dictionary constructed on WordNet.[2] Political dictionary is built upon political-related words in WordNet. As in this paper, we construct a political dictionary with 56 words and phrases, such as "liberal", "conservative", and "freedom" etc.

3 Case Study: DOMA

Our goal is to build and test classifiers that can distinguish political content between classes of interest. Particularly, we focus on classifying Tweets related to one of the most popular political topics, "Defence of Marriage Act" or DOMA, as the target. The techniques can be easily generalized to other political issues in Twitter.

3.1 Dataset

In order to obtain relevant Tweets, we use Twitter streaming API to track representative keywords which include "DOMA", "gay marriage", "Prop8", etc. We track all matched Tweets generated from June 16th to June 29th, immediately prior and subsequent to the DOMA decision, which results in more than 40 thousand Tweets per day on average.

3.2 Human Judgments

With more than 0.5 million potential DOMA relevant Tweets collected, we randomly sampled 100 Tweets per day from June 16th to June 29th, and 1,400 Tweets were selected in total. Three research assistants were trained and they showed high agreement on assigning labels of relevance, support, emotional intensity, and sentiment polarity after training. Each Tweet in our samples was labeled by all three annotators. After the labeling, we first removed "irrelevant" Tweets (if the Tweet was assigned "irrelevant" label by at least one annotator), and then the tweets with no major agreement among annotators on any of the sentiment dimensions were removed. As a result, 1,151 tweets with what we consider to be reliable labels remained in our dataset (which we expect to share with the research community).

3.2.1 Annotator Agreement

The Fleiss' Kappa agreement for each scale is reported in Table 1 and shows that labelers have an almost perfect agreement on relevance. Support, emotional intensity, and sentiment polarity, show either moderate or almost perfect agreement.

Measure	Fleiss' Kappa
Relevance	0.93
Support	0.84
Intensity	0.54
Polarity	0.49

Table 1: Agreement (Fleiss' Kappa) of Human Labels.

3.3 Classification Performance Results

We reproduce the same feature types as previous work and develop the political dictionary feature for this particular task. We experimented with a variety of automated classification algorithms, and for this preliminary experiment report the performance of Naïve Bayes algorithm (simple, fast, and shown to be surprisingly robust to classification tasks with sparse and noisy training data). 10-fold cross validation are performed to test the generalizability of the classifiers. Table 2 reports the average precision, recall and accuracy for all measures. Sarcasm is challenging to detect in part due to the lack of positive instances. One goal in this study is to build a model that captures trends among the different classes. In Section 3.4, we will show that the trends of different measures estimated by the trained classifier align with the human annotated ones over time.

3.4 Visualizing Sentiment Before and After DOMA

One natural application of the automated political sentiment analysis proposed in this paper is tracking public sentiment around landmark U.S. Supreme Court decisions. To provide a more reliable estimate, we apply our trained classifier on all relevant Tweets in our collection. More than

[1]http://sentiwordnet.isti.cnr.it/
[2]http://wordnet.princeton.edu/

Value	Prec. (%)	Rec. (%)	Accuracy(%)
Supportive (48%)	73	74	
Neutral (45%)	76	67	68
Opposed (7%)	17	30	
Intense (31%)	56	60	73
Dispassionate (69%)	81	79	
Pleased (10%)	48	31	
Neutral (79%)	84	78	69
Angry (11%)	24	45	

Table 2: Performance of Classifiers on Each Class.

2.5 million Tweets are estimated in four proposed measures. Figure 1 shows the distribution of on-topic Tweet count over time. The Supreme Court decision triggered a huge wave of Tweets, and the volume went down quickly since then.

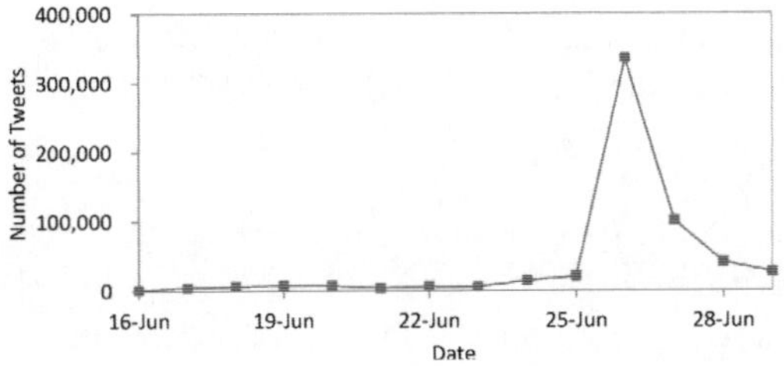

Figure 1: Number of "Gay Marriage" Tweets Over Time.

Figures 2 and 3 visualize both the human labeled trends and the ones obtained by the classifier for the classes "Supportive" and "Intense". In both figures, the peaks in the predicted labels generally align with the human-judged ones. We can see the supportiveness and intensity are both relatively high before the decision, and then they decline gradually after the Supreme Court decision.

Figure 3 shows the volume of intensive Tweets detected by our trained model has a burst on June 22rd, which is not captured by human labeled data. To investigate this, we manually checked all Tweets estimated as "intensive" on June 22rd. It turns out most of the Tweets are indeed intensive. The reason of the burst is that one Tweet was heavily retweeted on that day. We do not disclose the actual tweet due to its offensive content.

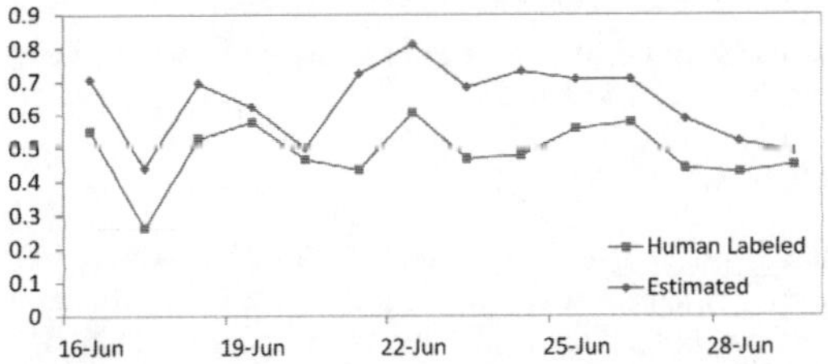

Figure 2: Percentage of "Supportive" Tweets Over Time.

Figure 4 plots the trends of "supportive" and

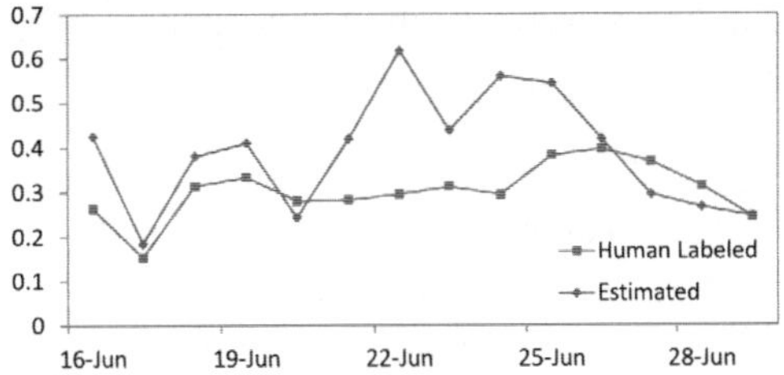

Figure 3: Percentage of "Intense" Tweets Over Time.

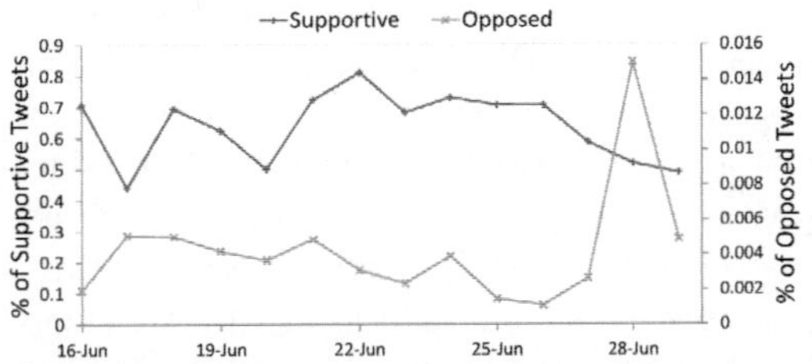

Figure 4: Comparison between "Supportive" and "Opposed" Trends.

"opposed" Tweets in different scales. According to the Supreme Court decision, the "supportive" group wins the debate. Interestingly, instead of responding immediately, the "loser" group react and start Tweeting 2 days after the decision. These trends indicate that "winner" and "loser" in the debate react differently in time and intensity dimensions.

We believe that our estimates of sentiment can be used in various ways by political scientists. The "positivity bias" (Gibson and Caldeira, 2009) model of Supreme Court opinion suggests that the Court can move public opinion in the direction of its decisions. Our results possibly indicate the opposite, the "polarizing" model suggested by (Franklin and Kosaki, 1989) and (Johnson and Martin, 1998), where more negative opinions are observed after the decision (in Figure 4), at least for a short period. By learning and visualize political sentiments, we could crystalize the nature of the decision that influences the degree to which the Supreme Court can move opinion in the direction of its decisions.

4 An Open Platform for Sharing and Analyzing Political Sentiments

Figure 5 shows a website[3] that visualizes political sentiments over time. The website shows several popular U.S. Supreme Court cases, such as "gay marriage", "voting right act", "tax cases",

[3]http://www.courtometer.com

etc., and general topics, such as "Supreme Court" and "Justices". Each of the topics is represented by a list of keywords developed by political science experts. The keywords are also used to track relevant Tweets through Twitter streaming API. To let users go deeper in analyzing public opinions, the website provides two types of real-time filtering: keywords and location of Tweet authors. After applying filters, a subset of matched Tweets are generated as subtopics and their sentiments are visualized. The example filtering in Figure 5 shows the process of creating subtopic "voting right act" out of a general topic "Supreme Court" by using keyword "VRA". We can see that the volume of negative Tweets of "voting right act" is higher than the positive ones, compared to the overall sentiment of the general Supreme Court topic. Once an interesting subtopic is found, users can download the corresponding data and share with other users.

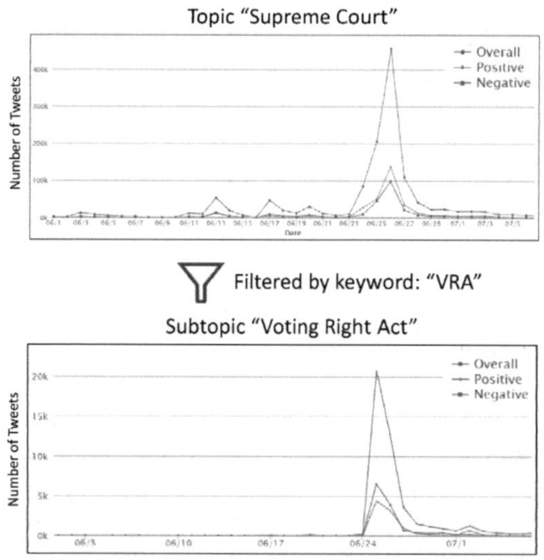

Figure 5: We build a website that visualizes political sentiments over time and let users create "subtopics" by using keyword and location filters.

5 Conclusions

In this paper we considered the problem of political sentiment analysis. We refined the notion of sentiment, as applicable to the political domain, and explored the features needed to perform automated classification to these dimensions, on a real corpus of tweets about one U.S. Supreme Court case. We showed that our existing classifier can already be useful for exploratory political analysis, by comparing the predicted sentiment trends to those derived from manual human judgments, and then applying the classifier on a large sample of tweets – with the results providing additional evidence for an important model of Supreme Court opinion formation from political science.

This work provides an important step towards robust sentiment analysis in the political domain, and the data collected in our study is expected to serve as a stepping stone for subsequent exploration. In the future, we plan to refine and improve the classification performance by exploring additional features, in particular in the latent topic space, and experimenting with other political science topics.

ACKNOWLEDGMENTS The work of Yu Wang and Eugene Agichtein was supported in part by DARPA grants N11AP20012 and D11AP00269, and by the Google Research Award.

References

Apoorv Agarwal, Boyi Xie, Ilia Vovsha, Owen Rambow, and Rebecca Passonneau. 2011. *Sentiment Analysis of Twitter Data.* In Proceedings of the Workshop on Language in Social Media (LSM).

Paula Carvalho, Luís Sarmento, Mário J. Silva, and Eugénio de Oliveira. 2009. *Clues for detecting irony in user-generated contents: oh...!! it's "so easy" ;-).* In Proceedings of the 1st international CIKM workshop on Topic-sentiment analysis for mass opinion.

M.D. Conover, B. Goncalves, J. Ratkiewicz, A. Flammini, and F. Menczer. 2011. *Predicting the Political Alignment of Twitter Users* In Proceedings of IEEE third international conference on social computing

Robert Dahl. 1957. *Decision-Making in a Democracy: The Supreme Court as National Policy-Maker.* Journal of Public Law.

Dmitry Davidov, Oren Tsur, and Ari Rappoport. 2010. *Semi-supervised Recognition of Sarcastic Sentences in Twitter and Amazon.* In Proceedings of the Fourteenth Conference on Computational Natural Language Learning (CoNLL).

Charles H. Franklin, and Liane C. Kosaki. 1989. *Republican Schoolmaster: The U.S. Supreme Court, Public Opinion, and Abortion.* The American Political Science Review.

James L Gibson, and Gregory A Caldeira. 2009. *Citizens, courts, and confirmations: Positivity theory and the judgments of the American people.* Princeton University Press.

James L Gibson, Gregory A Caldeira, and Lester Kenyatta Spence. 2003. *Measuring Attitudes toward the*

United States Supreme Court. American Journal of Political Science.

Valerie Hoekstra. 2003. *Public Reaction to Supreme Court Decisions*. Cambridge University Press.

Bernard J. Jansen, Mimi Zhang, Kate Sobel, and Abdur Chowdury. 2009. *Micro-blogging As Online Word of Mouth Branding*. in CHI '09 Extended Abstracts on Human Factors in Computing Systems.

Timothy R. Johnson, and Andrew D. Martin. 1998. *The Public's Conditional Response to Supreme Court Decisions*. American Political Science Review 92(2):299-309.

Haewoon Kwak, Changhyun Lee, Hosung Park, and Sue Moon. 2010. *What is Twitter, a Social Network or a News Media?*. in Proceedings of the 19th International Conference on World Wide Web (WWW).

Yu-Ru Lin, Drew Margolin, Brian Keegan, and David Lazer. 2013. *Voices of Victory: A Computational Focus Group Framework for Tracking Opinion Shift in Real Time*. In Proceedings of International World Wide Web Conference (WWW).

Bing Liu. 2012. *Sentiment analysis and opinion mining*. Synthesis Lectures on Human Language Technologies.

Yelena Mejova, Padmini Srinivasan, and Bob Boynton. 2013. *GOP Primary Season on Twitter: "Popular" Political Sentiment in Social Media*. In Proceedings of the Sixth ACM International Conference on Web Search and Data Mining (WSDM).

B. O'Connor, R. Balasubramanyan, B. R. Routledge, and N. A. Smith. 2010. *From tweets to polls: Linking text sentiment to public opinion time series*. In Proceedings of International AAAI Conference on Weblogs and Social Media (ICWSM).

Bo Pang, and Lillian Lee. 2008. *Opinion mining and sentiment analysis*. Foundations and Trends in Information Retrieval.

Bo Pang, Lillian Lee, and Shivakumar Vaithyanathan. 2002. *Thumbs up? sentiment classification using machine learning techniques*. In Proceedings of the Conference on Empirical Methods in Natural Language Processing (EMNLP).

Antonio Reyes, Paolo Rosso, and Tony Veale. 2012. *A multidimensional approach for detecting irony in Twitter*. Language Resources and Evaluation.

Swapna Somasundaran, Galileo Namata, Lise Getoor, and Janyce Wiebe. 2009. *Opinion Graphs for Polarity and Discourse Classification*. TextGraphs-4: Graph-based Methods for Natural Language Processing.

Aline A. Vanin, Larissa A. Freitas, Re-nata Vieira, and Marco Bochernitsan. 2013. *Some clues on irony detection in tweets*. In Proceedings of International World Wide Web Conference (WWW).

Theresa Wilson, Janyce Wiebe, and Paul Hoffmann. 2009. *Recognizing Contextual Polarity: an exploration of features for phrase-level sentiment analysis*. Computational Linguistics.

Theresa Wilson, Janyce Wiebe, and Rebecca Hwa. 2004. *Just how mad are you? Finding strong and weak opinion clauses*. In Proceedings of Conference on Artificial Intelligence (AAAI).

Andranik Tumasjan, Timm O. Sprenger, Philipp G. Sandner, and Isabell M. Welpe. 2010. *Predicting Elections with Twitter: What 140 Characters Reveal about Political Sentiment*. In Proceedings of the Fourth International AAAI Conference on Weblogs and Social Media (ICWSM).

Innovation of Verbs in Hebrew

Uzzi Ornan
Hebrew University f Jerusalem
Hebrew Linguistics
Technion, I.I.T. Haifa
Computer Science
Technion City, Haifa, 32000, Israel
ornanu@gmail.com, ornan@cs.technion.ac.il

Absract

In modern time a lot of connections developed among various nations, and people became acquainted with several languages. New conceptions move from their origin in a certain language to another surrounding. Hebrew also adopted many new words from foreign origin, but there is a difficulty to adopt foreign verbs in Hebrew, since a Hebrew verb must be in a certain pattern. This short paper explains how a special device has developed in the Hebrew grammar to cope with this need.

1 Hebrew words in array

Most Hebrew words are arranged in a "root pattern array". Each line contains a root, which is a sequence of three or more consonants, and each column contains a pattern built as a sequence of vowels, sometimes accompanied by one consonant or two. Each pattern also contains three or four slots in which the consonants of the root should enter (**Figure 1**).

Thus a word appears in each square containing the consonants of the root interwoven into the pattern (**Figure 2**). There are several thousands roots, and 100 – 120 patterns of nouns but only seven patterns of verbs. Nouns may be of foreign origins, but verbs should be in the seven patterns only.

2 Empty squares for innovations

Many squares in the array are actually empty. They may become full if new words are needed to be introduced into the language. Usually it happens if a speaker does not find a word that expresses his/her idea. He/She chooses a proper root, and by looking for proper pattern, a new word is produced and from here it shifts into the dictionary (described in **Figure 2**).

3 Verbal and nominal expressions

Languages have both verbal and nominal expressions. Speakers sometimes need both. In order to express an idea which contains both a noun and a verb, it is possible to use a "general purpose" verb, which expresses a general meaning of doing, such as *do*, *make*, or *act* etc., and relate it to the noun. Here are some expressions in Hebrew: First, general purpose Hebrew verbs:

lipˁol= to act,
le-bacceˁ =to perform,
la-ˁsot= to do, to make.

And some examples of actual use:
la-ˁśot ma`amaççim = to make efforts,
le-harim telepon = to pick up a telephone,
lišloaḥ mibraq = to send a telegram,
la-ˁrok biqqur = to pay a visit.

4 Same root for both

It is very common that both the verbal and the nominal expressions be of the same root, such as:

Proceedings of the Joint Workshop on Social Dynamics and Personal Attributes in Social Media, pages 94–97,
Baltimore, Maryland USA, 27 June 2014.

liktob miktab = to write a letter (root: *k't'b'*)
lsapper sippur = to tell a story (root: *s'p'r'*).

Such use of expression is specially significant in Hebrew for a need to add an adjective to the noun while the real meaning is to add an adverbial description to the verb. E.g., by the nominal phrase "important decision" such as in Hebrew : *le-haḥliṭ haḥlaṭa ḥašuba* (root: *ḥ ' l ' ṭ '*) = to decide an important decision. Here both noun and verb are of the same root. Sometimes the verbal expression itself includes the idea of the nominal expression, such as,

le-habriq = *lišloḥ mibraq* (to telegraph, or to send a telegram),
le-hištakker= *lištot le-šokra* (to drink up to toxication),
le-hitraggez = *le-habbiʿ rogez* (to express anger).

5 Foreign nouns need "squeezing"

But what about foreign nouns? Modern world offers a lot of contacts for speakers of various languages, and Hebrew also got a lot of foreign nouns from many languages. These nouns are not included in the array. and what is more important, they do not have roots, while Hebrew speakers are used to connect nouns and verbs, preferably through common roots. A special procedure developed in Hebrew grammar, which produces roots from foreign nouns. This procedure is "squeezing": We squeeze the noun and get its vowels out[1]. What remain is its consonants only.

This sequence of consonants is considered to be used as a new root. The new root is put in a new line in the list of roots at the root-pattern array, and of course on the spot a lot of new empty squares appear along the line of the new root. Some of them are verbal patterns. Now one can choose a proper verbal pattern and here a new Hebrew verb appears.

[1] See, Ornan 1976 (in Hebrew), Ornan 1990 p. 88.

6 Root is sequence of consonants

For example, a new instrument is invented somewhere in a foreign country and has been brought to the Hebrew speakers together with its name: It is the telephone. We have mentioned it above in the first appearance in the idiom *le-harim telepon*, but sometimes after that we find another word which conveys the same meaning, i.e., *le-talpen* = to phone. This verb may appear of course in various verbal structures, such as

tilpanti = I phoned,
talpenu elay = please phone me, etc.

The verb appeared as a result of the squeezing process. From telephone we got the sequence of consonants *t l p n* . and that was enough to add a new line in the root lines of the root-pattern array. ([p] and [f] relate to the same phoneme /p/ even in Modern Hebrew.)

7 Squeezing is original procedure

This procedure of squeezing has been active even in ancient times. It can be seen in the Greek word which entered into Hebrew as well as to many languages – *basis*. We have a Hebrew verb based on the root *b s s* , which was squeezed from *basis* in ancient time and is being used since Mishnaic Hebrew until modern time.

8 Squeezing in Hebrew increased

In Modern time squeezing seems to increase. Many new ideas appeared in the wide world, and Hebrew did not stay behind. Beside other ways of innovation of new words from wide world origin, we find a lot of new words, especially verbs, which have been coined by squeezing. See for example what happened to English words such as compilation, debug, format, fax, discuss, Pascal, Pasteur, Rentgen. They all passed through squeezing, even if some of them are not necessarily nouns. For example,

le-qampel = to compile (code),
le dabbeg = to debug,
le-farmet = to format,
le-faqses= to send a fax note
le-dasqes = to discuss, to talk
le-fasqel = run a Pascal code,
le-faster = pasterize,
le-rantgen = to X-ray.

9 Squeezing of Hebrew words

Next development of the squeezing procedure is that it began to work also on Hebrew words. It happened whenever a speaker feels that the old root does not satisfy his/her needs. A good example is the noun *mispar* which exists in the root-pattern array, with the root *s'p'r'* and pattern *mi—a-*. Its meaning is "a number", and the verb *sapar* means "to count". Now what happens when you need to express the idea of giving numbers to a bunch of pages or names in a long queue. The verb *sapar* "count" is not proper. So the noun *mispar* has been squeezed and a new root, *m ' s ' p ' r '* appeared in a new line at the array, producing a new verb *le-masper* = to give numbers. Another example is *himḥiz*. Its root *m ḥ z* squeezed from *maḥze* = stage play, a noun of root *ḥ ' z ' y '* (The m is from the pattern). The procedure is so strong that even a sequence of two adjacent words may be squeezed such as *"ˁad ka`n"* which means "up to the present". This idiom was squeezed, and we got a new root: *ˁ ' d ' k ' n '*, from which a verb as well as an adjective appeared:

> *le-ˁadken et ha-ḥadašot* = to update the news, or
> *ha-ti``ur lo` mˁudkan* = the description is not uptodate.[2]

---

[2] The squeezing procedure suggestion explains the connection between verbs and their origin much easier and nicer than the efforts done by Outi Bat-El, 1994. She speaks about "extracting", which is the exact "squeezing" described in Ornan, 1976 and Ornan, 1990 (without mentioning them), but tries to adopt it to another theory based on four elements (by McCarthy 1981) which includes adding vowels in a separate procedure, without including any formative consonant to a pattern, while the suggested approach here is based on two elements (pattern and root) only, and we include patterns which may contain consonants. Some needed procedures for correcting various new roots are dealt with in Ornan, 2003 pp. 110-116.

References

Bat-El Outi, 1994. Stem Modification and Cluster Transfer in Modern Hebrew. *Natural Language and a LinguisticTheory* 12, pp. 571-596

Bolozky, Shmuel 1978. Word Formation Strategies in the Hebrew Verb System, Denominative Verbs. *Afroasiatic Linguistics* 5:3 pp. 111-136.

McCarthy, John. J., 1981. A Prosodic Theory of Nonconcatenative Morphology. *Linguistic Inquiry* 12. pp. 373-418.

Ornan, Uzzi. 1976. על יצירת שורשים חדשים (on generating new roots). *Leshonenu- la-ˁam*, Academy of Hebrew Language, Jerusalem, Vol 27, pp 254-267.

Ornan, Uzzi. 1983. תצורת המילה העברית כיצד (How do we build a Hebrew word). Bar-Asher et al. (editors), *Studies in Hebrew dedicated to Ze`ev Ben-Haiim*, Magnes Press, Jerusalem, pp. 13-42.

Ornan, Uzzi. 1990. Machinery for Hebrew Word Formation, Martin Charles Golumbic (ed), *Advances in Artificial Intelligence,* Springer-Verlag, pp. *75-93.*

Ornan, Uzzi. 2003. *המילה האחרונה* (*The Final Word*), University of Haifa pub, pp. 103-126.

pattern root	_a_a_	_i__e_	ma__e_	hit_a__e-	__a_	ta__u_a	hi__i_
psq	pasaq	pisseq	mapseq	hitpasseq	psaq	-	hipsiq
gmr	gamar	gimmer	-	-	gmar	-	-
ḥbr	ḥabar	ḥibber	maḥber	hitḥabber	-	taḥbura	-
ˤbd	ˤabad	ˤibbed	-	-	-	-	hiˤbid
prsm	-	pirsem	-	hitparsem	-	-	-
ṭlgrp	-	ṭilgrep	-	-	-	-	-

Figure 1: Part of Root-Pattern Array

list of patterns: (ma—a- / ti—o-t)

list of roots: (gmr / ḥny / h'l'k') → MAhlAk → /mahlak/ → [mahalax]

phonemic word: /mahlak/

actual word: [mahalax]

Figure 2: Illustrating part of the generating algorithm

User Type Classification of Tweets with Implications for Event Recognition

Lalindra De Silva and **Ellen Riloff**
School of Computing
University of Utah
Salt Lake City, UT 84112
{alnds,riloff}@cs.utah.edu

Abstract

Twitter has become one of the foremost platforms for information sharing. Consequently, it is beneficial for the consumers of Twitter to know the origin of a tweet, as it affects how they view and interpret this information. In this paper, we classify tweets based on their origin, *exploiting only the textual content of tweets.* Specifically, using a rich, linguistic feature set and a supervised classifier framework, we classify tweets into two user types - *organizations* and *individual persons*. Our user type classifier achieves an 89% F_1-score for identifying tweets that originate from organizations in English and an 87% F_1-score for Spanish. We also demonstrate that classifying the user type of a tweet can improve downstream event recognition tasks. We analyze several schemes that exploit user type information to enhance Twitter event recognition and show that substantial improvements can be achieved by training separate models for different user types.

1 Introduction

Twitter has become one of the most widely used social media platforms, with users (as of March 2013) posting approximately 400 million tweets per day (Wickre, 2013). This public data serves as a potential source for a multitude of information needs, but the sheer volume of tweets is a bottleneck in identifying relevant content (Becker et al., 2011). De Choudhury et al. (2012) showed that the user type of a Twitter account is an important indicator in sifting through Twitter data. The knowledge of a tweet's origin has potential implications on the nature of the content to an end user (e.g., credibility, location, etc). Also, certain types of events are more likely to be reported by individual persons (e.g., local events) whereas organizations generally report events that are of interest to a wider audience.

The first part of our research focuses on user type classification in Twitter. De Choudhury et al. (2012) addressed this problem by examining meta-information derived from the Twitter API. In contrast, the goal of our work is to classify tweets, ***based solely on their textual content***. We highlight several reasons why this can be advantageous. One reason is that people frequently share content from other sources, but the shared content often appears in their Twitter timeline as if it was their own. Consequently, a tweet that was posted by an individual may have originated from an organization. Moreover, meta-information can sometimes be infeasible to obtain given the rate limits[1] and there are times when profile information for a user account is unavailable or ambiguous (e.g., users often leave their profile information blank or write vague entries). Therefore, we believe there is value in being able to infer the type of user who authored a tweet based solely on its textual content. Potentially, our methods for user type classification based on textual content can also be combined with methods that examine user profile data or other meta-data, since they are complementary sources of information.

In this paper, we present a classifier that tries to determine whether a tweet originated from an organization or a person using a rich, linguistically-motivated feature set. We design features to recognize linguistic characteristics, including sentiment and emotion expressions, informal language use, tweet style, and similarity with news headlines. We evaluate our classifier on both English and Spanish Twitter data and find that the classifier achieves an 89% F_1-score for identifying tweets that originate from organizations in English and a

[1] https://dev.twitter.com/docs/rate-limiting/1.1/limits

Proceedings of the Joint Workshop on Social Dynamics and Personal Attributes in Social Media, pages 98–108,
Baltimore, Maryland USA, 27 June 2014.

87% F_1-score for Spanish.

The second contribution of this paper is to demonstrate that user type classification can improve event recognition in Twitter. We conduct a study of event recognition for civil unrest events and disease outbreak events. Based on statistics from manually annotated tweets, we found that organization-tweets are much more likely to mention these events than person-tweets. We then investigate several approaches to incorporate user type information into event recognition models. Our best results are produced by training separate event classifiers for tweets from different user types. We show that user type information consistently improves event recognition performance for both civil unrest events and disease outbreak events and for both English and Spanish tweets.

2 Related Work

Our work is most closely related to that of De Choudhury et al. (2012), which proposed methods to classify Twitter users into three categories: 1) Journalists/media bloggers, 2) Organizations and 3) Ordinary Individuals. They employed features derived from social network structure, user activity and users' social interaction behaviors, and named entities and historical topic distributions in tweets. In contrast, our work classifies isolated tweets into two different user types, based on their textual content. Consequently, our work can produce different user type labels for different tweets by the same user, which can help identify shared content not authored by the user.

Another body of related work tries to classify Twitter users along other dimensions such as ethnicity and political orientation (Pennacchiotti and Popescu, 2011; Cohen and Ruths, 2013). Gender inference in Twitter has also garnered interest in the recent past (Ciot et al., 2013; Liu and Ruths, 2013; Fink et al., 2012). Researchers have also focused on user behaviors showcased in Twitter including the types of messages posted (Naaman et al., 2010), social connections (Wu et al., 2011), user responses to events (Popescu and Pennacchiotti, 2011) and behaviors related to demographics (Volkova et al., 2013; Mislove et al., 2011; Rao et al., 2010).

Event recognition is another area that continues to attract a lot of interest in social media. Previous work has investigated event identification and extraction (Jackoway et al., 2011; Becker et al., 2009; Becker et al., 2010; Ritter et al., 2012), event discovery (Benson et al., 2011; Sakaki et al., 2010; Petrović et al., 2010), tracking events over time (Kim et al., 2012; Sayyadi et al., 2009) and event retrieval over archived Twitter data (Metzler et al., 2012). While our work focuses on user type classification, we show that the user type of a tweet is an important piece of information that can be beneficial in event recognition models.

3 Twitter User Types

Twitter user types can be analyzed in different granularities and across different dimensions. We follow a high-level categorization of user types into organizations and individual persons. While we acknowledge the existence of other user types, such as automated bots, we focus only on the *organization* and *individual person* user types for our research.

Sample Tweets from Organizations

- *Banking Commission Split Over EU Bonus Cap http://t.co/GSSbmHAWsQ*
- *Apple likely to introduce smaller, cheaper iPad mini today http://t.co/TuKBHZ3z*
- *Diet Coke may be the new #2, but U.S. soda market is shrinking http://ow.ly/1bSNnh*

Sample Tweets from Individual Persons

- *@john It's a stress fracture. Nah, no dancing was involved!*
- *My gawd feels like my head's gonna explode*
- *Watching The Rainmaker. It has totally sucked me in :D #notsomuch lol*

Figure 1: Sample tweets from individual persons and organizations

From a linguistic point of view, we can observe several distinguishing characteristics between organization- and person-tweets. As shown in Figure 1, organization-tweets are often characterized by headline-like language usage, structured style, a lack of conversation with the audience (i.e., few reply-tweets), and hyperlinks to original articles. In contrast, person-tweets show significant language variability including shorthand terms, conversational behavior, slang and profanity, expressions of emotion, and an overall relaxed usage of language.

3.1 Data Acquisition for User Types

To create our data sets, we archived tweets (using Twitter Streaming API) for six months, beginning February 1st, 2013. We then used a language filter (Lui and Baldwin, 2012) to separate out the English and Spanish tweets. Also, in the data sets we created (see below), we removed duplicates, retweets and any tweet with less than 5 words. Given that large-scale human annotation is expensive, we explored several heuristics to reliably compile a large gold standard collection of person- and organization-tweets.

3.1.1 Acquiring Person-tweets

To acquire person-tweets, we devised a *person heuristic*, focusing on the *name* and the *profile description* fields in each user account corresponding to a tweet. We first gathered lists of **person names** (first names and surnames), for both English and Spanish, using census data[2] and online resources[3]. We also compiled a list of common **organization terms** (e.g., *agency, institute, company*, etc) in both English and Spanish.

The *person heuristic* labels a tweet as a person-tweet if [no organization term is in the name or the profile description fields] **AND** [all the words in the name field are person names *OR* the profile description field starts with either *'I'm'* or *'I am'*][4]. To assess the accuracy of the *person heuristic*, we also performed a manual annotation task. We employed two annotators and provided them with guidelines of what constitutes an individual person's Twitter account. We defined an individual person as someone who uses Twitter in their day-to-day life to post information about his/her daily activities, update personal status messages, comment about societal issues and/or interact with close social circles. The annotators were able to see the *name*, *profile description*, *location* and *url* fields of the Twitter user account and were asked to label each account as ***individual***, ***not individual*** or ***undetermined***. To calculate annotator agreement between the two annotators, we gave them 100 Twitter accounts, corresponding to English tweets collected using the *person heuristic*. The inter-annotator agreement (IAA) was .98 (raw agreement) and .97 (G-Index score). We did not use Cohen's Kappa (κ) as it is known to underestimate agreement (known as Kappa Paradox) when one category dominates. We then released another 250 accounts to each of the annotators, giving us a total of 600 manually labeled accounts[5].

In the distribution of labels assigned by the human annotators for these 600 accounts, 91.5% was confirmed as belonging to ***individual*** persons. 5% was identified as ***not individual*** whereas 3.5% was labeled as ***undetermined***. These numbers corroborate our claim that the *person heuristic* is a valid approximation for acquiring person-tweets.

However, limiting our person-tweets to those from accounts identified with the *person heuristic* could introduce bias (i.e., it may consider only the people who provided more complete profile information). To address this issue, we looked into additional heuristics that are representative of individual persons' Twitter accounts. We observed that applications designed specifically for hand-held devices (e.g., *twitter for iphone*) are frequently used to author tweets and used by individual persons. Organizations, on the other hand, primarily use the Twitter web tool and content management software applications to create, manage and post content to Twitter.

To further investigate our observation, we extracted the source information (i.e., the software applications used to author tweets) for a collection of 1.2 million English tweets from our tweet pool, for a random day, and identified those that were clearly *hand-held device apps* and covered at least 1% of the tweets. Table 1 shows the distribution of these *hand-held device apps*, which together accounted for approximately 66% of all tweets.

Hand-held Device App	**% of Tweets**
twitter for iphone	37.11
twitter for android	16.50
twitter for blackberry	5.50
twitter for ipad	2.55
mobile web (m2)	1.46
ios	1.36
echofon	1.29
ALL	**65.77**

Table 1: Percentage of (English) tweets authored from hand-held device apps

To evaluate our hypothesis that a high percentage of these tweets are person-tweets, we carried out another manual annotation task. We selected

[2] http://www.census.gov/genealogy/www/data/1990surnames/names_files.html

[3] http://genealogy.familyeducation.com/browse/origin/spanish

[4] Corresponding terms were used for Spanish

[5] We adjudicated the disagreements in the initial 100 Twitter accounts.

100 English Twitter accounts whose tweets were generated using one of the above *hand-held device apps* and asked the two annotators to label them using the same guidelines. For this task, the IAA was .84 (raw agreement) and .76 (G-Index score). As before, we released another 250 accounts to each of the annotators. In these 600 user accounts, 87.1% was confirmed to be ***individual*** persons. Only 1% was judged to be clearly ***not individual*** whereas 11.9% was labeled as ***undetermined***.

3.1.2 Acquiring Organization-tweets

Designing similar heuristics to identify organization-tweets proved to be difficult. Organizations describe themselves in numerous ways, making it difficult to automatically identify their names in user profiles. Furthermore, organization names often appear in individual persons' accounts because they mention their employers (e.g., *I'm a software engineer at Microsoft Corporation*). Therefore, to acquire organization-tweets, we relied on web-based directories of organizations (e.g., `www.twellow.com`) and gathered their tweets using the Twitter API. We used 58 organization accounts for English tweets and 83 accounts for Spanish.

3.1.3 Complete Data Set

We created a data set of 200,000 tweets for each language, consisting of 90% person-tweets and 10% organization-tweets. Among the 180,000 person-tweets, 132,000 (66% of 200,000) were tweets whose source was a *hand-held device app*. To collect the remaining 48,000 (24% of 200,000) of the person-tweets, we relied on the *person heuristic*. Finally, we gathered 20,000 organization-tweets using the web directories mentioned previously. In doing so, to ensure that we had a balanced mix of organizations, each organization contributed with a maximum of 500 tweets.

4 User Type Classification

To automatically distinguish person-tweets from organization-tweets, we trained a supervised classifier using N-gram features, an organization heuristic, and a linguistic feature set categorized into six classes. For the classification algorithm, we employed a Support Vector Machine (SVM) with a linear kernel, using the LIBSVM package (Chang and Lin, 2011). For the features that rely on part-of-speech (POS) tags, we used the English Twitter POS tagger by Gimpel et al. (2011) and another tagger trained on the CoNLL 2002 shared task data for Spanish (Tjong Kim Sang, 2002) using the OpenNLP toolkit (OpenSource, 2010).

4.1 N-gram Features

We started off by introducing N-gram features to capture the words in a tweet. Specifically, we trained a supervised classifier using unigram and bigram features encoded with binary values. In selecting the N-gram features, we discarded any N-gram that appears less than five times in the training data.

4.2 Organization Heuristic

Following observations by Messner et al. (2011), we combined two simple heuristic rules to flag tweets that are likely to be from an organization. The first observation is that 'replies' (i.e., @user mentions at the beginning of a tweet) are uncommon in organization-tweets. Hence, if a tweet is a reply, it is likely to be a person-tweet. The second observation is that organization-tweets frequently include a web link to external content.

Our ***organization heuristic***, therefore, combined these two properties. If the tweet is not a reply **AND** contains a web link, we labeled it as an organization-tweet. Otherwise, we labeled it as a person-tweet. In Section 5, we evaluate this heuristic as a classification rule on its own, and also incorporate its label as a feature in our classifier.

4.3 Linguistic Features

In the following sections, we describe our linguistic features and the intuitions in designing them.

4.3.1 Emotion and Sentiment

Twitter is a platform where individuals often express emotion. We detected emotions using four feature types: 1) interjections, 2) profanity, 3) emoticons and 4) overall sentiment of the tweet.

Interjections, profanity, and emoticons are widely used by individuals to convey emotion, such as anger, surprise, happiness, etc. To identify these three feature types, we used a combination of POS tags in the English tagger (which contains tags for interjections, emoticons, etc), compiled lists of interjections and profanity from the web for both English[6] and Spanish[7] and regular expression patterns for emoticons.

We also included sentiment features using the sentiment140 API[8] (Go et al., 2009). This API provides a sentiment label (positive, negative or neutral) for a tweet corresponding to its overall sentiment. We expect person-tweets to show more positive and negative sentiment and organization-tweets to be more neutral.

4.3.2 Similarity to News Headlines

Earlier, we observed that organization-tweets are often similar to news headlines. To exploit this observation, we introduced four features using language models and verb categories.

First, we collected 3 million person-tweets, for each language, using the *person heuristic* described in Section 3.1. Second, we collected another 3 million news headlines from each of the English and Spanish Gigaword corpora (Parker et al., 2009; Mendonca et al., 2009). Using these two data sets, we built unigram and bigram language models (with Laplace smoothing) for person-tweets and for news headlines. Given a new tweet, we calculated the probability of the tweet using both the person-tweet and headline language models. We defined a binary feature that indicates which unigram language model (person-tweet model *vs.* headline model) produced the highest probability. A similar feature is defined for the bigram language models.

We also observed that certain verbs are predominantly used in news headlines and are rarely associated with colloquial language (therefore, in person-tweets). Similarly, we observed verbs that are much more likely to be used by individual persons. To identify the most discriminating verbs, we ranked verbs appearing more than 5 times in the collected news headlines and person-tweets based on the following probabilities:

$$p(h|verb) = \frac{\text{Frequency of } verb \text{ in } \textit{headlines}}{\text{Frequency of } verb \text{ in } \textit{all instances}}$$

$$p(pt|verb) = \frac{\text{Frequency of } verb \text{ in } \textit{person-tweets}}{\text{Frequency of } verb \text{ in } \textit{all instances}}$$

The verbs were sorted by probability and we retained two disjoint sets of verbs, 1) the verbs most representative of headlines (i.e., *headline verbs*), selected by applying a threshold of $p(h|verb) > 0.8$ and 2) verbs most representative of person-tweets (i.e., *personal verbs*), with a similar threshold of $p(pt|verb) > 0.8$. We introduced two binary features that look for verbs in the tweet from these two learned verb lists. The top-ranked verbs for each category are displayed in Table 2. The learned headline verbs tend to be more formal and are often used in business or government contexts (e.g., *revoke*, *granting*, *etc*) whereas the personal verbs tend to represent personal activities, communications, and emotions (e.g., *hate*, *sleep*, *etc*). In total, we learned 687 headline verbs and 2221 personal verbs for English, and 1924 headline verbs and 5719 personal verbs for Spanish.

Headline verbs: aided, revoke, issued, broaden, testify, leads, postponing, forged, deepen, hijacked, raises, granting, honoring, pledged, departing, suspending, citing, compensate, preserved, weakening, differing
Personal verbs: raining, sleep, hanging, hate, marching, teaching, sway, having, risk, lurk, screaming, tagging, disturb, baking, exaggerate, pinch, enjoy, shredding, force, hide, wreck, saved, cooking, blur, told

Table 2: Top-ranked representative verbs learned from headlines and person-tweets

4.3.3 1st and 2nd Person Pronouns

Person-tweets often include self-references, in the form of first-person pronouns and their variant forms (e.g., possessive, reflexive), while organization-tweets rarely contain self-references. Also, organizations often address their audience using second-person pronouns in tweets (e.g., *Will **you** High Five the #Bruins or #Blackhawks? Sign up for a chance to win a trip to the Cup Final: http://t.co/XQP8ZDOINV*). To capture these characteristics, we included two binary features that look for 1st and 2nd person pronouns in a tweet.

4.3.4 NER Features

We hypothesized that organization-tweets will carry more named entities and proper nouns. For English tweets, we identified *Persons*, *Organizations* and *Locations* using the Named Entity Recognizer (NER) from Ritter et al. (2011). For Spanish tweets, we used NER models trained on CoNLL 2002 shared task data for Spanish. The features were encoded as three values, representing the frequency of each entity type in a tweet.

[6]http://www.noswearing.com/dictionary
[7]http://nawcom.com/swearing/mexican_spanish.htm
[8]http://help.sentiment140.com/api

	English			Spanish		
	P	**R**	**F_1**	**P**	**R**	**F_1**
ULM: Unigram Language Model	71.63	63.18	67.14	66.14	60.43	63.16
BLM: Bigram Language Model	81.46	49.17	61.32	80.03	51.08	62.36
NGR: SVM with N-grams	86.02	62.76	72.57	85.76	66.56	74.95
OrgH: Organization Heuristic	66.87	**91.08**	77.12	65.32	81.44	72.49
NGR + OrgH	82.26	86.82	84.48	83.85	85.17	84.50
NGR + OrgH + Linguistic Features	**89.01**	89.40	**89.20**†	**87.59**	**85.47**	**86.52**†

Table 3: User type classification results with **P**recision (%), **R**ecall (%) and **F_1**-Score (%). † denotes statistical significance at $p < 0.01$ compared to *NGR + OrgH*

4.3.5 Informal Language Features

Person-tweets often showcase erratic and casual use of language, whereas organization-tweets tend to have (relatively) more grammatical language usage. Hence, we introduced a feature to determine the *informality* of a tweet. Specifically, we check if a tweet begins with an uppercase letter or not, and whether sentences are properly separated with punctuation. To accomplish this, we used regular expression patterns that look for capitalized characters following punctuation and white-space characters. We also added a feature to check if all the letters in the tweet are lowercased. Use of elongated words (e.g., *cooooooool*) for emphasis, is another property of person-tweets and we captured this property by identifying words with three or more repetitions of the same character.

To comply with the 140 character length restriction of a tweet, person-tweets often employ ad-hoc short-hand usage of words that omit or replace characters with a phonetic substitute (e.g., *2mrw*, *good n8*). We used lists of common abbreviations found in social media[9] collected from the web and a binary feature was set if a tweet contained an instance from these lists.

4.3.6 Twitter Stylistic Features

One can also notice structural properties that are prevalent in either user type. News organizations often append a topic descriptor to the beginning of a tweet (e.g., ***Petraeus affair***: *Woman who complained of harassing emails identified http://t.co/hpyLQYeL*). To encode this behavior, we employed a simple heuristic that looked for a semicolon or a hyphen within the first three words of a tweet. Also, person-tweets employ heavy use of hashtags so we included the frequency of hashtags in a tweet as a single feature. We added two more features in the form of the length of the tweet and the frequency of @user mentions in the tweet.

[9] `http://www.noslang.com/dictionary/full/`

5 Evaluation of User Type Classification

In this section, we discuss and evaluate our user type classifier. All of the experiments were carried out using five-fold cross-validation, using data sets described in Section 3.1. In these experiments, we maintained the separation of organization-tweets at a user-account level in order to avoid tweets from one organization appearing in both train and test sets.

5.1 User Type Classifier Results

We first evaluated several baseline systems to assess the difficulty of the user type classification task. We report precision, recall and F_1-score with organization-tweets as the positive class.

To evaluate our hypothesis that organization-tweets are similar to news headlines, we first predicted user types using only the unigram and bigram language models described in Section 4.3.2. As shown in Table 3 (***ULM*** & ***BLM***), unigram models were capable of discerning organization-tweets with 71% and 66% precision on English and Spanish tweets, respectively. This is substantial performance given that the random chance of labeling an organization-tweet (i.e., precision) is merely 10%. The bigram models show $\geq$ 80% precision whereas the unigram models show higher recall.

As another baseline, we evaluated an SVM classifier that uses only N-gram features. As Table 3 shows, the N-gram classifier (***NGR***) achieved very high precision (86%) for both English and Spanish tweets. However, it yielded relatively moderate recall (63% for English and 67% for Spanish).

We then evaluated the organization heuristic (***OrgH***) all by itself. The heuristic identifies two common characteristics of organization-tweets and as expected, it achieved substantial recall (91% for English and 81% for Spanish) but

	English			Spanish		
	P	**R**	**F_1**	**P**	**R**	**F_1**
NGR + OrgH	82.26	86.82	84.48	83.85	85.17	84.50
+ Emotion and Sentiment Features	86.58	86.41	86.50	85.91	84.19	85.05
+ Features Derived from News Headlines	87.83	87.10	87.46	86.68	84.05	85.35
+ 1st and 2nd Person Pronouns	87.88	88.53	88.20	86.61	84.38	85.48
+ NER Features	88.05	88.75	88.40	86.71	84.69	85.69
+ Informal Language Features	88.39	89.14	88.77	86.89	85.31	86.09
+ Twitter Stylistic Features	89.01	89.40	89.20	87.59	85.47	86.52
NGR + OrgH + Linguistic Features	**89.01**	**89.40**	**89.20**	**87.59**	**85.47**	**86.52**

Table 4: Linguistic feature ablation with **P**recision (%), **R**ecall (%) and **F_1**-Score (%)

with mediocre precision.

These results show that the N-gram classifier achieved high precision whereas the organization heuristic achieved high recall. To exploit the best of both worlds, we evaluated another model (***NGR + OrgH***) that added the organization heuristic as an additional feature for the N-gram classifier. This system fares better than all the previous models, achieving 82% precision with 87% recall for English and 84% precision with 85% recall for Spanish.

Next, we show the benefits obtained from adding the linguistic feature set. As the final row in Table 3 shows, having incorporated all the linguistic features, our final system showed an improvement of 7% precision and 3% recall on English tweets for an overall F_1-score gain of approximately 5%. On Spanish tweets, the same increments were 4%, 0.3% and 2%, respectively. This final classifier is statistically significantly better than the model without linguistic features (***NGR + OrgH***) for both languages at the $p < 0.01$ level, analyzed using a paired booststrap test drawing 10^6 samples with repetition from test data, as described in Berg-Kirkpatrick et al. (2012).

5.2 Analysis of Linguistic Features

Having observed that linguistic features improved user type classification, we evaluated the impact of each type of linguistic feature using an ablation study. Table 4 shows the classifier performance when each of the features types was added cumulatively over the ***NGR + OrgH*** baseline.

We immediately see a 4% and 2% precision gain by adding emotion and sentiment features, for English and Spanish, respectively. Adding features derived from news headlines, we observe that the classifier fares better, improving precision for both languages and improving recall for English. 1st and 2nd person pronouns improved recall on English data but had little impact on Spanish data. The NER features produced very small gains in both languages. The informal language features increased recall from 84.69% to 85.31% on Spanish tweets. Finally, the Twitter stylistic features gained 0.7% more precision for both languages. Overall, the feature types that contributed the most were the emotion/sentiment features, the news headline features, and the Twitter stylistic features.

6 Twitter Event Recognition

Twitter provides a facility where users can search for tweets using keywords. However, keyword-based queries for events can often lead to myriad irrelevant results due to different senses of keywords (polysemy) and figurative or metaphorical use of keywords. For instance, a Twitter search for civil unrest events with a few representative keywords (e.g., *strike*, *rally*, *riot*, *etc.*) can often lead to results referring to sports events, such as a *bowling strike* or a *tennis rally* or where the keywords are used figuratively (e.g., *She's a riot!*). In this section, we investigate if the user type of a tweet can help cut through such ambiguity. Specifically, we hypothesize that event keywords may be used more consistantly and with less ambiguity in organization-tweets, and therefore user type information may be helpful in improving event recognition.

To explore our hypothesis that the user type can influence the event relevance of a tweet, we constructed a set of experiments using two types of events - civil unrest events and disease outbreaks. Civil unrest refers to forms of public disturbance that affect the order of a society (e.g., *strikes*, *protests*, *etc.*) whereas a disease outbreak refers to an unusual or widespread occurrence of a disease (e.g., *a measles outbreak*).

	English		Spanish	
	Civil Unrest	**Disease Outbreaks**	**Civil Unrest**	**Disease Outbreaks**
Person-tweets	5.27%	9.52%	9.32%	5.00%
Organization-tweets	36.54%	39.34%	51.66%	44.06%
All-tweets	**12.50%**	**20.07%**	**14.72%**	**13.22%**

Table 6: Percentage of event-relevant tweets in 4000 tweets with keywords for each category

English Civil Unrest: protest, protested, protesting, riot, rioted, rioting, rally, rallied, rallying, marched, marching, strike, striked, striking
English Disease Outbreaks: outbreak, epidemic, influenza, h1n1, h5n1, pandemic, quarantine, cholera, ebola, flu, malaria, dengue, hepatitis, measles
Spanish Civil Unrest: protesta, protestar, amotinaron, protestaron, protestaban, protestado, amotinarse, amotinaban, marcha, huelga, amotinando, protestando, amotinado
Spanish Disease Outbreaks: brote, epidemia, influenza, h1n1, h5n1, pandemia, cuarantena, sarampión, cólera, ebola, malaria, dengue, hepatitis, gripe

Table 5: Keywords used to query Twitter for two types of events in English and Spanish

	English	Spanish
Civil Unrest	.89, .88, .77	.74, .74, .67
Disease Outbreaks	.82, .73, .68	.84, .83, .80

Table 7: Pair-wise inter-annotator agreement (IAA) measured using Cohen's Kappa (κ) on 200 tweets among the three AMT annotators for each event type in each language

6.1 Data Acquisition for Event Recognition

We began by collecting tweets that *contained at least one of the keywords* listed in Table 5, using the Twitter search API, and we set up an annotation task using Amazon Mechanical Turk (AMT) annotators. First, we created guidelines to distinguish event-relevant tweets from irrelevant tweets and annotated 300 tweets for each of the four categories (i.e., English Civil Unrest, Spanish Civil Unrest, English Disease Outbreaks and Spanish Disease Outbreaks).

We released 200 tweets in each category for annotation to three AMT annotators[10]. We used these 200 tweets to calculate pair-wise IAA using Cohen's Kappa (κ) which we report in Table 7. The IAA scores were generally good, ranging from 0.67 to 0.89. Each annotator subsequently labeled 2000 tweets, yielding a total of 6000 tweets for each category. In each of these 6000 tweet sets, we randomly separated 2000 tweets as tuning data and 4000 as test data.

First, we applied our user type classifier to these tweets and analyzed the number of true event tweets for each user type. Table 6 shows the percentage of true event tweets in the entire test set, as well as the percentage of event tweets for each user type. Overall, the percentage of true event tweets in each test set is $\leq 20\%$. This means that most of the tweets ($> 80\%$) with event keywords ***do not*** discuss an event, confirming the unreliability of using event keywords alone.

However, there is a substantial difference in the density of true event tweets between the two user types. Across both civil unrest and disease outbreaks, and for both languages, we see a much higher percentage of organization-tweets with event keywords mentioning an event than person-tweets with event keywords. Table 6 shows that, in English civil unrest category, organization-tweets are 7 times more likely (36.54% as opposed to 5.27%) to report an actual event than person-tweets with the same keywords. In the English disease outbreaks category, organization-tweets are 4 times more likely to report an event (39.34% vs. 9.52%). We notice similar observations in the Spanish tweets too.

6.2 Event Recognition Results

In this section, we evaluate the impact of user type information by introducing a simple baseline experiment for Twitter event recognition followed by several schemes that we devised to incorporate user type information in more principled ways.

First, we trained a supervised classifier to predict the probability of a tweet being event-relevant using only unigrams and bigrams as features, encoded with binary values. This baseline system is *agnostic to the user type*. We used the SVM Platt method implementation of LIBSVM (Chang and Lin, 2011) and carried out experiments using five-fold cross-validation. As Table 8 shows, this ap-

[10] We first released 100 tweets in each category to AMT and enlisted 10 annotators. After calculating IAA on these 100 tweets, we retained 3 annotators who had the highest agreement with our annotations.

	English			Spanish		
	P	R	F_1	P	R	F_1
Civil Unrest Events						
User type-agnostic classifier	**80.97**	50.20	61.98	77.51	60.37	67.88
User type included as a feature	80.00	50.40	61.84	77.19	61.56	68.50
(θ_p, θ_o) optimized for F_1-score	60.50	**72.60**	66.00	64.97	78.57	71.13
User type-specific classifier	79.34	63.61	**70.61**†	**79.20**	**81.89**	**80.52**†
Disease Outbreak Events						
User type-agnostic classifier	83.15	55.99	66.92	80.49	56.14	66.15
User type included as a feature	**83.46**	55.36	66.57	80.93	59.36	68.48
(θ_p, θ_o) optimized for F_1-score	75.10	**66.58**	70.58	68.94	72.58	70.71
User type-specific classifier	80.35	66.07	**72.51**†	**82.20**	**74.26**	**78.03**†

Table 8: Event recognition results showing **P**recision (%), **R**ecall (%) and **F**$_1$-Score (%), for the two event types in English and Spanish. † denotes statistical significance at $p < 0.01$ compared to the baseline (*User type-agnostic classifier*)

proach achieved 62% F_1-score in English and 68% F_1-score in Spanish, for civil unrest events. For disease outbreak events, the corresponding values were 67% and 66%.

As our first attempt to incorporate user type information, we added the user type label as one additional feature. As shown in Table 8, the added feature yielded small gains for Spanish but made little difference for English.

Given our initial hypothesis (and evidence in Table 6) about events and organization-tweets, we would prefer to be aggressive in labeling organization-tweets as event-relevant. One way to accomplish this with a trained probabilistic classifier is to assign different probability thresholds to person- and organization-tweets. To acquire the optimal threshold parameters for person-tweets (θ_p) and organization-tweets (θ_o), we performed a grid-based threshold sweep on tuning data and optimized with respect to F_1-scores. Table 8 shows that this approach yielded substantial recall gains for all four categories and produced the best F_1-scores thus far.

A more principled approach is to create two completely different classifiers, one for each user type. Each classifier can then model the vocabulary and word associations that are most likely to occur in tweets of that type. Using five-fold cross-validation, we train separate models for person- and organization-tweets. During event recognition, we first apply our user type classifier to a tweet and then apply the appropriate event recognition model. As shown in the final rows in Table 8, this method consistently outperforms the other approaches. Compared to the best competing method, the user type-specific classifiers produced F_1-score gains of 4.6% and 9.4% for English and Spanish civil unrest events, and F_1-score gains of 2% and 7.3% for English and Spanish disease outbreak events.

7 Conclusion

In this work, we tackled the problem of classifying tweets into two user types, organizations and individual persons, based on their textual content. We designed a rich set of features that exploit different linguistic aspects of tweet content, and demonstrated that our classifier achieves F_1-scores of 89% for English and 87% for Spanish. We also presented results showing that organization-tweets with event keywords have a much higher density of event mentions than person-tweets with the same keywords and showed the benefits of incorporating user type information into event recognition models. Our results showed that creating separate event recognition classifiers for different user types yields substantially better performance than using a single event recognition model on all tweets.

8 Acknowledgments

This work was supported by the Intelligence Advanced Research Projects Activity (IARPA) via Department of Interior National Business Center (DoI/NBC) contract number D12PC00285. The U.S. Government is authorized to reproduce and distribute reprints for Governmental purposes notwithstanding any copyright annotation thereon. The views and conclusions contained herein are those of the authors and should not be interpreted as necessarily representing the official policies or endorsements, either expressed or implied, of IARPA, DoI/NBC, or the U.S. Government.

References

Hila Becker, Mor Naaman, and Luis Gravano. 2009. Event identification in social media. In *WebDB*.

Hila Becker, Mor Naaman, and Luis Gravano. 2010. Learning similarity metrics for event identification in social media. In *Proceedings of the Third ACM International Conference on Web Search and Data Mining*, WSDM '10, pages 291–300, New York, NY, USA. ACM.

H. Becker, M. Naaman, and L. Gravano. 2011. Selecting quality twitter content for events. In *Proceedings of the Fifth International AAAI Conference on Weblogs and Social Media (ICWSM11)*.

E. Benson, A. Haghighi, and R. Barzilay. 2011. Event discovery in social media feeds. In *The 49th Annual Meeting of the Association for Computational Linguistics, Portland, Oregon, USA. To appear*.

Taylor Berg-Kirkpatrick, David Burkett, and Dan Klein. 2012. An empirical investigation of statistical significance in nlp. In *Proceedings of the 2012 Joint Conference on Empirical Methods in Natural Language Processing and Computational Natural Language Learning*, pages 995–1005. Association for Computational Linguistics.

Chih-Chung Chang and Chih-Jen Lin. 2011. LIBSVM: A library for support vector machines. *ACM Transactions on Intelligent Systems and Technology*, 2:27:1–27:27. Software available at `http://www.csie.ntu.edu.tw/~cjlin/libsvm`.

Morgane Ciot, Morgan Sonderegger, and Derek Ruths. 2013. Gender inference of twitter users in non-english contexts. In *Proceedings of the 2013 Conference on Empirical Methods in Natural Language Processing, Seattle, Wash*, pages 18–21.

Raviv Cohen and Derek Ruths. 2013. Classifying political orientation on twitter: Its not easy! In *Seventh International AAAI Conference on Weblogs and Social Media*.

M. De Choudhury, N. Diakopoulos, and M. Naaman. 2012. Unfolding the event landscape on twitter: classification and exploration of user categories. In *Proceedings of the ACM 2012 conference on Computer Supported Cooperative Work*, pages 241–244. ACM.

Clayton Fink, Jonathon Kopecky, and Maksym Morawski. 2012. Inferring gender from the content of tweets: A region specific example. In *ICWSM*.

K. Gimpel, N. Schneider, B. O'Connor, D. Das, D. Mills, J. Eisenstein, M. Heilman, D. Yogatama, J. Flanigan, and N.A. Smith. 2011. Part-of-speech tagging for twitter: annotation, features, and experiments. In *Proceedings of the 49th Annual Meeting of the Association for Computational Linguistics: Human Language Technologies: short papers-Volume 2*, pages 42–47. Association for Computational Linguistics.

Alec Go, Richa Bhayani, and Lei Huang. 2009. Twitter sentiment classification using distant supervision. *CS224N Project Report, Stanford*, pages 1–12.

A. Jackoway, H. Samet, and J. Sankaranarayanan. 2011. Identification of live news events using twitter. In *Proceedings of the 3rd ACM SIGSPATIAL International Workshop on Location-Based Social Networks*, page 9. ACM.

M. Kim, L. Xie, and P. Christen. 2012. Event diffusion patterns in social media. In *Sixth International AAAI Conference on Weblogs and Social Media*.

Wendy Liu and Derek Ruths. 2013. Whats in a name? using first names as features for gender inference in twitter.

Marco Lui and Timothy Baldwin. 2012. langid. py: An off-the-shelf language identification tool. In *Proceedings of the ACL 2012 System Demonstrations*, pages 25–30. Association for Computational Linguistics.

Angelo Mendonca, David Andrew Graff, Denise DiPersio, Linguistic Data Consortium, et al. 2009. *Spanish gigaword second edition*. Linguistic Data Consortium.

M. Messner, M. Linke, and A. Eford. 2011. Shoveling tweets: An analysis of the microblogging engagement of traditional news organizations. In *International Symposium on Online Journalism, UT Austin, available at: http://online. journalism. utexas. edu/2011/papers/Messner2011. pdf (last accessed April 3, 2011)*.

D. Metzler, C. Cai, and E. Hovy. 2012. Structured event retrieval over microblog archives. In *Proceedings of the 2012 Conference of the North American Chapter of the Association for Computational Linguistics: Human Language Technologies*, pages 646–655.

Alan Mislove, Sune Lehmann, Yong-Yeol Ahn, Jukka-Pekka Onnela, and J Niels Rosenquist. 2011. Understanding the demographics of twitter users. *ICWSM*, 11:5th.

M. Naaman, J. Boase, and C.H. Lai. 2010. Is it really about me?: message content in social awareness streams. In *Proceedings of the 2010 ACM conference on Computer supported cooperative work*, pages 189–192. ACM.

OpenSource. 2010. Opennlp. *http : //opennlp.sourceforge.net/*.

Robert Parker, Linguistic Data Consortium, et al. 2009. *English gigaword fourth edition*. Linguistic Data Consortium.

Marco Pennacchiotti and Ana-Maria Popescu. 2011. A machine learning approach to twitter user classification.

Saša Petrović, Miles Osborne, and Victor Lavrenko. 2010. Streaming first story detection with application to twitter. In *Human Language Technologies: The 2010 Annual Conference of the North American Chapter of the Association for Computational Linguistics*, pages 181–189. Association for Computational Linguistics.

A.M. Popescu and M. Pennacchiotti. 2011. Dancing with the stars, nba games, politics: An exploration of twitter users response to events. In *Proceedings of the International AAAI Conference on Weblogs and Social Media*.

Delip Rao, David Yarowsky, Abhishek Shreevats, and Manaswi Gupta. 2010. Classifying latent user attributes in twitter. In *Proceedings of the 2nd international workshop on Search and mining user-generated contents*, pages 37–44. ACM.

Alan Ritter, Sam Clark, Mausam, and Oren Etzioni. 2011. Named entity recognition in tweets: An experimental study. In *Proceedings of the Conference on Empirical Methods in Natural Language Processing*, EMNLP '11, pages 1524–1534, Stroudsburg, PA, USA. Association for Computational Linguistics.

A. Ritter, O. Etzioni, S. Clark, et al. 2012. Open domain event extraction from twitter. In *Proceedings of the 18th ACM SIGKDD international conference on Knowledge discovery and data mining*, pages 1104–1112. ACM.

T. Sakaki, M. Okazaki, and Y. Matsuo. 2010. Earthquake shakes twitter users: real-time event detection by social sensors. In *Proceedings of the 19th international conference on World wide web*, pages 851–860. ACM.

H. Sayyadi, M. Hurst, and A. Maykov. 2009. Event detection and tracking in social streams. In *Proceedings of International Conference on Weblogs and Social Media (ICWSM)*.

Erik F. Tjong Kim Sang. 2002. Introduction to the conll-2002 shared task: Language-independent named entity recognition. In *Proceedings of the 6th Conference on Natural Language Learning - Volume 20*, COLING-02, pages 1–4, Stroudsburg, PA, USA. Association for Computational Linguistics.

Svitlana Volkova, Theresa Wilson, and David Yarowsky. 2013. Exploring demographic language variations to improve multilingual sentiment analysis in social media. In *Proceedings of the 2013 Conference on Empirical Methods on Natural Language Processing*.

K Wickre. 2013. Celebrating #twitter7. `https://blog.twitter.com/2013/celebrating-twitter7`. Accessed: 03/20/2014.

S. Wu, J.M. Hofman, W.A. Mason, and D.J. Watts. 2011. Who says what to whom on twitter. In *Proceedings of the 20th international conference on World wide web*, pages 705–714. ACM.

Collective Stance Classification of Posts in Online Debate Forums

Dhanya Sridhar
Computer Science Dept.
UC Santa Cruz
dsridhar@soe.ucsc.edu

Lise Getoor
Computer Science Dept.
UC Santa Cruz
getoor@soe.ucsc.edu

Marilyn Walker
Computer Science Dept.
UC Santa Cruz
maw@soe.ucsc.edu

Abstract

Online debate sites are a large source of informal and opinion-sharing dialogue on current socio-political issues. Inferring users' stance (PRO or CON) towards discussion topics in domains such as politics or news is an important problem, and is of utility to researchers, government organizations, and companies. Predicting users' stance supports identification of social and political groups, building of better recommender systems, and personalization of users' information preferences to their ideological beliefs. In this paper, we develop a novel collective classification approach to stance classification, which makes use of both structural and linguistic features, and which collectively labels the posts' stance across a network of the users' posts. We identify both linguistic features of the posts and features that capture the underlying relationships between posts and users. We use probabilistic soft logic (PSL) (Bach et al., 2013) to model post stance by leveraging both these local linguistic features as well as the observed network structure of the posts to reason over the dataset. We evaluate our approach on 4FORUMS (Walker et al., 2012b), a collection of discussions from an online debate site on issues ranging from gun control to gay marriage. We show that our collective classification model is able to easily incorporate rich, relational information and outperforms a local model which uses only linguistic information.

1 Introduction

Modeling user stance (PRO, CON) in discussion topics in online social media debate is of interest to researchers, corporations and governmental organizations alike. Predicting a user's stance towards a given issue can support the identification of social or political groups (Gawron et al., 2012; Abu-Jbara et al., 2012; Anand et al., 2011; Qiu et al., 2013; Hasan and Ng, 2013), help develop better recommendation systems, or tailor users' information preferences to their ideologies and beliefs. Stance classification problems consist of a collection of debate-style discussions by authors on different controversial, political topics.

While these may be spoken as in the Congressional Debates corpus (Thomas et al., 2006; Burfoot, 2008), we focus on forum posts on social media debate sites. Users on debate sites share their opinions freely, using informal and social language, providing a rich and much more challenging domain for stance prediction.

Social media debate sites contain online discussions with posts from various authors, where each post is either a response to another post or the root of the discussion (Anand et al., 2011; Walker et al., 2012a). Posts are linked to one another by either rebuttal or agreement links and are labelled for stance, either PRO or CON, depending on the framing of the issue under discussion. Each post reflects the stance and sentiment of its author. Authors may participate in multiple discussions in the same topic, and may discuss multiple topics. For example consider the sample posts from the online discussion forum `4forums.com` shown in Fig. 1. Here, we see discussion topics, together with sample quotes and responses, where the response is a direct reply to the quote text. The annotations for stance were gathered using Amazon's Mechanical Turk service with an interface that allowed annotators to see complete discussions. Quotes provide additional context that were used by human annotators in a separate task for annotating agreement and disagreement (Misra and Walker, 2013). Responses can be labeled as either PRO or CON toward the topic. For the example shown in Fig. 1,

Proceedings of the Joint Workshop on Social Dynamics and Personal Attributes in Social Media, pages 109–117,
Baltimore, Maryland USA, 27 June 2014.

Quote **Q**, Response **R**	**Stance**	**Topic**
Q: I thought I'd start a new thread for those newcomers who don't want to be shocked by sick minded nazi XXXX. Anyway... When are fetuses really alive, and how many fetuses are actually aborted (murdered) before that time? **R**: The heart starts beating 3 weeks after conception, and you can't live without a beating heart, but me personally, I think that as soon as the miracle starts, (egg and sperm combine) that is when life begins. I know it's more of a spiritual thing for me instead of a fact. :)	CON	**Abortion**
Q2: Most americans support a Federal Marriage Amendment. Defining Marriage as a union between a man and a woman. Federal Marriage Amendment. This is the text of the Amend: Marriage in the United States shall consist only of the union of a man and a woman. Neither this constitution or the constitution of any state, nor state or federal law, shall be construed to require that marital status or the legal incidents thereof be conferred upon unmarried couples or groups. **R2**: Debator, why does it bother you so much that some people are gay? Its a sexual prefference. People like certain things when they have sex. Example: A man likes a women with small boobs. Or, a man likes a women with nice legs. People like the way certain things feel (I'm not giving te example for that one;)). So why does it bother people that someone's sexual prefference is just a little kinkier than thiers?	PRO	**Gay Marriage**

Figure 1: Sample Quote/Response Pair from `4forums.com` with Mechanical Turk annotations for stance. Both response posts are from the same author.

both response posts are from the same author. We describe the dataset further in Section 4.1.

We believe that models of post stance in online debate should capture both the content and the context of author posts. By jointly reasoning over both the content of the post and its relationships with other posts in the discussion, we perform collective classification, as we further define in Section 3 (Sen et al., 2008). Previous work has shown that collective classification models often perform better than content-only approaches. (Burfoot et al., 2011; Hasan and Ng, 2013; Thomas et al., 2006; Bansal et al., 2008; Walker et al., 2012c). Here, we develop a collective classification approach for stance prediction which leverages the sentiment conveyed in a post through its language, and the reply links consisting of agreements or rebuttals between posts in a discussion. We implement our approach using *Probabilistic Soft Logic* (PSL) (Bach et al., 2013), a recently introduced tool for collective inference in relational data. We evaluate our model on data from the 4FORUMS online debate site (Walker et al., 2012b).

Section 2 first presents an overview of our approach and then in Section 3.1 we describe the PSL framework in more detail. Section 4 describes the evaluation data and our results showing that the PSL model improves prediction of post stance in the `4Forums` dataset. In Section 5 we describe related work, and compare with our proposed approach. Section 6 summarizes our approach and results.

2 Overview of Approach

Given a set of topics $\{t_1 \dots t_n\}$, where each topic t_i consists of a set of discussions $\{d_{i1} \dots d_{ij}\}$, we model each discussion d_k as a collection of posts $\{p_{k0}, \dots, p_{km}\}$, where each post p_{ki} is mapped to its author a_i.

A discussion $d_i \in \mathcal{D}$ is a tree of posts, starting with the initial post p_{i0}. We distinguish between posts that start a new thread (root) and others (non-root). Each non-root post p_{ij} is the response to some previous post p_{ik}, where $k < j$, and we refer to p_{ik} as the parent of p_{ij}. For a subset of the posts, p_{ij} has been annotated with a real valued number in the interval $[-5, 5]$ that denotes whether the post disagrees or agrees with its parent. Values ≤ 0 are considered disagreement and values ≥ 1, as agreement. We discard the posts where the annotations are in the interval $(0, 1)$ since those indicate high annotator uncertainty about agreement.

Fig. 2 illustrates an example of three discussion trees for two topics where author a_2 participates in multiple discussions of the same topic and a_3 and a_4 participate in multiple topics. An author directly replies with a post to another author's post and either disagrees or agrees.

Each post p_{ij} in discussion d_i is also mapped to $\{x_{ij_1}, \dots, x_{ij_N}\}$ linguistic features as described in Section 3.2.1 as well as y_{ij}, the stance label (PRO, CON) towards the discussion topic t_i.

We say that a_j participates in topic t_i if there exist any posts $p_j \in d_i$ with author a_j.

Using the tree structure and posts that have annotations for agreement or disagreement, we con-

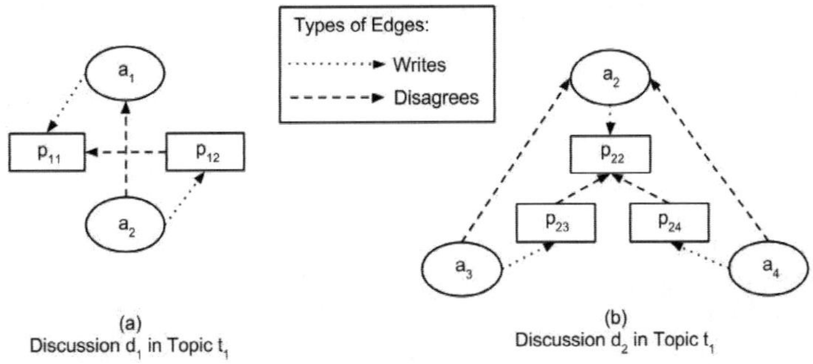

Figure 2: Example of 3 discussions in (a), (b) and (c). Dotted lines denote the 'writes' relation between authors and posts and dashed lines denote the 'disagrees' relation between posts and between authors. Authors can participate in multiple discussions of the same topic, shown by a_2 in both (a) and (b). Moreover, authors may post in multiple topics, as shown by a_3 and a_4 in both (b) and (c), and may interact with the same authors multiple times, as shown again in (b) and (c).

sider the network graph $\mathcal{G}$ of disagreement and agreement between posts and between authors, where the vertices are posts $\{p_0, \ldots, p_m\}$ and authors $\{a_0, \ldots, a_n\}$. A disagreement edge exists from post p_u to p_v if p_u disagrees with p_v.

A disagreement edge exists from a_w to a_y if any of the posts $\{p_w, \ldots, p_x\}$ mapped to a_w disagree with any posts $\{p_y, \ldots p_z\}$ mapped to a_y. We similarly define agreement edges for both posts and authors.

3 Collective Classification of Stance

Given the discussion structure defined in the previous section, our task is to infer the stance of each post. We make use of both linguistic features and the relational structure in order to *collectively* or *jointly* infer the stance labels. This corresponds to a collective classification setting (Sen et al., 2008), in which we are given a multi-relational network and some partially observed labels, and we wish to infer all of the unobserved labels, conditioned on observed attributes and links. Collective classification refers to the combined classification of a set of interdependent objects (posts, in our domain) using information given by both the local features of the objects and the properties of the objects' neighbors in a network. For the stance classification problem, we infer stance labels for posts using both the correlation between a post and its linguistic attributes $\{x_{ij_1}, \ldots, x_{ij_N}\}$, and the labels and attributes of its neighbors in observed network graph $\mathcal{G}$. We use PSL, described below, to perform collective classification.

3.1 Probabilistic Soft Logic

Probabilistic soft logic (PSL) is a framework for probabilistic modeling and collective reasoning in relational domains (Kimmig et al., 2012; Bach et al., 2013). PSL provides a declarative syntax and uses first-order logic to define a templated undirected graphical model over continuous random variables. Like other statistical relational learning methods, dependencies in the domain are captured by constructing rules with weights that can be learned from data.

But unlike other statistical relational learning methods, PSL relaxes boolean truth values for atoms in the domain to soft truth values in the interval [0,1]. In this setting, finding the *most probable explanation* (MPE), a joint assignment of truth values to all random variable ground atoms, can be done efficiently.

For example, a typical PSL rule looks like the following:

$$P(A, B) \wedge Q(B, C) \rightarrow R(A, C)$$

where P, Q and R are *predicates* that represent observed or unobserved attributes in the domain, and A, B, and C are *variables*. For example, in our 4FORUMS domain, we consider an observed attribute such as *writesPost*(A, P) and infer an unobserved attribute (or label) such as *isProPost*(P, T). Instantiation of predicates with data is called grounding (e.g. *writesPost(A2, P7)*), and each ground predicate, often called ground atom, has a soft truth value in the interval [0,1]. To build a PSL model for stance classification, we represent posts

isProPost(P, T) ∧ *writesPost(A, P)*	→	*isProAuth(A, T)*
¬ *isProPost(P, T)* ∧ *writesPost(A, P)*	→	¬ *isProAuth(A, T)*
agreesPost(P, P2) ∧ *isProPost(P, T)*	→	*isProPost(P2, T)*
agreesPost(P, P2) ∧¬ *isProPost(P, T)*	→	¬ *isProPost(P2, T)*
disagreesPost(P, P2) ∧ *isProPost(P, T)*	→	¬ *isProPost(P2, T)*
disagreesPost(P, P2) ∧¬ *isProPost(P, T)*	→	*isProPost(P2, T)*
agreesAuth(A, A2) ∧ *isProAuth(A, T)*	→	*isProAuth(A, T)*
agreesAuth(A, A2) ∧¬ *isProAuth(A, T)*	→	¬ *isProAuth(A2, T)*
disagreesAuth(A, A2) ∧ *isProAuth(A, T)*	→	¬ *isProAuth(A2, T)*
disagreesAuth(A, A2) ∧¬ *isProAuth(A, T)*	→	*isProAuth(A2, T)*
hasLabelPro(P, T)	→	*isProPost(P, T)*
¬ *hasLabelPro(P, T)*	→	¬ *isProPost(P, T)*

Table 1: Rules for PSL model, where P = post, T = Topic, and A = Author.

and authors as variables and specify predicates to encode different interactions, such as *writes*, between them. Domain knowledge is captured by writing rules with weights that govern the relative importance of the dependencies between predicates. The groundings of all the rules result in an undirected graphical model that represents the joint probability distribution of assignments for all unobserved atoms, conditioned on the observed atoms.

Triangular norms, which are continuous relaxations of logical AND and OR, are used to combine the atoms in the first-order clauses. As a result of the soft truth values and the triangular norms, the underlying probabilistic model is a *hinge-loss Markov Random Field* (HL-MRF). Inference in HL-MRFs is a convex optimization, which leads to a significant improvement in efficiency over discrete probabilistic graphical models. Thus, PSL offers a very natural interface to compactly represent stance classification as a collective classification problem, along with methods to reason about our domain.

3.2 Features

We extract both linguistic features that capture the content of a post and features that capture multiple relations from our dataset.

3.2.1 Linguistic Features

To capture the content of a post, on top of a *bag-of-words* representation with unigrams and bigrams, we also consider basic lengths, discourse cues, repeated punctuation counts and counts of lexical categories based on the Linguistic Inquiry and Word Count tool (LIWC) (Pennebaker et al., 2001). Basic length features capture the number of sentences, words, and characters, along with the average word and sentence lengths for each post. The discourse cues feature captures frequency counts for the first few words of the post, which often contain discourse cues. To capture the information in repeated punctuation like "!!", "??" or "?!" we include the frequency count of the given punctuation patterns as a feature of each post (Anand et al., 2011). LIWC counts capture sentiment by giving the degree to which the post uses certain categories of subjective language.

3.2.2 Relational Information

As our problem domain contains relations between both authors and posts, for our PSL model, we consider the relations between authors, between posts and between authors and posts. As described above, in PSL, we model these relations as first-order predicates. In Section 3.3, we describe how we populate the predicates with observations from our data.

Author Information We observe that authors participate in discussions by writing posts. For a subset of authors, we have annotations for their interactions with other authors as either disagreement or agreement, as given by network graph $\mathcal{G}$. We encode this with the following predicates: *writesPost*(A, P), *disagreesAuth*(A1, A2), *agreesAuth*(A1, A2).

Post Information Posts are linked to the topic of their given discussion, and to other posts in their discussion through disagreement or agreement. Additionally, we include a predicate for post stance towards its topic as predicted by a classifier that only uses linguistic features, as described in Section 3.3, as prior information. We capture these relations with the following predicates: *hasLabelPro*(P, T), *hasTopic*(P, T), *disagreesPost*(P1, P2), *agreesPost*(P1, P2).

3.2.3 Target attributes

Our goal is to 1) predict the stance relation between a post and its topic, namely, PRO or CON and 2) predict the stance relation between an author and a topic. In our PSL model, our target predicates are *isProPost*(P, T) and *isProAuth*(A, T).

3.3 PSL Model

We construct our collective stance classification model in PSL using the predicates listed above. For disagreement/agreement annotations in the interval [-5, 5], we consider values [-5,0] as evidence for the *disagreesAuth* relation and values [1, 5] as evidence for the *agreesAuth* relation. We discard observations with annotations in the interval [0,1] because it indicates a very weak signal of agreement, which is already rare on debate sites. We populate *disagreesPost* and *agreesPost* in the same way as described above.

For each relation, we populate the corresponding predicate with all the instances that we observe in data and we fix the truth value of each observation as 1. For all such predicates where we observe instances in the data, we say that the predicate is closed. For the relations *isPostPro* and *isAuthPro* that we predict through inference, a truth value of 1 denotes a PRO stance and a truth value of 0 denotes a CON stance. We say that those predicates are open, and the goal of inference is to jointly assign truth values to groundings of those predicates.

We use our domain knowledge to describe rules that relate these predicates to one another. We follow our intuition that agreement between nodes implies that they have the same stance, and disagreement between nodes implies that they have opposite stances. We relate post and author nodes to each other by supposing that if a post is PRO towards its topic, then its author will also be PRO towards that topic.

We construct a classifier that takes as input the linguistic features of the posts and outputs predictions for stance label of each post. We then consider the labels predicted by the local classifier as a prior for the inference of the target attributes in our PSL model. Table 1 shows the rules in our PSL model.

Topic	Authors	Posts
Abortion	385	8114
Evolution	325	6186
Gun Control	319	3899
Gay Marriage	316	7025
Death Penalty	170	572

Table 2: Overview of topics in 4FORUMSdataset.

4 Experimental Evaluation

We first describe the dataset we use for evaluation and then describe our evaluation method and results.

4.1 Dataset

We evaluate our proposed approach on discussions from `https://www.4forums.com`, an online debate site on social and political issues. The dataset is publicly available as part of the Internet Argument Corpus, an annotated collection of 109,533 forum posts (Walker et al., 2012b; Walker et al., 2012c). On 4FORUMS, a user initiates a discussion by posting a new question or comment under a topic, or participate in an ongoing discussion by replying to any of the posts in the thread. The discussions were given to English speaking Mechanical Turk annotators for a number of annotation tasks to get labels for the stances of discussion participants towards the topic, and scores for each post in a discussion indicating whether it is in agreement or disagreement with the preceding post.

The scores for agreement and disagreement were on a 11 point scale [-5, 5] implemented using a slider, and annotators were given quote/response pairs to determine if the response text agreed or disagreed with the quote text. We use the mean score across the 5-7 annotators used in the task. A more negative value indicates higher inter-annotator confidence of disagreement, and a more positive value indicates higher confidence of agreement. The gold-standard annotation used for the stance label of each post is given by the majority annotation among 3-8 Mechanical Turk annotators performed as a separate task, using entire discussions to determine the stance of the authors in the discussion towards the topic. We use the stance of each post's author to determine the post's stance. For our experiments, we use all posts with annotations for stance, and about 90% of these posts also have annotations for agreement/disagreement.

The discussions span many topics, and Table 2 gives a summary of the topics we consider in our experiments and the distribution of posts across these topics. Each post in a discussion comes as a quote-response pair, where the quote is the text that the post is in response to, and the response is the post text. We refer to (Walker et al., 2012b) for a full description of the corpus and the annotation process.

4.2 Evaluation

In order to evaluate our methods, we split the dataset into training and testing sets by randomly selecting half the authors from each topic and their posts for the training set and using the remaining authors and their posts for the test set. This way, we ensure that no two authors appear in both training and test sets for the same topic, since stance is topic-dependent. We create 10 randomly sampled train/test splits for evaluation. Each split contains about 18,000 posts. For each train/test split, we train a linear SVM for each topic, with the L2-regularized-L1-loss SVM implemented in the LibLINEAR package (Fan et al., 2008). We use only the linguistic features from the posts, for each topic in the training set. We refer to the baseline model which only uses the the output of the SVM as the LOCAL model. We output the predictions from LOCAL model and get stance labels for posts in both the training and test sets. We use the predictions as prior information for the true stance label in our PSL model, with the *hasLabel* predicate.

We use the gold standard stance annotation (PRO, CON) for each post as ground truth for weight learning and inference. A truth value of 1 for *isPostPro* and *isAuthPro* denotes a PRO stance and a truth value of 0 denotes a CON stance. We learn the weights of our PSL model (initially set to 1) for each of our training sets and perform inference on each of the test sets.

Table 3 shows averages for F1 score for the positive class (PRO), area under the precision-recall curve (AUC-PR) for the negative class (CON) and area under the ROC curve (AUROC) over the 10 train/test splits. For the PSL model, the measures are computed for joint inference over all topics in the test sets. For the per-topic linear SVMs (LOCAL model), we compute the measures individually for the predictions of each topic in the test sets and take a weighted average over the topics. Our PSL model outperforms the LOCAL model, with statistically significant improvements in the F1 score and AUC-PR for the negative class. Moreover, our model completes weight learning and inference on the order of seconds, boasting an advantage in computational efficiency, while also maintaining model interpretability.

Table 4 shows the weights learned by the PSL model for the rules in one of the train/test splits of the experiment. The first two rules relating post stance and author stance are weighted more heavily, in part because the *writesPost* predicate has a grounding for each author-post pair and contributes to lots of groundings of the rule. The rules that capture the alternating disagreement stance also have significant weight, while the rules denoting agreement both between posts and between authors are weighted least heavily since there are far fewer instances of agreement than disagreement. This matches our intuition of political debates.

We also explored variations of the PSL model by removing the first two rules relating post stance and author stance and found that the weight learning algorithm drove the weights of the other rules close to 0, worsening the performance. We also removed rules 3-10 that capture agreement/disagreement from the model, and found that the model performs poorly when disregarding the links between nodes entirely. The PSL model learns to weight the first and second rule very highly, and does worse than when considering the prior alone. Thus, the combination of the rules gives the model its advantage, allowing the PSL model to make use of a richer structure that has multiple types of relations and more information.

5 Related Work

Over the last ten years, there has been significant progress on modeling stance. Previous work covers three different debate settings: (1) congressional debates (Thomas et al., 2006; Bansal et al., 2008; Yessenalina et al., 2010; Balahur et al., 2009); (2) company-internal discussion sites (Murakami and Raymond, 2010; Agrawal et al., 2003); and (3) online social and political public forums (Somasundaran and Wiebe, 2009; Somasundaran and Wiebe, 2010; Wang and Rosé, 2010; Biran and Rambow, 2011; Walker et al., 2012c; Anand et al., 2011). Debates in online public forums (e.g. Fig. 1) differ from debates in congress and on company discussion sites because the posts are

Classifier	F1 Score	AUC-PR negative class	AUROC
LOCAL	0.66 ± 0.015	0.44 ± 0.04	0.54 ± 0.02
PSL	0.74 ± 0.04	0.511 ± 0.04	0.59 ± 0.05

Table 3: Averages and standard deviations for F1 score for the positive class, area under PR curve for the negative class, and area under ROC curve for post stance over 10 train/test splits.

isProPost(P, T) $\wedge$ *writesPost(A, P)*	$\rightarrow$	*isProAuth(A, T)* : 10.2
$\neg$ *isProPost(P, T)* $\wedge$ *writesPost(A, P)*	$\rightarrow$	$\neg$ *isProAuth(A, T)* : 8.5
agreesPost(P, P2) $\wedge$ *isProPost(P, T)*	$\rightarrow$	*isProPost(P2, T)* : 0.003
agreesPost(P, P2) $\wedge\neg$ *isProPost(P, T)*	$\rightarrow$	$\neg$ *isProPost(P2, T)* : 0.003
disagreesPost(P, P2) $\wedge$ *isProPost(P, T)*	$\rightarrow$	$\neg$ *isProPost(P2, T)* : 0.06
disagreesPost(P, P2) $\wedge\neg$ *isProPost(P, T)*	$\rightarrow$	*isProPost(P2, T)* : 0.11
agreesAuth(A, A2) $\wedge$ *isProAuth(A, T)*	$\rightarrow$	*isProAuth(A, T)* : 0.001
agreesAuth(A, A2) $\wedge\neg$ *isProAuth(A, T)*	$\rightarrow$	$\neg$ *isProAuth(A2, T)* : 0.0
disagreesAuth(A, A2) $\wedge$ *isProAuth(A, T)*	$\rightarrow$	$\neg$ *isProAuth(A2, T)* : 0.23
disagreesAuth(A, A2) $\wedge\neg$ *isProAuth(A, T)*	$\rightarrow$	*isProAuth(A2, T)* : 0.6
hasLabelPro(P, T)	$\rightarrow$	*isProPost(P, T)* : 2.2
$\neg$ *hasLabelPro(P, T)*	$\rightarrow$	$\neg$ *isProPost(P, T)* : 4.8

Table 4: Weights learned by the model for the PSL rules in train/test split 2 of experiments

shorter and the language is more informal and social. We predict that this difference makes it more difficult to achieve accuracies as high for 4FORUMS discussions as can be achieved for the congressional debates corpus.

Work by (Somasundaran and Wiebe, 2009) on idealogical debates very similar to our own show that identifying argumentation structure improves performance; their best performance is approximately 64% accuracy over all topics. Research by (Thomas et al., 2006; Bansal et al., 2008; Yessenalina et al., 2010; Balahur et al., 2009) classifies the speaker's stance in a corpus of congressional floor debates. This work combines graph-based and text-classification approaches to achieve 75% accuracy on Congressional debate siding over all topics. Other work applies MaxCut to the reply structure of company discussion forums (Malouf and Mullen, 2008; Murakami and Raymond, 2010; Agrawal et al., 2003). Murakami & Raymond (2010) show that rules for identifying agreement, defined on the textual content of the post improve performance.

More recent work has explicitly focused on the benefits of collective classification in these settings (Burfoot et al., 2011; Hasan and Ng, 2013; Walker et al., 2012c), and has shown in each case that collective classification improves performance. The results reported here are the first to apply the PSL collective classification framework to the forums conversations from the IAC corpus (Anand et al., 2011; Walker et al., 2012c).

6 Discussion and Future Work

Here, we introduce a novel approach to classify stance of posts from online debate forums with a collective classification framework. We formally construct a model, using PSL, to capture relational information in the network of authors and posts and our intuition that agreement or disagreement between users correlates to their stance towards a topic. Our initial results are promising, showing that by incorporating more complex interactions between authors and posts, we gain improvements over a content-only approach. Our approach is ideally suited to collective inference in social media. It easily extendable to use additional relational information, and richer behavioral and linguistic information.

Acknowledgments

Thanks to Pranav Anand for providing us with the stance annotations for the `4forums` dataset. This work is supported by National Science Foundation under Grant Nos. IIS1218488, CCF0937094 and CISE-RI 1302668.

References

Amjad Abu-Jbara, Mona Diab, Pradeep Dasigi, and Dragomir Radev. 2012. Subgroup detection in ideological discussions. In *Association for Computational Linguistics (ACL)*, pages 399–409.

R. Agrawal, S. Rajagopalan, R. Srikant, and Y. Xu. 2003. Mining newsgroups using networks arising from social behavior. In *International Conference on World Wide Web (WWW)*, pages 529–535. ACM.

Pranav Anand, Marilyn Walker, Rob Abbott, Jean E. Fox Tree, Robeson Bowmani, and Michael Minor. 2011. Cats Rule and Dogs Drool: Classifying Stance in Online Debate. In *ACL Workshop on Sentiment and Subjectivity*.

Stephen H. Bach, Bert Huang, Ben London, and Lise Getoor. 2013. Hinge-loss markov random fields: Convex inference for structured prediction. In *Uncertainty in Artificial Intelligence (UAI)*.

A. Balahur, Z. Kozareva, and A. Montoyo. 2009. Determining the polarity and source of opinions expressed in political debates. *Computational Linguistics and Intelligent Text Processing*, pages 468–480.

M. Bansal, C. Cardie, and L. Lee. 2008. The power of negative thinking: Exploiting label disagreement in the min-cut classification framework. *COLING*, pages 13–16.

O. Biran and O. Rambow. 2011. Identifying justifications in written dialogs. In *IEEE International Conference on Semantic Computing (ICSC)*, pages 162–168.

Clinton Burfoot, Steven Bird, and Timothy Baldwin. 2011. Collective classification of congressional floor-debate transcripts. In *Association for Computational Linguistics (ACL)*, pages 1506–1515.

C. Burfoot. 2008. Using multiple sources of agreement information for sentiment classification of political transcripts. In *Australasian Language Technology Association Workshop*, volume 6, pages 11–18.

Rong-En Fan, Kai-Wei Chang, Cho-Jui Hsieh, Xiang-Rui Wang, and Chih-Jen Lin. 2008. LIBLINEAR: A library for large linear classification. *Journal of Machine Learning Research*, 9:1871–1874.

J.M. Gawron, D. Gupta, K. Stephens, M.H. Tsou, B. Spitzberg, and L. An. 2012. Using group membership markers for group identification in web logs. In *AAAI Conference on Weblogs and Social Media (ICWSM)*.

Kazi Saidul Hasan and Vincent Ng. 2013. Stance classification of ideological debates: Data, models, features, and constraints. *International Joint Conference on Natural Language Processing*.

Angelika Kimmig, Stephen H. Bach, Matthias Broecheler, Bert Huang, and Lise Getoor. 2012. A short introduction to probabilistic soft logic. In *NIPS Workshop on Probabilistic Programming: Foundations and Applications*.

R. Malouf and T. Mullen. 2008. Taking sides: User classification for informal online political discourse. *Internet Research*, 18(2):177–190.

Amita Misra and Marilyn A Walker. 2013. Topic independent identification of agreement and disagreement in social media dialogue. In *Conference of the Special Interest Group on Discourse and Dialogue*, page 920.

A. Murakami and R. Raymond. 2010. Support or Oppose? Classifying Positions in Online Debates from Reply Activities and Opinion Expressions. In *International Conference on Computational Linguistics (ACL)*, pages 869–875.

J. W. Pennebaker, L. E. Francis, and R. J. Booth, 2001. *LIWC: Linguistic Inquiry and Word Count*.

Minghui Qiu, Liu Yang, and Jing Jiang. 2013. Modeling interaction features for debate side clustering. In *ACM International Conference on Information & Knowledge Management (CIKM)*, pages 873–878.

Prithviraj Sen, Galileo Mark Namata, Mustafa Bilgic, Lise Getoor, Brian Gallagher, and Tina Eliassi-Rad. 2008. Collective classification in network data. *AI Magazine*, 29(3):93–106.

S. Somasundaran and J. Wiebe. 2009. Recognizing stances in online debates. In *ACL and AFNLP*, pages 226–234.

S. Somasundaran and J. Wiebe. 2010. Recognizing stances in ideological on-line debates. In *NAACL HLT 2010 Workshop on Computational Approaches to Analysis and Generation of Emotion in Text*, pages 116–124.

M. Thomas, B. Pang, and L. Lee. 2006. Get out the vote: Determining support or opposition from Congressional floor-debate transcripts. In *Conference on Empirical Methods in Natural Language Processing (EMNLP)*, pages 327–335.

Marilyn Walker, Pranav Anand, Rob Abbott, Jean E. Fox Tree, Craig Martell, and Joseph King. 2012a. That's your evidence?: Classifying stance in online political debate. *Decision Support Sciences*.

Marilyn Walker, Pranav Anand, Robert Abbott, and Jean E. Fox Tree. 2012b. A corpus for research on deliberation and debate. In *Language Resources and Evaluation Conference, LREC2012*.

Marilyn Walker, Pranav Anand, Robert Abbott, and Richard Grant. 2012c. Stance classification using dialogic properties of persuasion. In *Meeting of the North American Association for Computational Linguistics. NAACL-HLT12*.

Y.C. Wang and C.P. Rosé. 2010. Making conversational structure explicit: identification of initiation-response pairs within online discussions. In *Human Language Technologies: The 2010 Annual Conference of the North American Chapter of the Association for Computational Linguistics*, pages 673–676.

A. Yessenalina, Y. Yue, and C. Cardie. 2010. Multi-level structured models for document-level sentiment classification. In *Conference on Empirical Methods in Natural Language Processing (EMNLP)*, pages 1046–1056.

Author Index

Association for Computational Linguistics
209 N. Eighth Street
Stroudsburg, Pennsylvania 18360

CURRAN ASSOCIATES INC
proceedings.com